Apple Training Series:

# Mac OS X Support Essentials v10.6

**A Course on Supporting and Troubleshooting
Mac OS X v10.6 Snow Leopard**

## Student Workbook

**Apple Training Series: Mac OS X Support Essentials v10.6 Student Workbook**
Courseware Version 10.6.1
September 17, 2009

Published by Peachpit Press
Peachpit Press is a division of Pearson Education.
Copyright © 2010 by Apple Inc.

Apple Training Series Editor: Rebecca Freed
Project Lead/Development Editor: Kevin M. White
Production Editors: Danielle Foster, Becky Winter
Contributors: Simon Wheatley, Patrick Gallagher
Apple Editor: Shane Ross
Technical Editor: Gordon Davisson
Copyeditor: Rachel Fudge
Proofreader: Naomi Adler-Dancis
Compositor: Danielle Foster
Cover design: Mimi Heft
Cover illustrator: Kent Oberheu
Interior design: Danielle Foster

**Notice of Rights**

All rights reserved. No part of this course may be reproduced or transmitted in any form by any means, electronic, mechanical, photocopying, recording, or otherwise, without the prior written permission of the publisher. For information on getting permission for reprints and excerpts, contact permissions@peachpit.com.

**Trademarks**

Many of the designations used by manufacturers and sellers to distinguish their products are claimed as trademarks. Where those designations appear in this book, and Peachpit was aware of a trademark claim, the designations appear as requested by the owner of the trademark. All other product names and services identified throughout this book are used in editorial fashion only and for the benefit of such companies with no intention of infringement of the trademark. No such use, or the use of any trade name, is intended to convey endorsement or other affiliation with this book.

ISBN 13: 978-0-321-68049-5
ISBN 10:     0-321-68049-9
9 8 7 6 5 4 3 2 1
Printed and bound in the United States of America

IMPORTANT: The exercises described within this book should be used in connection with classroom computing facilities that are used solely in support of classroom instruction in a noncommercial environment. It is possible that use of the exercises could lead to the unintentional loss or corruption of data and the interruption of network services. Therefore the exercises should NOT be performed using commercial or personal equipment.

The information in this book is distributed on an "As Is" basis without warranty. While every precaution has been taken in the preparation of the book, neither the authors nor Peachpit shall have any liability to any person or entity with respect to any loss or damage caused or alleged to be caused directly or indirectly by the instructions contained in this book or by the computer software and hardware products described in it.

# Contents

Contents

# 6   Applications and Boot Camp

# 7   Network Configuration

Contents

# 10 System Startup

# 1

# Installation and Initial Setup

# 1.1  Installing Mac OS X

Although all new Mac computers are shipped with a version of Mac OS X installed, there are certainly many older Macs that don't have the latest version, Mac OS X 10.6. For this reason alone you should be familiar with the Mac OS X installation process. Also, there are occasions, where on a newer Mac, you may need to install the system software again. In this lesson you will learn about the Mac OS X installation process. Further, there are several extremely useful administration and troubleshooting utilities available from the Mac OS X Install DVD. In this lesson you will also learn how to access and use these utilities.

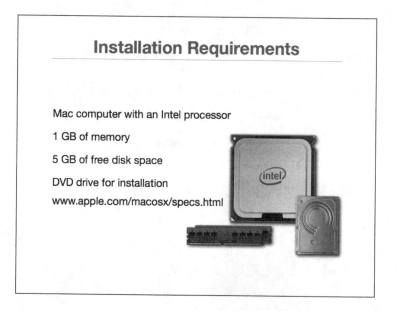

## Installation Requirements

Mac computer with an Intel processor

1 GB of memory

5 GB of free disk space

DVD drive for installation

www.apple.com/macosx/specs.html

For detailed instructions, see "Before You Install Mac OS X" in Chapter 1 of *Apple Training Series: Mac OS X Support Essentials v10.6*.

## Before You Install Mac OS X

Back up data

Read documentation in DVD "Instructions" folder

Collect information

Check firmware and update if needed

Decide on installation method

For detailed instructions, see "Before You Install Mac OS X" in Chapter 1 of *Apple Training Series: Mac OS X Support Essentials v10.6.*

## Mac OS X Install DVD Utilities

Extremely useful menu of Mac utilities

Reset Password is only available from this disc

Use Disk Utility to erase or partition system volume

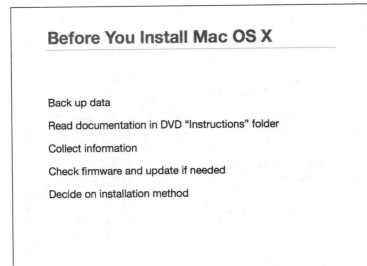

For detailed instructions, see "Using Installer Disc Utilities" in Chapter 1 of *Apple Training Series: Mac OS X Support Essentials v10.6.*

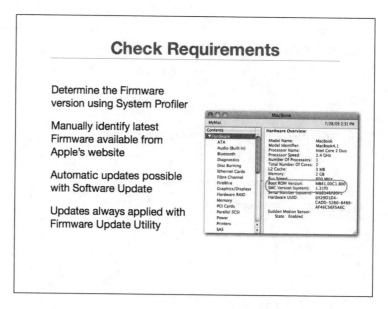

For detailed instructions, see "Before You Install Mac OS X" in Chapter 1 of *Apple Training Series: Mac OS X Support Essentials v10.6.*

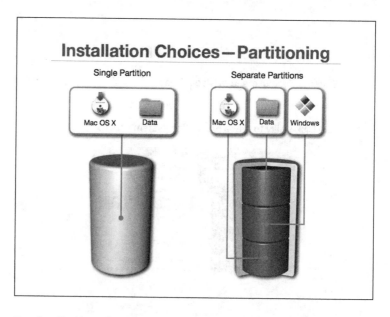

For detailed instructions, see "Preparing the System Drive" in Chapter 1 of *Apple Training Series: Mac OS X Support Essentials v10.6.*

## System Volume Formats

Mac OS X system volume:

- Mac OS Extended (Journaled)—Default for Mac clients
- Mac OS Extended (Journaled, Case-sensitive)—Mac servers

Boot Camp system volume:

- MS-DOS (FAT32)—Default for Boot Camp setup
- NTFS—Mac support is read only, but this format is required for installing Windows Vista and Windows 7
- When using multiple partitions, Boot Camp only recognizes the last Windows-formatted volume on an internal drive

For detailed instructions, see "Preparing the System Drive" in Chapter 1 of *Apple Training Series: Mac OS X Support Essentials v10.6.*

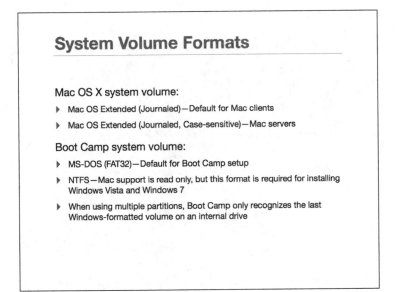

For detailed instructions, see "Preparing the System Drive" in Chapter 1 of *Apple Training Series: Mac OS X Support Essentials v10.6.*

Installation—Select Destination

Install Mac OS X

Select the disk where you want to install Mac OS X

Backup
At least 39.35 GB free
40.01 GB total

Macintosh HD
At least 159.4 GB free
159.7 GB total

Mac OS X will be installed on the "Macintosh HD" disk.

To change the items you want to install, click Customize.

Customize          Go Back    Install

For detailed instructions, see "Installing Mac OS X" in Chapter 1 of *Apple Training Series: Mac OS X Support Essentials v10.6.*

Installation—Customize

| | |
|---|---|
| ☑ Essential System Software | 7.94 GB |
| ▼ ☑ Printer Support | Zero KB |
| ☑ Printers Used by This Mac | |
| ■ Nearby and Popular Printers | |
| ☐ All Available Printers | |
| ☑ Additional Fonts | 114 MB |
| ▶ ☑ Language Translations | 1.18 GB |
| ☑ X11 | 159.1 MB |
| ☐ Rosetta | 3.5 MB |
| ☐ QuickTime 7 | 32.5 MB |

9.4 GB required for installation          154.17 GB free after installation

Select to install software for commonly used printers, including printers from Canon, Epson, Lexmark, HP, and other manufacturers. This also includes supported printers nearby on your network.

Restore Defaults                    OK

Customize          Go Back    Install

For detailed instructions, see "Installing Mac OS X" in Chapter 1 of *Apple Training Series: Mac OS X Support Essentials v10.6.*

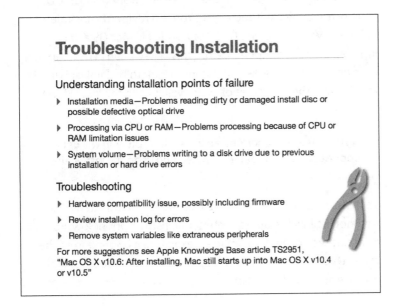

## View the Installer Log File

Accessible from menu Window > Installer Log

Remains open during entire installation

Prevents automatic restart after installation

For detailed instructions, see "Installer Troubleshooting" in Chapter 1 of *Apple Training Series: Mac OS X Support Essentials v10.6.*

## Troubleshooting Installation

Understanding installation points of failure

▸ Installation media—Problems reading dirty or damaged install disc or possible defective optical drive

▸ Processing via CPU or RAM—Problems processing because of CPU or RAM limitation issues

▸ System volume—Problems writing to a disk drive due to previous installation or hard drive errors

Troubleshooting

▸ Hardware compatibility issue, possibly including firmware

▸ Review installation log for errors

▸ Remove system variables like extraneous peripherals

For more suggestions see Apple Knowledge Base article TS2951, "Mac OS X v10.6: After installing, Mac still starts up into Mac OS X v10.4 or v10.5"

For detailed instructions, see "Installer Troubleshooting" in Chapter 1 of *Apple Training Series: Mac OS X Support Essentials v10.6.*

Exercise 1.1.1

# Using the Mac OS X Install DVD

## Objectives

- Start up from the Install DVD

- Understand the functionality of the available utilities

- Verify that the computer meets the system requirements for Mac OS X v10.6

- Understand the installation options for Mac OS X

## Summary

In this exercise you will boot your computer from a Mac OS X installer. This installer could be in the form of a Mac OS X Install DVD or it might be a NetBoot image created from the install DVD. Your instructor will tell you which. You will review the included utilities as well as the Mac OS X Installer itself. Mac OS X was installed on your computer before this class began in order to save class time for other tasks, but it is important to be familiar with the installer and the robust set of tools available on the Install DVD.

> **Note** You will not perform an installation, but you will get an opportunity to look at the steps leading up to the installation.

Your instructor will tell you which bootup technique to use: DVD or NetBoot. Follow the appropriate set of instructions below. Booting from this type of NetBoot image is exactly like booting from the install DVD, so once you have booted, the rest of the steps in the exercise are exactly the same.

# Boot Using a Mac OS X Install DVD (DVD Method)

To access the Installer and other utilities, you need to boot from the installation disc. Only perform these steps if your instructor passes out DVDs.

1 Insert the Mac OS X Install DVD provided by your instructor.

 If your computer is a Mac Pro and is off, you can hold down the mouse button while you turn on the computer to eject the DVD. Just turn on the computer and hold down the mouse button until it opens. For slot-loading drives, just turn on the computer and insert the disc.

2 Restart your computer.

3 Press and hold the C key until the gray Apple appears on the screen.

 When the C key is held down during startup, the computer attempts to boot using the disc that is in the internal optical drive.

4 After the installation disc has booted, you will see an initial installation screen where you select the interface language. If the Welcome music and video play, you probably pressed the C key too late or did not hold it down long enough. Try again by repeating steps 2 and 3.

# NetBoot the Computer from an Install Image (NetBoot Method)

To access the Installer and other utilities, you need to boot from the installation disc. Only perform these steps if your instructor tells you to NetBoot.

1 Turn on your computer.

2   Press and hold the N key until the gray Apple appears on the screen.

When the N key is held down during startup, the computer attempts to boot from an image that resides on a server. Your instructor has prepared a special disk image from the install disc. It resides on the classroom server.

3   After the computer has booted, you will see an initial installation screen where you select the interface language. If the Welcome music and video play, you probably pressed the N key too late or did not hold it down long enough. Try again by repeating steps 1 and 2.

## Select the Main Language

Mac OS X supports a variety of languages. The first step in running the Mac OS X Installer is to select the user interface language.

1   In the language selection screen, ensure that "Use English for the main language" is selected.

2   Click the arrow button to open the Installer.

## Examine the Utilities Available During Installation

While booted from the Mac OS X Install DVD, you have access to some utilities in addition to the Installer. You can use these utilities to check the system configuration and perform maintenance or troubleshooting tasks. In this part of the exercise you will look at some of these utilities in order to become more familiar with them. You will use them later in the course.

## Open System Profiler

You will use System Profiler to examine your computer.

1   From the Utilities menu, choose System Profiler.

The System Profiler utility opens, scans your computer, and creates a report detailing the computer's hardware and software configuration. Below is an example of what you will see. What you see on the screen of your computer will vary.

*Question 1*  *What is the processor type and amount of RAM in the example above?*

*Question 2*  *Does this computer meet the qualifications to run Mac OS X v10.6?*

*Question 3*  *Which BootROM version is installed on this computer?*

*Question 4*  *What SMC version is installed on this computer?*

*Question 5  What is the minimum amount of hard drive space necessary to install Mac OS X?*

---

*Question 6  What is the minimum amount of memory required by Mac OS X?*

---

2   Depending on your hardware, you may have an ATA drive or a Serial ATA drive. Look at both to find your hard drive. Most likely, it is a Serial ATA drive.

In the Contents list on the left side of the System Profiler window, select either ATA or Serial ATA to determine what size hard drive is installed in your computer.

3   Quit System Profiler to return to the Installer.

## Examine Your Startup Disk

The Startup Disk utility allows you to select which device from which to boot. If you are having problems booting from a disk drive, you could connect a second disk drive with Mac OS X installed and use Startup Disk to configure the computer to boot from the new drive.

1   Choose Startup Disk from the Utilities menu. Notice that Startup Disk shows you a list of all bootable volumes. One of the options is Network Startup or one or more NetBoot images, depending on what it finds on your network.

12

2   You don't need to change the startup disk now, so quit
    Startup Disk.

## Examine Disk Utility

Disk Utility is provided on the Mac OS X Install DVD to allow you to
image, reformat, or repartition your hard drive before you install
Mac OS X. It also allows you to diagnose and fix some disk problems when booted from the installation disc.

1   Choose Disk Utility from the Utilities Menu.

    In the Device List on the left, you will see your hard drive and
    the Mac OS X Install DVD or NetBoot image. Note there is a
    primary entry for each physical device and an indented list of
    volumes on each device.

2   Select the entry that represents your hard drive (as opposed to
    your boot volume).

    Notice the options available to perform on the drive itself: First
    Aid, Erase, Partition, RAID, and Restore. One of the main reasons
    Disk Utility is provided on the installation disc is to allow you to
    partition a drive before installing Mac OS X.

3   In the list of devices on the left, select the entry that represents
    the boot volume on your hard drive. It will typically be named
    Macintosh HD.

    Notice the options available to perform on volumes: First Aid,
    Erase, RAID, and Restore.

4   Quit Disk Utility to return to the Installer.

## Password Reset Utility

The Password Reset Utility on the Mac OS X Install DVD can be
used to reset passwords after booting from the disc. At this time,
you have not created any user accounts, but the System Administrator account (root) still exists. You will examine this feature
without actually changing any passwords.

1   Choose Utilities > Reset Password.

2   Select the boot volume on your hard drive, typically named Macintosh HD.

Under "Select the user account," notice that "System Administrator (root)" is selected in the pop-up menu. If you were to reset a user's password, you would choose the user from the pop-up menu and then enter their password, confirm their password, optionally provide a password hint, and then click Save.

The Reset Password utility also allows you to correct home folder permissions for the selected user. You would do this by clicking the Reset button at the bottom of the window.

3   Return to the Installer by quitting Reset Password.

## Continue the Initial Installation Steps

Now you will proceed through the rest of the Installer screens, but you will not perform the installation. You do not want to reinstall the operating system. By going through the following steps, you can experience the configuration of an installation without actually waiting for the Mac OS X software to be copied to your system.

1   In the Install Mac OS X introductory screen, click Continue.

You will walk through the start of the installation process, but you will not install the operating system. That has already been done for you.

The Software License Agreement sheet slides down from the top of the window.

2   Click Agree.

3   The next screen prompts you to "Select the disk where you want to install Mac OS X." Select the icon that represents your disk drive (usually labeled Macintosh HD).

4   Click Customize.

The Customize button lets you choose which packages will be
installed. If the target disk is blank, the Installer will perform
a simple installation. If Mac OS X is already on the disk, the
Installer will install the version of Mac OS X that is on the install
disc. This is similar to the Archive and Install feature that existed
in earlier versions of Mac OS X.

By default, only parts of Printer Support are installed.
Specifically, Printers Used by This Mac and Nearby and Popular
Printers will be installed. If you want to install All Available
Printers, you will need to make the appropriate selection here.

Also note that, by default, all Language Translations are
installed and Rosetta and QuickTime 7 are not installed. If later
you attempt to open an application that requires Rosetta or
QuickTime 7, the system will attempt to fetch it from Software
Update for you.

5   Click OK.

> **Note**  Do not click the Install button; otherwise the Installer
> will install Mac OS X, which you do not want to do at this time.

6   Quit the Installer by choosing Quit Mac OS X Installer from the
Mac OS X Installer menu.

7   In the dialog, click Restart.

The computer will reboot.

8   If you booted from an optical disc, eject the Mac OS X Install
DVD after the computer has finished booting.

# 1.2  Configuring and Updating Mac OS X

The initial Mac OS X configuration is made very simple thanks to the Setup Assistant. However, in this lesson you will learn how a few of these initial configurations have a fundamental and widespread effect on the system. In this lesson you will also be introduced to a few tools that you will use throughout this training for both administrative and troubleshooting purposes: System Preferences, System Profiler, and Console. Finally, you will explore and apply methods for updating your Mac with the latest Apple software.

## Setup Assistant

Welcome & select country

Keyboard language

Migration Assistant *

Network configuration **

Your Internet connection **

Bind to Mac server **

Apple ID & registration info *

Account creation

Account picture

MobileMe subscription **

Select time zone & time **

### Create Your Account

Enter a name and password to create your user account. You need this password to administer your computer, change settings, and install software.

Full Name:  Client Administrator
Account Name:  cadmin
            This will be used as the name for your home folder and can't be changed.
Password:  ••••••••••••
Verify:  ••••••••••••
Password Hint:

Enter a hint to help you remember your password. Anyone can use the hint, so choose a hint that won't make it easy to guess your password.

( Go Back )  ( Continue )

* Steps that can be skipped

** Steps that may not appear, can also be skipped

For detailed instructions, see "Initial Mac OS X Setup" in Chapter 1 of *Apple Training Series: Mac OS X Support Essentials v10.6.*

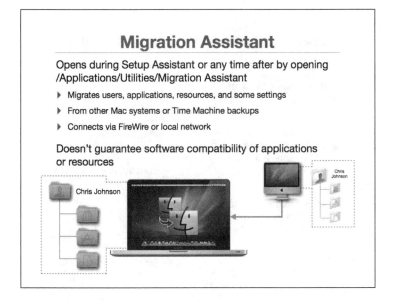

For detailed instructions, see "Initial Mac OS X Setup" in Chapter 1 of *Apple Training Series: Mac OS X Support Essentials v10.6.*

For detailed instructions, see "Configure Mac OS X" in Chapter 1 of *Apple Training Series: Mac OS X Support Essentials v10.6.*

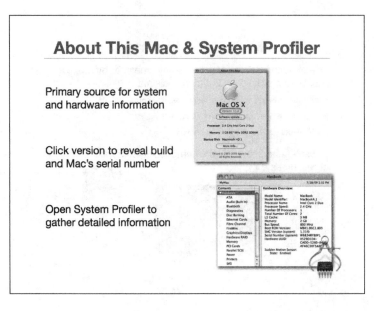

For detailed instructions, see "Configure Mac OS X" in Chapter 1 of *Apple Training Series: Mac OS X Support Essentials v10.6.*

For detailed instructions, see "Install Software and Updates" in Chapter 1 of *Apple Training Series: Mac OS X Support Essentials v10.6.*

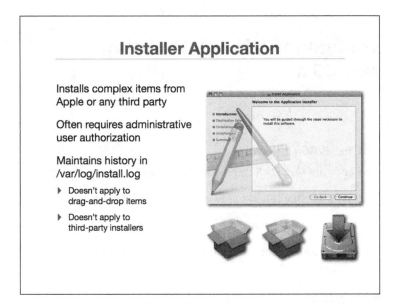

For detailed instructions, see "Install Software and Updates" in
Chapter 1 of *Apple Training Series: Mac OS X Support Essentials v10.6.*

## View Logs via Console

Mac OS X provides feedback via logs

Console monitors messages as they happen

Keep Console open to continually monitor

For detailed instructions, see "Install Software and Updates" in
Chapter 1 of *Apple Training Series: Mac OS X Support Essentials v10.6.*

Exercise 1.2.1

# Configuring a New Installation of Mac OS X

## Objectives

- Configure Mac OS X using Setup Assistant

- Configure sharing and network interfaces for class use

- Use Software Update to check for updates to Mac OS X

- Download Student Materials from the classroom server

## Summary

In this exercise you will configure a clean installation of Mac OS X on your class computer. Configuring Mac OS X for this class entails answering a few basic questions, setting up the initial administrator user account, and configuring several preferences. Completing these tasks will acquaint you with the Setup Assistant application; the Sharing, Network, and Accounts panes of System Preferences; the Finder's Connect to Server command; and an Apple installer.

## Configure Mac OS X with Setup Assistant

The following steps will walk you through the basic setup of Mac OS X using the Setup Assistant:

1   In the Welcome screen, select the appropriate region and click Continue.

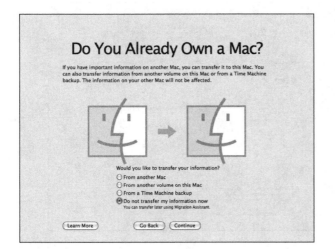

2   In the Select Your Keyboard screen, select the appropriate keyboard layout and click Continue.

3   In the "Do You Already Own a Mac?" screen, select "Do not transfer my information now" and click Continue.

    If you were replacing a computer, the other options would assist you in migrating user data and system information from the old computer to the new one.

    The Setup Assistant will evaluate your network environment and try to determine if you are connected to the Internet. This can take a few moments.

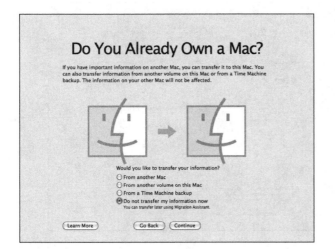

4   If asked about Your Internet Connection, choose "Using DHCP for the TCP/IP Connection Type." If you are asked about Wireless Networks, please ask your instructor how you should configure your computer.

5   If asked to Enter Your Apple ID, do not enter anything and click Continue.

6   When asked for Registration Information, click Continue.

A dialog sheet opens informing you that some of your registration information is missing.

7   Click Continue.

Your computer discovers the classroom server (mainserver.
pretendco.com) and offers to allow you to bind to it.

8   In the Connect to Mac OS X Server window, ensure "Use the
following Mac OS X Server" is not selected and click Continue.

9   In the Create Your Account screen, enter the following information:

> **Note**  It is important that you create this account as specified
> here. If you do not, future exercises may not work as written.
> Highlighted text is used throughout this guide to indicate
> text that you should enter exactly as shown.

- Full Name: `Client Administrator`
- Account Name: `cadmin`
- Password: `cadmin`
- Verify: `cadmin`
- Password Hint: Not Required

**Create Your Account**

Enter a name and password to create your user account. You need this password to administer your computer, change settings, and install software.

Full Name: Client Administrator

Account Name: cadmin

This will be used as the name for your home folder and can't be changed.

Password: ••••••

Verify: ••••••

Password Hint:

Enter a hint to help you remember your password. Anyone can see the hint, so choose a hint that won't make it easy to guess your password.

Go Back   Continue

10 Click Continue.

The assistant does not advance and places an exclamation point badge next to the password hint. It is trying to encourage you to give a password hint. Notice that the assistant tells you that password hints can be viewed by anyone. For that reason, more security-conscious environments will not want to provide password hints.

11 Click Continue again.

This time the assistant creates your account.

The assistant will ask you to Select a Picture for This Account. If your computer has an available camera, you can take a snapshot.

12 Either take a snapshot or select a picture from the library and then click Continue.

13 If offered a free trial of MobileMe, select "I don't want to try MobileMe for free right now" and click Continue.

14 In the Select Time Zone screen, choose your correct time zone. Once your time zone is selected, choose the nearest location from the pop-up menu.

If your classroom has Internet access, you can select "Set time zone automatically using current location" and the system will attempt to discover which time zone you are in.

15 Click Continue.

16 If you are presented with the Thank You screen, click Go. If you
are reminded to register, click the Done button to continue.

## Set the Computer Name

Because every student has entered the same account name
information, all student computers have the same computer name.
To distinguish your computer on the network, you need to set a
unique computer name. Mac OS X will not allow duplicate local
host names, so you may see an error message indicating your local
host name has been incremented from "Client-Administrators-
*computer model*.local" to "Client-Administrators-*computer model-n*.
local," where *n* is a unique number based on when you configured
your computer relative to other students. You will also set a local
host name associated with your student number.

1 If any dialogs open asking, "Do you want to use <some
volume> to back up with Time Machine?" click Don't Use in
each such dialog.

> **Do you want to use "Mac OS X Install DVD" to back up with Time Machine?**
>
> Time Machine keeps an up-to-date copy of everything on your Mac. It not only
> keeps a spare copy of every file, it remembers how your system looked, so you
> can revisit your Mac as it appeared in the past.
>
> (?)     ( Decide Later )          ( Don't Use )  ( Use as Backup Disk )

2 Open System Preferences by clicking its icon in the Dock.

3  Click Sharing in System Preferences.

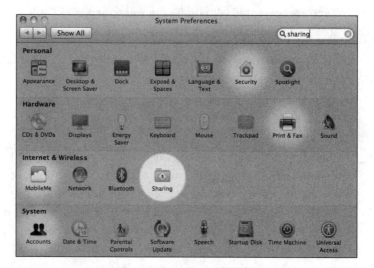

4  Set the Computer Name text field to `clientn`, replacing *n* with your student number. For example, if your student number is 17, the computer name should be client17, all lowercase letters and no spaces, as shown in the following image.

5   Press the Return key.

Notice that your local host name (.local name) displayed under your computer name updates to match your new computer name.

6   Select the Remote Management checkbox.

A dialog sheet slides down from the toolbar asking you what you want users to be able to do using Remote Management.

7   Hold down the Option key while clicking the checkbox next to Observe. This should select all the options in the dialog.

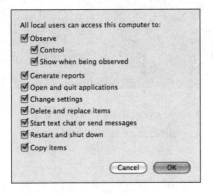

8   Click OK.

> **Note**  By selecting Remote Management and all subsequent checkboxes, you are allowing your instructor to control the keyboard and mouse, gather information, and update your Mac throughout this course, enabling him or her to assist you with steps and exercises if necessary.

9   Click Show All to return to the main System Preferences view.

## Turn Off All Interfaces Except Ethernet

Your computer configuration might have additional network interfaces, such as an extra Ethernet connector or an AirPort Card. You should disable these interfaces for this course. This will prevent possible confusion as we look at networking and other features of the operating system.

1   In System Preferences, click the Network icon.

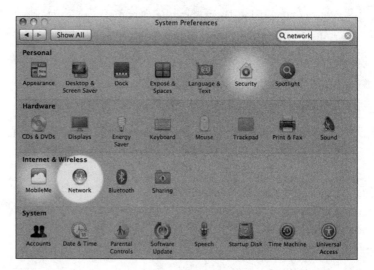

2   Look at the list of network services on the left. Verify that Ethernet has a green status indicator next to it, and says Connected.

3  For each service in the list after (not including) Ethernet:

   a.  Select the service in the service source list.

   b.  From the Action (gear) menu below the service list, choose Make Service Inactive.

```
Duplicate Service...
Rename Service...
Make Service Inactive

Set Service Order...

Import Configurations...
Export Configurations...

Manage Virtual Interfaces...
```

4  If you made any changes, save them by clicking Apply.

5  Select the Ethernet service.

6   Verify that your Ethernet network service is configured to use DHCP to obtain an IP address.

7   Quit System Preferences.

Exercise 1.2.2
# Installing Apple Updates

## Objectives

- Download Student Materials from classroom server

- Install a package

- Understand how to work with Software Update

## Summary

In this exercise you will download the student materials required for the rest of the exercises in the course. You will also install a package and then install software updates using the Software Update service. Your instructor will tell you if any updates are available. Your instructor may give you alternative directions for installing updates, depending on your classroom environment.

## Download the Student Materials from the Classroom File Server

You will now connect to the classroom file server (called mainserver) to download the student materials. The details of networking, connecting to, and providing network services will be covered in later chapters.

1   If necessary, open a new Finder window. You can do this by choosing File > New Finder Window or typing Command-N.

    Notice the mainserver in the shared section of the sidebar (under SHARED). If mainserver is not shown, click All to view all the shared items.

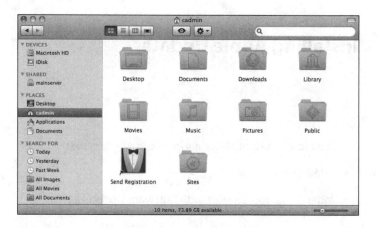

2  Select mainserver. If you had to click All in the previous step, you will have to double-click the mainserver icon.

3  Double-click on the Public folder.

4  Open a second Finder window (Command-N).

5  In the new Finder window, click Macintosh HD in the sidebar on the left.

6  Open the Users folder.

7  Open the Shared folder.

8  Drag the StudentMaterials folder from mainserver's Public share point (the first Finder window) to /Users/Shared (the second Finder window).

   This will create a copy of the student materials on your computer. If your instructor has included software updates in the student materials, it may take several minutes to download them.

9  After copying is complete, unmount mainserver by selecting it in the sidebar and choosing File > Eject (Command-E).

   You may want to drag the StudentMaterials folder to the Finder's sidebar in the Places section. You will be accessing the StudentMaterials folder frequently and this will give you an easy shortcut to it.

## Install Software Updates (Package Install Method)

If your instructor has chosen to distribute any available software updates as part of the student materials, you will need to follow these steps to install them. Your instructor will tell you if you need to do this.

1   In the Finder, open the Mac OS X Updates folder inside the StudentMaterials folder.

2   For each software update your instructor says should be installed (your instructor may additionally specify an order in which they should be installed):

   a.   Double-click the disk image file.

         After a short while a new volume will mount on the desktop. It contains the update package.

   b.   Double-click on the new volume and then double-click on the update package to install it.

   c.   Authenticate as Client Administrator again. Software updates require administrative privileges to install.

   d.   When each update has installed, click Done or Restart as appropriate.

3   Repeat these steps until all of the updates have been installed.

## Install Software Updates (Software Update Server Method)

If your instructor has chosen to distribute any available software updates through the classroom software update server, you will need to follow these steps to install them. Your instructor will tell you if you need to do this.

1   In the Chapter1 folder of the student materials, select the file ConfigureSUS.command.

2   Press the Space bar.

This will open the file in a preview mode called Quick Look. This file is a small shell script (a built-in way of automating tasks). It will run a couple of commands to configure your computer to use the classroom software update server. Previewing the file in Quick Look will not run those commands.

```
#!/bin/bash

# the sudo defaults write portion sets the preference for the location of the
# software update server.  The rest is just dressing to make it work.

echo "cadmin" | sudo -S /usr/bin/defaults write /Library/Preferences/com.apple.SoftwareUpdate CatalogURL "http://
mainserver.pretendco.com:8088/index-leopard-snowleopard.merged-1.sucatalog"
```

3  Press the Space bar again to quit Quick Look.

4  Open the ConfigureSUS.command file by double-clicking it.

   The Terminal application opens and the script is run.

5  When the command is finished, quit Terminal.

6  From the Apple menu, choose Software Update.

7  Your instructor will give you a list of updates to install. Select all of the updates he or she specifies and deselect any other updates.

8  Click Install.

9  If you are prompted to restart, do so.

You may need to do this procedure several times. Your instructor will tell you if this is necessary and which updates to install each time.

# 2

# User Accounts

# 2.1 Managing User Accounts

Mac OS X v10.6 delivers a robust, secure, and highly polished multiple-user environment. Mac OS X's UNIX foundation is primarily responsible for providing such a sophisticated multiple-user environment. In this lesson, you will explore the fundamental technologies that allow individuals to log in and use the Macintosh. You will learn how to recognize various user account types and user attributes. Further, you will learn how to create and manage multiple user accounts in Mac OS X.

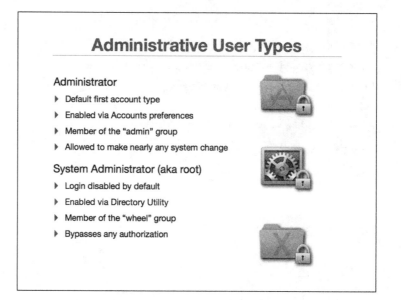

### Administrative User Types

**Administrator**
▸ Default first account type
▸ Enabled via Accounts preferences
▸ Member of the "admin" group
▸ Allowed to make nearly any system change

**System Administrator (aka root)**
▸ Login disabled by default
▸ Enabled via Directory Utility
▸ Member of the "wheel" group
▸ Bypasses any authorization

For detailed instructions, see "Understanding User Accounts" in Chapter 2 of *Apple Training Series: Mac OS X Support Essentials v10.6.*

## Restricted User Types

**Standard**

▸ Safest option for general use

▸ Can open most applications

▸ Cannot make system changes

**Guest (aka everyone)**

▸ Enabled by default for file sharing

▸ Optionally enabled for login

▸ Automatically deleted home folder

**Sharing**

▸ Created for file sharing

▸ No home folder, thus no login

For detailed instructions, see "Understanding User Accounts" in Chapter 2 of *Apple Training Series: Mac OS X Support Essentials v10.6.*

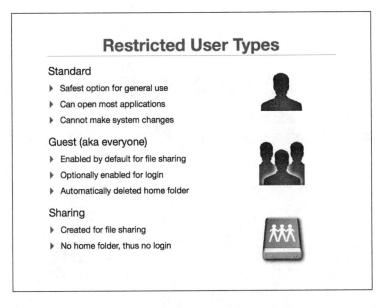

## Creating User Accounts

For detailed instructions, see "Managing User Accounts" in Chapter 2 of *Apple Training Series: Mac OS X Support Essentials v10.6.*

For detailed instructions, see "Managing User Accounts" in Chapter 2 of *Apple Training Series: Mac OS X Support Essentials v10.6.*

For detailed instructions, see "Managing User Accounts" in Chapter 2 of *Apple Training Series: Mac OS X Support Essentials v10.6.*

For detailed instructions, see "Managing User Accounts" in Chapter 2 of *Apple Training Series: Mac OS X Support Essentials v10.6*.

For detailed instructions, see "Managing User Accounts" in Chapter 2 of *Apple Training Series: Mac OS X Support Essentials v10.6*.

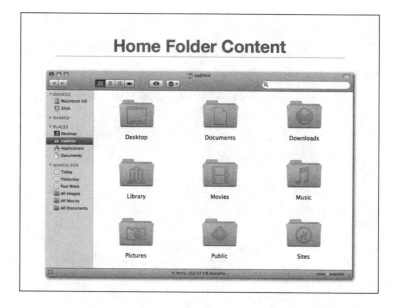

For detailed instructions, see "Managing User Home Folders" in
Chapter 2 of *Apple Training Series: Mac OS X Support Essentials v10.6*.

For detailed instructions, see "Managing User Home Folders" in
Chapter 2 of *Apple Training Series: Mac OS X Support Essentials v10.6*.

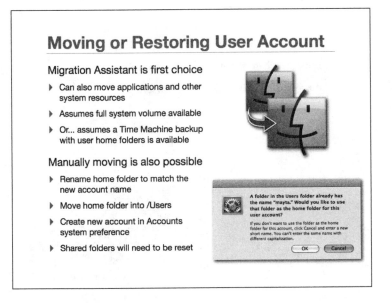

For detailed instructions, see "Managing User Home Folders" in Chapter 2 of *Apple Training Series: Mac OS X Support Essentials v10.6.*

For detailed instructions, see "Login Options and Fast User Switching" in Chapter 2 of *Apple Training Series: Mac OS X Support Essentials v10.6.*

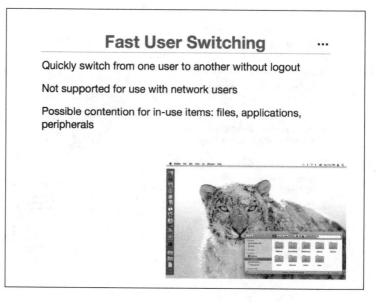

For detailed instructions, see "Login Options and Fast User Switching" in Chapter 2 of *Apple Training Series: Mac OS X Support Essentials v10.6*.

## Exercise 2.1.1
# Creating User Accounts

## Objective

- Create and test a standard user account

## Summary

You already created an administrator account during the initial configuration of your computer. You will now be creating additional accounts to gain a better understanding of the user experience. The first user account will be a standard user. It is a best practice to use a standard user account for your day-to-day use. The Client Administrator account should only be used for system administration tasks such as software installation and system configuration.

## Creating a Standard User Account

These steps will guide you through account creation.

1   Open System Preferences and click Accounts. It may be necessary to unlock the Accounts pane by clicking the Lock button and authenticating as the admin user.

2   Click the New User button (+) beneath the accounts list and enter the following information:

a.   New Account: Standard

b.   Full Name: `Chris Johnson`

c.   Account Name: `chris`

d.   Password: `chris`

e.   Verify: `chris`

Do not select "Turn on FileVault protection." Do not provide a
password hint. Click the Create Account button.

3   When prompted that automatic login is turned on, click Turn
Off Automatic Login.

4   Verify that Chris's account is selected in the account list.

5   Click the Picture button (the "image well" next to the Reset Password button) and select a picture from the menu that pops up.

## Test the New User Account

You will now log in to Chris's user account to verify that it was created correctly.

1   Choose Log Out Client Administrator from the Apple menu.

2   In the dialog asking if you are sure, click Log Out.

3   In the login window, select Chris Johnson and enter the password you entered above (chris).

4   Click the Log In button.

    You are now logged in as Chris Johnson.

5   Open System Preferences and then click the Desktop & Screen Saver icon to open that preference pane.

6   Select a desktop picture from the Plants collection.

7  Click the Show All button and then open the Accounts preferences.

Mac OS X defaults to a one-button mouse configuration. To access contextual menus and the like, hold down the Control key while clicking the single mouse or trackpad button. If your computer has a trackpad, you may be able to enable a couple of secondary click options using Trackpad preferences. If you have a recent Apple mouse, you can enable Right Clicking using Mouse preferences. If you have a third-party multibutton mouse, the right mouse button probably already works as a right click.

8  Click the Lock button in the bottom-left corner and then authenticate as Client Administrator (you can use either the Full Name or the Account Name cadmin) to unlock the Accounts preferences. This will allow you to make changes to accounts while remaining logged in as Chris.

9  Control-click Chris's account and choose Advanced Options from the pop-up menu.

Record the following:

a.  User: _____

b.  User ID:_____

c.  Group: _____

d.  Account name: _____

e.  Login shell:_____

f.  Home directory: _____

g.  UUID: _____

10 When you're done, click Cancel. It is always a good idea to cancel a settings dialog when you have not made changes to it.

11 Log out.

Exercise 2.1.2

# Restoring a Deleted User Account

## Objective

- Restore files from a deleted user's home folder that has been saved as a disk image

## Summary

You will create a user account and populate the home folder for the user. Then you will delete the account, preserving the contents of the home folder. Finally, you will create a new account, ensuring that the new user gets the old user's home folder contents. HR asked you to create an account for Marta Mishtuk. Her real name is Mayta Mishtuk, so you'll need to fix their error. Besides illustrating how to restore a deleted user account, this technique can also be used for changing a user's short name.

## Creating Marta Mishtuk's Home Folder

You will create an account and a home folder for Marta Mishtuk.

1  Log in as the Client Administrator (cadmin).

2  Open Accounts preferences in System Preferences.

3  Click the lock icon to authenticate as Client Administrator.

4  Create a new user account for Marta Mishtuk:

   a. New Account: Standard

   b. Full Name: `Marta Mishtuk`

   c. Account Name: `marta`

   d. Password: `marta`

   e. Verify: `marta`

   Do not provide a password hint. Do not select "Turn on FileVault protection." Click the Create Account button.

5  Control-click Marta's account and choose Advanced Options from the pop-up menu.

Record the following:

a.  User:_____

b.  User ID:_____

c.  Group: _____

d.  Account name: _____

e.  Login shell:_____

f.  Home directory: _____

g.  UUID: _____

6  Cancel the Advanced Options dialog sheet.

7  Log out as Client Administrator.

8  Log in as Marta Mishtuk (marta).

9  Open TextEdit from the Applications folder.

10 In the Untitled document, enter the text "This is Mayta's project document." ("Mayta" is not a typo.)

11 Save the file to Marta's desktop with the filename Project.

12 Log out.

## Deleting Marta's Account

You will delete Marta's account, preserving her home folder in a disk image file. A disk image is like a virtual floppy disk. It is a file that contains a file system.

1  Log in as the Client Administrator.

2  Open Accounts preferences in System Preferences. Unlock the preference pane, if necessary.

3  Delete Marta's account by clicking on her name and then clicking the (-) button.

4   In the "Are you sure you want to delete the user account 'Marta Mishtuk'?" dialog, select "Save the home folder in a disk image" and click OK.

The computer pauses briefly while it copies Marta's home folder into a disk image.

## Restoring Marta's Account for Mayta

Marta's files (actually Mayta's) have been preserved in a disk image. Now you need to copy them to Mayta's new home folder so that when the new account is created she gets her old (the Marta account's) files.

1   Create a folder named "mayta" on the Desktop.

You can do this from the Desktop's contextual menu or by clicking the desktop and choosing New Folder from the Finder's File menu. Then type the name of the folder and press Return.

**50**

2   Drag the mayta folder into the Users folder. You can find the
    Users folder in a Finder window by clicking Macintosh HD in the
    Finder's sidebar and then double-clicking Users.

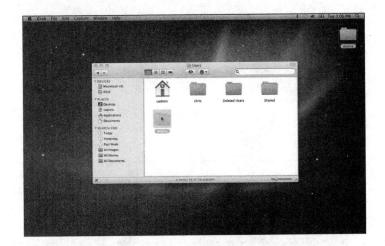

3   You are given a notice that the folder cannot be moved. Click
    Authenticate and authenticate as the Client Administrator.

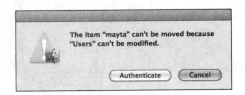

4   Verify that there is now a folder called mayta in the Users folder.

5   In the Finder, choose New Finder Window from the File menu.
    In the new window, click Macintosh HD in the sidebar. Then
    open the Users folder and open the Deleted Users folder inside
    Users. You should see marta.dmg in Deleted Users.

6  Open the marta.dmg disk image file in the Deleted Users.

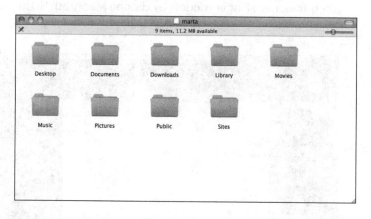

7  Drag the contents of the mounted image marta into the mayta folder you created in the Users folder.

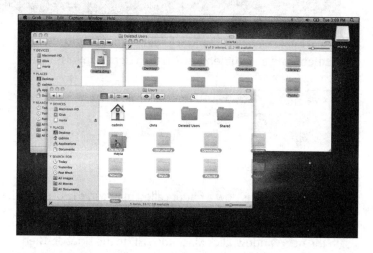

8  Open the Desktop folder inside the new mayta folder so you can see Mayta's Project document (Project.rtf if filename extensions are visible).

9   After verifying that Mayta's documents are in place, unmount the marta volume from the desktop by clicking the eject icon next to its icon in the sidebar or by ejecting it from the Desktop.

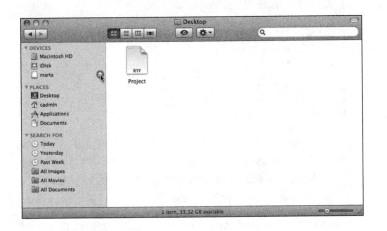

## Creating and Verifying Mayta Mishtuk's Account

You will now create the Mayta Mishtuk user account, using the restored home folder as the new account's home folder.

1   If necessary, open System Preferences and click Accounts. Authenticate if necessary.

2   Click the New User button (+) to create another account:

   a.  New Account: Standard

   b.  Full Name: `Mayta Mishtuk`

   c.  Account Name: `mayta`

   d.  Password: `mayta`

   e.  Verify: `mayta`

   Do not select "Turn on FileVault protection." Do not provide a password hint. Click the Create Account button.

3 A dialog appears that asks if you would like to use "mayta" as the home folder for this user account. Click OK.

> **A folder in the Users folder already has the name "mayta." Would you like to use that folder as the home folder for this user account?**
>
> If you don't want to use the folder as the home folder for this account, click Cancel and enter a new short name. You can't enter the same name with different capitalization.
>
> OK    Cancel

4 Control-click Mayta's account and choose Advanced Options from the pop-up menu. Notice that Mayta's UUID is different from Marta's, which you recorded under "Creating Marta Mishtuk's Home Folder." The User ID may not have changed.

5 Try to open the Desktop folder in Mayta's home folder now. If your Finder window was still displaying the Desktop folder, click on Documents and then click on Desktop again. You no longer have permission because the files are now owned by Mayta's new account.

6 Log out as the Client Administrator and log in as mayta.

7 In the "The system was unable to unlock your login keychain" dialog, click "Continue log in." We will look at this feature shortly.

8 Verify that the Project file is on the desktop.

9 Log out of the Mayta account.

Exercise 2.1.3
# Fast User Switching

## Objectives

- Enable fast user switching

- Understand the effects of having two users logged in at the same time

## Summary

In this exercise you will enable fast user switching and switch between two users. You will observe that there can be resource contention issues between users.

1   Log in as Client Administrator. Then open System Preferences and select Accounts. Authenticate as necessary.

2   Click Login Options.

3   Check "Show fast user switching menu as" and ensure Name is selected in the pop-up list.

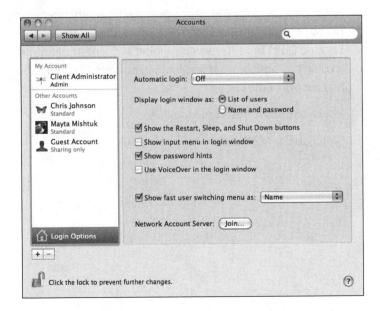

4  Quit System Preferences.

5  From the Applications folder, launch QuickTime Player.

6  From QuickTime Player's File menu, choose New Screen Recording.

You will begin recording video of your screen and then switch to chris's account to see what happens.

7  In the Screen Recording window, click the record button (white circle with a red dot in the center). In the dialog sheet that opens, click Start Recording.

8  Use Fast User Switching to switch to chris's account.

9  Use Fast User Switching to switch back to cadmin's account.

QuickTime Player will open the movie file to which it captured the screen.

10  In the Screen Recording.mov window, click the play button that appears in a box in the lower portion of the window.

Notice that QuickTime Player captured what was happening on the screen up to the point at which you authenticated as chris. Because QuickTime Player was running as Client Administrator, it could not capture what was happening once Chris Johnson had control of the screen.

11  Switch to Chris Johnson and log out.

12  Switch to Client Administrator and log out.

# User Account Security

# 2.2

Again, Mac OS X's UNIX foundation is primarily responsible for providing a secure multiple-user environment. However, there are also some uniquely Mac security mechanisms in place that help your users maintain security. In this lesson you will learn about the various password types used in Mac OS X, and you will learn several methods for resetting these passwords. You'll also learn about protecting a user's home folder using FileVault. Finally, you will explore and manage the Keychain system for storing users' important secrets, like saved resource passwords.

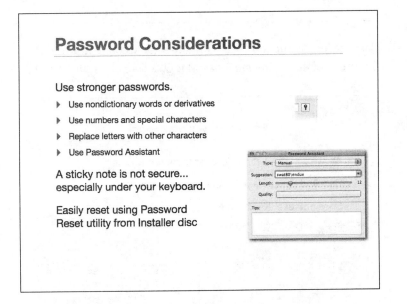

For detailed instructions, see "Using Password Assistant" in Chapter 2 of *Apple Training Series: Mac OS X Support Essentials v10.6.*

## Password Types

**Account**
▶ User login and primary authentication

**Master Password**
▶ Resets local account passwords

**Keychain**
▶ Secures access to saved secrets

**Resource Password**
▶ General use, can be saved to keychains

**Firmware**
▶ Secures system during startup

For detailed instructions, see "Fundamental Account Security" in Chapter 2 of *Apple Training Series: Mac OS X Support Essentials v10.6.*

## Master Password

Allows you to reset any local account passwords

Required by interface to set up local FileVault accounts

Does not reset Keychain Access

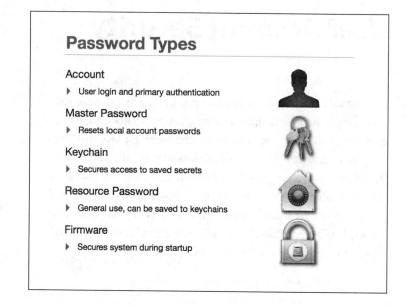

For detailed instructions, see "Understanding Password Types" in Chapter 2 of *Apple Training Series: Mac OS X Support Essentials v10.6.*

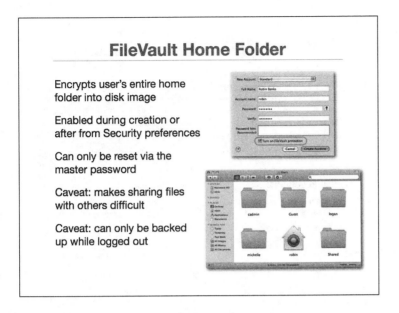

For detailed instructions, see "Using FileVault Accounts" in Chapter 2 of *Apple Training Series: Mac OS X Support Essentials v10.6.*

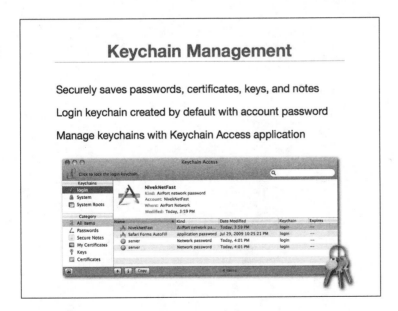

For detailed instructions, see "Managing Keychains" in Chapter 2 of *Apple Training Series: Mac OS X Support Essentials v10.6.*

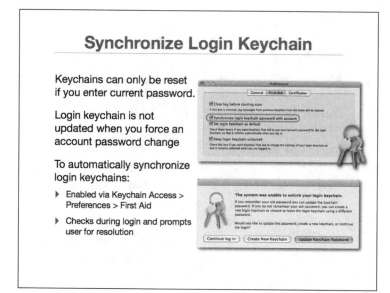

For detailed instructions, see "Resetting Account Passwords" in Chapter 2 of *Apple Training Series: Mac OS X Support Essentials v10.6*.

For detailed instructions, see "Understanding Password Types" in Chapter 2 of *Apple Training Series: Mac OS X Support Essentials v10.6*.

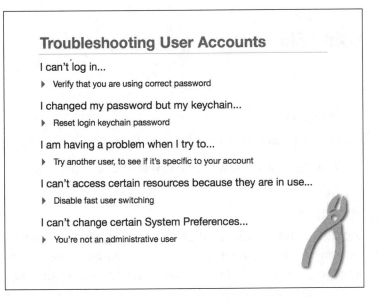

**Troubleshooting User Accounts**

I can't log in...

▶ Verify that you are using correct password

I changed my password but my keychain...

▶ Reset login keychain password

I am having a problem when I try to...

▶ Try another user, to see if it's specific to your account

I can't access certain resources because they are in use...

▶ Disable fast user switching

I can't change certain System Preferences...

▶ You're not an administrative user

For detailed instructions, see "Resetting Account Passwords" in Chapter 2 of *Apple Training Series: Mac OS X Support Essentials v10.6.*

Exercise 2.2.1

# Using FileVault

## Objectives

- Enable FileVault and set the master password

- Create a user account with an encrypted home folder

## Summary

Encrypting a folder increases the level of security for a user's files. This can keep the data in that folder secure if the computer is ever stolen, or prevent access to an account even if the login password is changed using the Install DVD.

In this exercise you will set the master password for the computer and then enable FileVault for a new user, Robin Banks. FileVault securely encrypts and decrypts the contents of your home folder while you use it.

## Set the Master Password

The master password helps when passwords are forgotten. Setting a master password is required in order to enable FileVault. If a user forgets their login password, the master password provides a quick way to reset the user's password and still allow them access to their encrypted home folder. When used with FileVault, entering the master password allows the user to access their information even though their login password is forgotten. Otherwise the data stored in the FileVault-encrypted account would be lost forever. You will do this as Chris Johnson, a normal user, to illustrate that normal users can perform administrative functions as long as they have administrator credentials available to them.

1   Log in as Chris Johnson, open System Preferences, and click Security.

2   Click the FileVault button.

3   Click Set Master Password.

4   Authenticate as Client Administrator when requested.

5   Enter the password as: `apple#main`

6   In the verify field type: `apple#main`

7   Do not provide a password hint. Click OK.

You have now set the computer's master password.

> **Note**  The master password is set for the computer. You can change it later by clicking Change in the Security pane.

## Create and Encrypt a Home Folder

To encrypt a home folder using FileVault, create a new user with an encrypted home folder.

1   In System Preferences, click Show All, and then click the Accounts icon.

2   Unlock the Accounts pane, if necessary, authenticating as Client Administrator.

3   Create a new user, Robin Banks (Short Name: robin, Password: robin).

4   Select the Turn on FileVault protection checkbox.

If you are using a desktop computer (Mac Mini, iMac, or Mac Pro), you will get an additional option to "Use secure virtual memory." Select that checkbox as well.

Secure virtual memory is on by default on notebook computers and off by default on desktop computers.

5   Click Create Account.

A progress indicator (looks like a spinning gear) indicates that Robin's home folder is being created and encrypted.

## Verify the Home Folder Encryption

Once a home folder is encrypted, its contents are inaccessible unless the owner of the folder logs in. Do the following to verify that the system encrypted Robin's home folder:

1   Log out as chris and log in as Client Administrator.

2   Navigate to the Users folder.

3   You will see the No Access indicator on Robin's home folder.

4   Log out as Client Administrator and log in as Robin.

5  Navigate to Robin's home folder.

Notice that the contents of the home folder display normally. FileVault encryption is transparent to the end user. The home folder icon in the sidebar shows a security icon to indicate the encrypted status for Robin's home folder.

6  Using Fast User Switching, switch to Client Administrator.

7  Navigate to the Users folder.

8  Notice Robin's home folder now appears as an alias of the folder. Double-click it. You still have no access to her home folder.

9  Switch users to Robin Banks and log out.

Notice that when logging out, the system recovers disk space used by her account.

10  Switch to Client Administrator and log out.

Exercise 2.2.2
# Password Management

## Objectives

- Reset a user's password
- Understand how password resets affect user keychains
- Use the Password Assistant

## Summary

In this exercise you will reset a user password first from the administrator account, then from the user's account, and note the implications for the user's keychain. You will use the Keychain Access utility to resolve the issues arising from the user password being reset while the user's keychain password remained unchanged. After completing these tasks you will be acquainted with the distinctions between the user password and the keychain password, how these two passwords can get out of sync, and some ways to fix synchronization issues. Finally, you will reset a user's password using the master password and change the master password to see the effect of changing it on FileVault users.

## Reset User Passwords as an Administrator

While any administrator account can change another user's account password, this will not change that user's original keychain password. To experience changing a standard user's password from an administrator account, you will change Chris's password from the Client Administrator account.

1   Log in as Chris Johnson.

2   Choose Connect to Server from the Go menu in the Finder.

3  Enter mainserver.pretendco.com and click Connect.

4  Ensure Registered User is selected for "Connect as" and enter the following information:

   a.  Name: studentn (where *n* is your student number)

   b.  Password: student

   c.  Select "Remember this password in my keychain."

> **Note**  Please verify that you have selected "Remember this password in my keychain."

5  Click Connect.

6  Select the volume Public.

7  Disconnect from the server by ejecting mainserver in the Shared section of the Finder's sidebar.

8  Log out of Chris Johnson's user account.

9  Log in using the Client Administrator account.

10 Open the Accounts preferences.

11 Click the lock button and authenticate using the administrator account Client Administrator.

**12** Select the Chris Johnson account and click Reset Password.

The Password Change dialog appears.

The message at the top of the dialog indicates that this will not update the keychain password. You must log in as the user Chris Johnson to synchronize the user password and the keychain password.

> **Note**  You can also reset any user password when booted from the Mac OS X Installer DVD using the Password Reset Utility.

**13** In the New Password and Verify fields type: p4$$w0rd

Use a zero instead of an O.

**14** Click Reset Password.

## Change a User Password from the User Account

Chris has decided that the password created by the Client Administrator is not as secure as he would like it to be. It is standard practice for users to be able to change their assigned passwords to a password of their own. You will use the Chris account to accomplish this change, showing how users can administer their own passwords.

1    Log out of the Client Administrator user account.

2    Log in as user Chris Johnson (new password p4$$w0rd).

     A dialog appears indicating "The system was unable to unlock your login keychain." You will look at this dialog shortly.

3    For now, click "Continue log in."

     This dialog is a new feature of Mac OS X v10.6 and is the result of Chris Johnson's password being changed by an administrator. The administrator didn't have Chris's old keychain password, so the keychain password could not be changed.

4    Change Chris Johnson's password in the Accounts pane of System Preferences by selecting Chris Johnson and then clicking Change Password.

     a.  Enter the old password: p4$$w0rd

     b.  Click the Password Assistant button (key icon).

     c.  In the Password Assistant, change the Length slider to 9.

     d.  Enter the new password: macOS:101

         This password is rated fair and happens to refer to the name of the class. Note the use of the capital letters O and S as well as a punctuation mark and numerals. Password Assistant does not give any tips for this password.

e.  In the Verify field type `macOS:101`

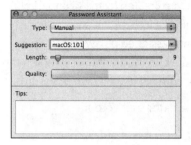

5  Click the Change Password button.

6  When notified that the keychain password will change, click OK.

> **Note**  Because the previous password (p4$$w0rd) did not match the existing keychain password (chris), the keychain password is not updated and Chris is at risk of losing his keychain data. If a user forgets the keychain password when the account and keychain passwords are out of sync, the login keychain cannot be unlocked and items contained in that keychain will be inaccessible until the user remembers the keychain password. There is no password recovery mechanism for keychains.

7  Quit System Preferences.

## Unlock the Login Keychain

When you did the exercise on fast user switching, you should have added an entry to the keychain when you connected to main-server. We are now going to view a keychain password.

1  Still logged in as Chris Johnson, open Keychain Access. It is located in the Utilities folder, which is inside the Applications folder.

In the upper left of the Keychain Access window, you will see a list of keychains. The login keychain is locked because your account password was not the same as your keychain password when you logged in. This is because you changed the password for Chris's account as the Client Administrator. This caused the login password and keychain password to be out of sync. The system was unable to unlock the keychain at login because the account password and keychain password didn't match. The keychain password was not changed when you updated the password from within Chris's account, once again because the account and keychain passwords did not match.

Note also that you can still see which items are on the keychain, even though it is locked. You should have an item for mainserver that you created when you logged into the server earlier. You cannot, however, recover the password unless you unlock the keychain.

2  Your login keychain is locked. Click the lock on the top left to unlock it. You will be prompted for your login keychain password.

3  Enter your original password, `chris`, to unlock your keychain. The lock icon in the toolbar and the lock icon next to the login keychain will open.

> **Note**  At this point you might not be clear about Chris's password state. Here is a summary of what you have done. You will simplify this situation shortly.
>
> `chris` was the original password for the Chris Johnson account. This is still the current keychain password.
>
> `p4$$w0rd` is what the Client Administrator changed Chris's account password to.
>
> `macOS:101` was the password set using the Chris Johnson account, changing it from `p4$$w0rd`. This is the current account password.

## Reset the Keychain Password

In some cases, the keychain password might not be the same as the login password. This often happens when a user has multiple keychain files, or if an administrator changes a user's password. If a user's password is changed because the user forgot the password, the user's keychain data will not be accessible. If the user later remembers the password, the user can unlock the keychain and reset the password to match the login password. There are three ways to reset the password: The first two are through the use of Keychain Access, the third is through the dialog you saw when Chris first logged in after Client Administrator reset the password. All three techniques basically reduce to a) provide the old password and b) reset it to the new password. A keychain cannot be recovered without its current password.

1  Still logged in as Chris Johnson, in Keychain Access, verify that the login keychain is unlocked.

2  Choose Edit > Change Password for Keychain "login."

3  In the dialog enter the following information:

  a.  Current Password: `chris`

  b.  New Password: `macOS:101`

  c.  Verify: `macOS:101`

Note that the Password Assistant automatically rates the strength of your password.

4  Click OK to save the new password.

Your keychain password is now synchronized with your login password.

If Chris changes his login password again, the keychain password would also be changed because the login password and the keychain password are now the same.

5  Quit Keychain Access.

## Verify the Synchronization

Use Keychain Access to verify that the login and keychain passwords are in sync.

1 Log out of the Chris Johnson account.

2 Log back into the Chris Johnson account.

   This way you will verify the keychain state after a successful login by Chris.

3 Open Keychain Access from /Applications/Utilities.

   Note that this time, it is unlocked even though you did not unlock it by clicking the lock icon. This is evidence that the passwords are in sync when Chris logs in.

4 Quit Keychain Access.

5 Open System Preferences and go to the Accounts pane.

6 Click Change Password and change Chris's password from macOS:101 to chris once again.

7 Quit System Preferences.

8 Open Keychain Access again.

   Notice that the login keychain is still unlocked.

9 Lock the login keychain by selecting it and then clicking the open padlock icon in the toolbar.

10 Click the lock in the toolbar again to unlock the login keychain.

*Question 1   Which password unlocks the keychain now? Why?*

_____

_____

_____

_____

11 Log out as Chris Johnson.

## Reset a FileVault User's Password with the Master Password

When a FileVault user forgets their password, you can reset it using the master password. This will allow the user to regain access to their files.

1   At the login window, select Robin Banks. Provide an incorrect password (i.e., not robin) for her account three times.

The login window changes to ask for the master password.

2   Enter the master password (apple#main).

A dialog is presented telling you that if you use the master password to reset the user's password, a new login keychain will be created for the user.

3   Click OK. The login window changes again to ask for Robin's new password.

4   Enter banks for both the New Password and Verify Password fields. Do not provide a Password Hint.

5   Click the Log In button.

6   When the "The system was unable to unlock your login key-chain" dialog appears, click Create New Keychain.

As before, this dialog is presented because the account password (banks) doesn't match the keychain password (robin).

7 Open Keychain Access in the Utilities folder.

In the upper-left corner of the Keychain Access window, you see that the login keychain is unlocked. This is a new login keychain and will have no items in it.

8 Log out as Robin Banks.

## Reset the Master Password

The master password allows you to reset a FileVault user's password and preserve their access to their home folder. It can be changed without affecting the FileVault users on the system.

1 Log in as Client Administrator.

2 Open the Security pane of System Preferences.

3 Click the FileVault tab and then click Change to change the master password. Authenticate as necessary.

Enter the current master password (`apple#main`) and the new master password `main#apple`.

4 Click OK.

The master password has been reset. This change is transparent to FileVault users.

5 Log out as Client Administrator.

6 Log in as Robin Banks to verify that nothing has changed for her.

7 Log out when you are done.

# Keychain Management

## Objectives

- Change keychain password so it no longer matches the login password

- Retrieve passwords from a keychain

- Sync the keychain and login passwords

- Create additional keychains

- Use a keychain to store notes securely

- View and edit keychain entries

## Summary

As you've seen, typically a user's keychain password and login password are the same. When you create a user account, the login keychain file is created to store the user's passwords and is secured with their account password. However, in environments where more security is desired, a user can decouple his or her keychain password from his or her login password by using the Keychain Access application to change the login keychain's password. In this case, the user will have to enter the login keychain's password before applications such as Mail and Safari can access stored passwords. The system provides various features to help the user keep their account and keychain passwords synchronized. Users may also create additional keychains. The default storage location for keychains is ~/Library/Keychains (the Keychains folder inside the Library folder in the user's home folder (~)). You can however, put keychains in other locations, too.

In this exercise, you will explore various keychain management techniques.

## Show Keychain Status in the Menu Bar

You will prepare the keychain environment for more advanced users using Keychain Access.

1   Log in as Chris Johnson (chris).

2   Open Keychain Access from the Utilities folder.

3   Open the Keychain Access preferences by selecting Preferences from the Keychain Access menu and then selecting Show Status in Menu Bar.

This places a lock icon in the menu bar, making it more convenient to perform various security-related functions.

Command-, (Command-comma) is a shortcut for Preferences that works in most applications.

4   Select Edit > Change Password for Keychain "login."

5   Enter the current password (chris), a new password (keychain), and verify the new password.

> **Note**  Normally you would want to test the strength of your passwords by clicking the key icon to invoke the Password Assistant. We are using simple passwords in the classroom for academic purposes only.

6   Click OK, then log out and log back in.

Notice that the "The system was unable to unlock your login keychain" dialog did not appear this time. Last time you chose to "Continue log in." The system has remembered this selection and will not present that dialog again when it finds that your account and keychain passwords don't match.

Look at the Keychain menu bar item. Notice that the lock icon appears locked, not open. This means that although you logged in successfully to your account, your keychain did not automatically unlock.

Normally, when the keychain and login passwords are the same, the login keychain unlocks to allow applications to access the passwords stored on it. Because the account and login passwords don't match, Chris will have to enter his login keychain password in order for applications to access stored passwords.

## Retrieve a Password with the Keychain Password

Even though passwords are stored to make them conveniently available for applications, there may be times when a user needs to retrieve a password that has been stored. For example, a user who wants to use webmail on a different computer may want to retrieve his or her email password in order to do so. You will use the keychain to retrieve a forgotten password.

1  Ensure you are logged in as Chris Johnson.

2  Open Keychain Access from /Applications/Utilities.

3  Double-click the mainserver password entry. This entry was created at the beginning of Exercise 2.2.2 when you logged into mainserver and checked the checkbox telling the system to store the credentials in your keychain.

   A mainserver window will appear.

4  In the Attributes pane, select Show Password.

   A dialog informs you that Keychain Access wants to use the "login" keychain. You see this because the keychain is still locked.

5  Enter your login keychain's password (keychain) and click OK.

   Another dialog informs you that Keychain Access wants to use your confidential information stored in mainserver.pretendco. com in your keychain. Even though your keychain is unlocked, you still have to provide the keychain's password to access this item.

   Each item has an access control list associated with it that determines which applications have access to the item.

6   Enter your keychain password (keychain) and click Allow.

Notice that your mainserver password is now visible. This demonstrates how, even if an administrator or other user resets your login password, they would not be able to find your other passwords that are safely stored in your keychain without your original password.

7   Close the mainserver window.

## Sync Keychain Password with Login Password

If you want to resynchronize the login keychain password with the login password, you can use Keychain First Aid to synchronize the two. In addition to the synchronization feature, Keychain First Aid can repair certain application issues with stored passwords, such as when Microsoft Entourage erroneously asks for a password that has previously been stored.

1   Still logged in as Chris Johnson, go to Keychain Access's Preferences, then click First Aid.

2   Select "Synchronize login keychain password with account."

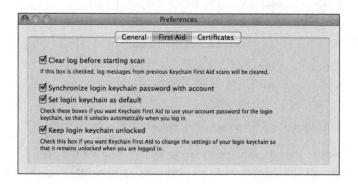

3   Close the Preferences window.

4   Choose Keychain First Aid from the Keychain Access menu.

5   Enter Chris's account password (chris), select Repair, and
    click Start.

6   If asked to provide the keychain password for the login key-
    chain, enter it (keychain) and click OK.

7   Once repair completes, log out.

8   Log in as Chris Johnson, and check the keychain item in the
    menu bar. Note that it now appears unlocked.

## Create Another Keychain

Since the login keychain typically unlocks automatically when a user logs in, all stored passwords are automatically available. However, users may want more security for certain types of stored passwords. In order to increase the security of stored items, create additional keychains for items like web form passwords, secure notes, AirPort network passwords, client site passwords, etc. that may require more security. Storing passwords in separate key-chains requires an additional entry of that keychain's password.

1  Still logged in as Chris Johnson, open Keychain Access and choose New Keychain from the File menu.

2  Save the keychain as Secure Notes and click Create.

3  Set the password as keychain. Normally, you would want to use the password assistant to choose a good, unique password for your new keychain.

The new keychain is added to the Keychains list. It is unlocked.

You can drag items from one keychain to another or create items on your new keychain. When the system tries to use those keychain items, you will need to provide the password for the keychain that contains the item.

## Create a Secure Note in a Keychain

Now that you have a separate keychain for secure notes, create some secure note items. Secure notes are like locked sticky notes for passwords, user names, or any type of information you would want to save on a sticky note, with the addition of keychain security. For example, you could create a secure note to keep track of additional keychain passwords.

1  Ensure you are logged in as Chris Johnson, open Keychain Access, and select the Secure Notes keychain.

2  Unlock the Secure Notes keychain if necessary.

3  Select File > New Secure Note Item.

4  Fill in the Keychain Item Name and Note as follows:

   Keychain Item Name: `Bank PINs`

   Note: `First Bank of Nowhere: 387466`

   When complete, click Add.

5  Lock the Secure Notes Keychain by clicking the lock icon in the toolbar.

6  To retrieve the note, select the Secure Notes keychain, unlock it, and double-click the note item you wish to open in the list.

7  Click the "Show note" checkbox and enter the password when prompted.

8  When you are done viewing the contents, you can relock the keychain by clicking the open lock on the toolbar.

9  Log out.

## Regain Access to a Keychain

A few exercises ago, you had the system create a new keychain for Robin Banks after her password was reset. The system did not delete her old keychain. It simply renamed it. Robin has since remembered her old password and would like access to the contents of her old keychain.

1  Log in as Robin Banks (banks).

2  In the Finder, navigate to <Robin's home folder>/Library/
   Keychains (~/Library/Keychains).

3  Double-click the file login_renamed_1.keychain. This will cause
   Keychain Access to open and login_renamed_1.keychain to be
   available in the Keychains list.

4  Select login_renamed_1 in the list of keychains and click the
   lock in the toolbar.

5  Enter the old password for Robin's account and login keychain
   (robin). Her old keychain unlocks and you could retrieve any

items that were on it. You did not previously place any items on this keychain. You can also use the techniques you have already used to change the password on this keychain.

6  Use System Preferences to change Robin's password back to `robin`.

7  Log out.

# 3

# Command Line and Automation

# 3.1  Command-Line Essentials

You can't expect to truly understand the power of Mac OS X's UNIX foundation without experiencing it firsthand. This lesson will guide you through a formal introduction to the command-line environment. Topics include command-line navigation, file manipulation, and basic text editing. While you will only be scratching the surface of what's possible at the command line, this lesson provides a starting point for those who are new to the command line.

## Why Learn the Command Line?

**Work around limitations**

▶ Many options not in the graphical interface

▶ Bypass Finder restrictions to file system

**Additional administrative access**

▶ Administrators can act as root

▶ Invisible (to the user) remote access via SSH

**Powerful administrative automation**

▶ Built-in automation via simple text scripts

▶ Combine with Apple Remote Desktop to simultaneously send UNIX commands to multiple remote computers

For detailed instructions, see "Command-Line Essentials" in Chapter 3 of *Apple Training Series: Mac OS X Support Essentials v10.6.*

## Access the Command Line

Terminal application

>console at login screen

Single-user mode startup

Remotely via SSH

Default "shell" is /bin/bash

Mac OS X

Name: >console

Password:

Sleep    Restart    Shut Down    Log In

For detailed instructions, see "Command-Line Essentials" in Chapter 3 of *Apple Training Series: Mac OS X Support Essentials v10.6*.

## At the Command Line

Command prompt          Command entry

Terminal — bash — 80×24

```
Last login: Sat Aug  1 14:39:01 on ttys000
MyMac:~ cadmin$ ls -lA
total 48
-rw-------   1 cadmin  staff      3 Jul 29 22:22 .CFUserTextEncoding
-rw-r--r--@  1 cadmin  staff  12292 Aug  1 14:42 .DS_Store
drwx------   2 cadmin  staff     68 Aug  1 14:41 .Trash
-rw-------   1 cadmin  staff    115 Aug  1 16:58 .bash_history
-rw-------   1 cadmin  staff     38 Aug  1 16:58 .lesshst
drwx------+  4 cadmin  staff    136 Jul 31 21:41 Desktop
drwx------+  4 cadmin  staff    136 Jul 29 22:22 Documents
drwx------+  6 cadmin  staff    204 Jul 29 22:25 Downloads
drwx------+ 29 cadmin  staff    986 Jul 29 22:25 Library
drwx------+  3 cadmin  staff    102 Jul 29 22:22 Movies
drwx------+  3 cadmin  staff    102 Jul 29 22:22 Music
drwx------+  4 cadmin  staff    136 Jul 29 22:22 Pictures
drwxr-xr-x+  5 cadmin  staff    170 Jul 29 22:22 Public
drwxr-xr-x+  5 cadmin  staff    170 Jul 29 22:22 Sites
MyMac:~ cadmin$ cd Desktop/
MyMac:Desktop cadmin$
```

Command results

Computer name

Working directory     User account     Awaiting your next command...

For detailed instructions, see "Command-Line Essentials" in Chapter 3 of *Apple Training Series: Mac OS X Support Essentials v10.6*.

# Anatomy of a Command

| 1. **ls** | 2. **-lRA** | 3. **~/Documents** | 4. **> list.txt** |

| | |
|---|---|
| 1 **Command Name** | In this example the ls command displays a list of a folder's contents. |
| 2 **Command Options** | Options add conditions, limits, or other modifiers to the command. |
| 3 **Arguments** | This is the recipient of the action, often specified as a file or folder path. |
| 4 **Extras** | Redirected output, or other commands, as needed. In this example a text file is created from the list output. |

For detailed instructions, see "Command-Line Essentials" in Chapter 3 of *Apple Training Series: Mac OS X Support Essentials v10.6.*

# Command-Line Manuals

Nearly every command has a "man page"

Simple to access: man *commandname*

Search all manual pages: man –k *searchkeyword*

Search text inside page: /*searchkeyword*

```
● ○ ○                  Terminal — less — 80×24
LS(1)                    BSD General Commands Manual                    LS(1)

NAME
     ls -- list directory contents

SYNOPSIS
     ls [-ABCFGHLOPRSTUWabcdefghiklmnopqrstuwx1] [file ...]

DESCRIPTION
     For each operand that names a file of a type other than directory, ls
     displays its name as well as any requested, associated information.  For
     each operand that names a file of type directory, ls displays the names
     of files contained within that directory, as well as any requested, asso-
     ciated information.

     If no operands are given, the contents of the current directory are dis-
     played.  If more than one operand is given, non-directory operands are
     displayed first; directory and non-directory operands are sorted sepa-
     rately and in lexicographical order.

     The following options are available:

     -@      Display extended attribute keys and sizes in long (-l) output.
:
```

For detailed instructions, see "Command-Line Essentials" in Chapter 3 of *Apple Training Series: Mac OS X Support Essentials v10.6.*

## Common Commands

**ls** *path*
▸ List the contents of a directory

**cd** *path*
▸ Change your working directory

**pwd**
▸ Show path of working directory

**cp** *src dest*
▸ Copy a file

**cp –R** *src dest*
▸ Copy a folder and its contents

**mv** *src dest*
▸ Move or rename an item

**rm –R** *path*
▸ Remove a file or folder

**touch** *path*
▸ Change an item's modification date or create an empty file

**sudo** *command*
▸ Execute following command as root or "superuser"
▸ Must be an admin and provide your password

For detailed instructions, see "Command-Line Essentials" in Chapter 3 of *Apple Training Series: Mac OS X Support Essentials v10.6.*

## Command-Line Paths

A *path* is directions to an item in the file system.

UNIX uses forward slash / to delineate folders.
▸ The "root" of the system volume: /
▸ Logan's desktop folder:  /Users/logan/Desktop

The tilde ~ is shorthand for your home folder.
▸ Your desktop folder:  ~/Desktop

Spaces in pathnames use backslash space "\ ".
▸ Local screen savers:  /Library/Screen\ Savers

Nonsystem volumes mount in /Volumes.
▸ The mainserver public share:  /Volumes/Public

For detailed instructions, see "Command-Line Navigation" in Chapter 3 of *Apple Training Series: Mac OS X Support Essentials v10.6.*

## Command-Line Shortcuts

| Shortcut | Action |
| --- | --- |
| Tab | Completes path being typed |
| Drag folder to Terminal | Enters absolute path |
| open . | Opens working folder in Finder |
| Control-C | Terminates command in progress |
| Up and Down Arrow keys | Accesses prior commands |
| Control-L or clear | Clears screen |
| Option-click | Moves cursor to mouse location |
| Control-A | Moves cursor to beginning of the line |
| Control-E | Moves cursor to end of the line |
| Esc-F | Moves forward one word |
| Esc-B | Moves backward one word |

For detailed instructions, see "Command-Line Tips and Tricks" in Chapter 3 of *Apple Training Series: Mac OS X Support Essentials v10.6.*

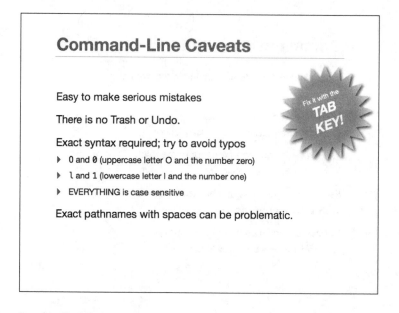

## Command-Line Caveats

Easy to make serious mistakes

There is no Trash or Undo.

Exact syntax required; try to avoid typos

▸ O and 0 (uppercase letter O and the number zero)

▸ l and 1 (lowercase letter l and the number one)

▸ EVERYTHING is case sensitive

Exact pathnames with spaces can be problematic.

Fix it with the TAB KEY!

For detailed instructions, see "Command-Line Tips and Tricks" in Chapter 3 of *Apple Training Series: Mac OS X Support Essentials v10.6.*

Exercise 3.1.1
# Command-Line Navigation

## Objectives

- Navigate the command-line environment using absolute and relative paths
- Compare file visibility in the Finder and at the command line
- Get help in the command-line environment

## Summary

In this exercise, you will become acquainted with basic UNIX command-line tools used for navigation. You will use these tools to see some of the file system objects that are not visible in the Finder. You will also learn how to access the built-in manual to get more information about a command.

## View a Home Folder Using Command-Line Tools

You will open the Terminal application (found in the Utilities folder) and list the contents of your home folder, comparing what you see there against what you see in the Finder.

1   Log in as Client Administrator (cadmin).

2   In the Finder, open the Utilities folder inside the Applications folder. The Finder provides a keyboard shortcut for access to this folder: Command-Shift-U.

3  Open the Terminal application. You can type the first few letters of the application name until it is selected and then use the Open command in the File menu (Command-O) to open the application.

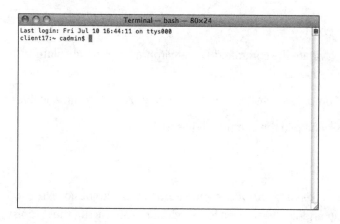

The second line of output includes your prompt information, for example:

```
client17:~ cadmin$
```

In this example, client17 is the name of the computer you logged into. The colon separates the computer name from the path to your current working directory, where you are in the file system. When you first open a Terminal window, this will be your home folder. ~ is UNIX shorthand for your home folder. After the space is the short name of the user you are logged in as. Finally, the $ character is the actual prompt. Essentially it means "type your commands here."

4  At the prompt, type `ls` and press the Return key.

You will see output that looks something like the following, followed by another prompt:

```
Desktop      Library    Pictures
Documents    Movies     Public
Downloads    Music      Sites
```

If your computer is not connected to the Internet, you may also see a file named Send Registration.

5   Switch to Finder. If there is not a Finder window open, open one by choosing New Finder Window from the File menu.

6   Select cadmin's home folder in the Finder sidebar and compare the contents of the home folder as seen in the Finder and in the Terminal window.

What you saw at the command line is the same as what you saw in the Finder.

7   Switch back to your Terminal window and type `ls  -A` at the prompt. Generally speaking, the command-line environment is case-sensitive. The A option is not the same as the a option.

You will notice a few extra files in the listing, all beginning with a period. By UNIX convention, these "dot files" are hidden in directory listings unless you ask for them, which you did by providing the A option to `ls`. The Finder follows this convention by not showing you dot files.

## Examine and Change Your Current Working Directory

You can think of your current working directory as the place you are in the file system. When you open a new Terminal window, your current working directory is your home folder. You can use the `cd` command to change your current working directory.

1   At the prompt, type `pwd`. The period (.) ends the sentence and is not part of the command, so do not type it. This book will note if a trailing . is part of the command. Generally, this book will not tell you specifically when to press the Return key. It will tell you not to press Return if there is more coming, so go ahead and press Return.

Many basic UNIX commands are derived from the first few letters of their full names. So "pwd" is short for print working directory, "ls" is short for list, and "cd" is short for change directory.

You will see:

`/Users/cadmin`

This is where Client Administrator's home folder exists in the file system and is the folder you are currently "in" in this Terminal window.

2  At the prompt, type `cd Library`. This will change your current working directory to the Library folder inside your home folder.

This command uses a relative path. A relative path means "start in my current working directory."

Notice that your prompt changes to something like this:

`client17:Library cadmin$`

The path component of the prompt only indicates the folder you are immediately in, not the entire path.

Also notice that `cd` did its work (changing your working directory) successfully without providing any feedback. The prompt changed, but `cd` didn't say something like "Working directory successfully changed." By UNIX tradition, a command that completes successfully and doesn't need to provide any information (like `ls`, whose job it is to provide you with information about the contents of a directory) will exit silently. That is, it won't provide unnecessary feedback in non-error situations. On the other hand, if you weren't expecting output and you get an error message, you should probably investigate its cause before continuing.

3  At the prompt, type `pwd`. The Terminal displays:

`/Users/cadmin/Library`

You can see that you have "moved" into the Library folder that was inside your previous working directory.

4  Use `ls` to view what files and folders are in this Library folder.

5  At the prompt, type `cd /Library`. Note the / that precedes Library this time.

6   At the prompt, type `pwd`. You will see output like this:

`/Library`

This is a different folder entirely.

A path that starts with a leading / is called an absolute path. It means "Start at the root folder and navigate from there." A path that does not start with a leading / is a relative path. It means "Start in your current working directory and navigate from there."

7   Use `ls` to view the files and folders that are in this Library folder.

There is a fair amount of overlap in terms of the names of the items in this Library and the one in cadmin's home folder, but they are not exactly the same.

8   At the prompt, type `cd` and a space character. Do not press the Return key.

Terminal provides some nice integration between the graphical environment and the command-line environment, including the ability to drag and drop items from the Finder into a Terminal window and have the path to the item appear on your command line. In this case, you are going to use Finder to find a folder to which you want to change your Terminal window's working directory.

9   Switch to Finder.

Sometimes, especially when you don't know exactly what you are looking for, it is faster and easier to find a file or folder graphically.

10  Open a new Finder window if necessary and click Macintosh HD in the sidebar.

11  Open the Users folder.

12  Select the Shared folder and drag it to your Terminal window. You can use Exposé to move from one window to the other if you can't see your Terminal window.

**13** Drop Shared onto the content area of your Terminal window.

Notice that it fills in the path (/Users/Shared) for you. Also notice that "Macintosh HD" does not appear in the path that Terminal fills in for you. Finder shows you volume names to make locating a particular volume easier and for historical reasons. The underlying UNIX system does not use these volume names in the same way.

**14** Switch to the Terminal and press the Return key.

**15** Type `pwd` at the prompt.

You see that you are now in the Shared folder.

## Examine the Manual for ls

One of the nice things about the UNIX environment is that the manual is built-in. The `ls` command turns out to be a very flexible and feature-rich command. To find out more about it, you will use the built-in manual by way of the `man` command.

**1** At the prompt in your Terminal window, type `man ls`. This will open the manual page ("man page") for the `ls` command.

Each manual page is divided into various parts. The number in parentheses on the top line indicates in which section of the manual this command is documented. In this case, `ls` is documented in section 1, which is for general use commands. Next you see the name of the command and a very terse summary of what the command does, "list directory contents." The synopsis is supposed to be a formal representation of how to use the command. Anything contained in square brackets is optional. The synopsis isn't always completely accurate. For example, a few options for `ls` are mutually exclusive of each other, but this synopsis does not indicate that. Generally speaking, options or switches (which change the behavior of a command) immediately follow the command and arguments (which tell the command what to operate on) follow options or switches. The description, which describes the various uses of the command, follows the synopsis.

man uses a tool called a pager to display multiple screen pages of text and allow you to navigate a man page. The tool that man uses is called less. Let's find out how to use the pager.

2   Press the Q key to quit viewing the man page for ls.

3   At the prompt, type man less.

4   Use the Space key to read through the manual for less one screen page at a time. As you read about various other commands that are possible when viewing a file with less, try them out.

5   Once you have some familiarity with less, review the man page for ls.

6   Because the manual is accessible through the man command, it perhaps makes sense that man has a manual page, too. Review it by using the man command (man man).

Exercise 3.1.2
# Command-Line File Manipulation

## Objective

- Explore various file-manipulation commands

## Summary

In this exercise you will learn about various file-manipulation commands, including how to copy, move, rename, and delete files and folders.

## Create Some Files to Manipulate

Using TextEdit, you will create a couple of files that you will use in future steps. You should still be logged in as Client Administrator.

1   Open TextEdit. It can be found in the /Applications folder.

2   In TextEdit's Format menu, choose Make Plain Text.

3   Add the following to the Untitled (default) document.

    MacBook Pro

    Xserve

    Mac Pro

    iPhone

    MacBook

    iMac

    Mac Mini

```
● ● ●                    Untitled
MacBook Pro
Xserve
Mac Pro
iPhone
MacBook
iMac
Mac Mini
```

4  Save the document as Comps in your Documents folder.

```
Save As: Comps                    ▼
Where:  📁 Documents              ⬍

Plain Text Encoding: Unicode (UTF-8)     ⬍
                    ☑ If no extension is provided, use ".txt".
                              Cancel    Save
```

5  Open a new document in TextEdit.

6  In TextEdit's Format menu, choose Make Plain Text.

7  Save the new document as Empty in your Documents folder.

## Copy and Move Files and Create a Folder

You will work with a variety of commands to manipulate files and folders at the command line.

1  Switch to Terminal if it is still running or open it from the Utilities folder. If there is not a Terminal window open, open a new one.

2  Use cd to change into your Documents folder.

3   Use `ls` to view the files in your Documents folder. The file About Stacks.pdf already existed in your Documents folder. At the command line, you can open it graphically using the open command. For more information, see the man page for open.

Notice that TextEdit automatically added a filename extension of txt to the files it saved.

4   Make a copy of Comps.txt, naming it MacModels.txt (do not type the prompt):

```
client17:Documents cadmin$ cp Comps.txt MacModels.txt
```

Many commands that take a source and a destination list the source first.

The command-line interface requires you to type filenames and the like correctly. Fortunately, most shells have built-in features to help you type correctly. For example, in the above command, if you type the `C` at the beginning of Comps.txt and press the Tab key, the shell looks in your current working directory for files that start with C. Because there is only one such file, Comps.txt, it fills in the full name for you. If more than one file matches what you typed, it will complete as much as it can (all the characters that are the same across the matching files). It then beeps at you when you have more than one completion option. When it does this, pressing Tab again will cause it to show you all the matching options. This "tab completion" can save you a great deal of typing and correcting using the Delete key. Tab completion is one of the tricks that those proficient at UNIX use in order to make their use of the environment fast and accurate. Try it out in future steps of these exercises.

5   Use `less` to view both files. MacModels.txt is an exact copy of Comps.txt.

**Create a Folder and Copy a File to It**

cp can also be used to copy files into a folder or directory, retaining the same filename as the original or giving the copy a new name in the process.

6  Create a new folder in your documents folder:

client17:Documents cadmin$ `mkdir AppleInfo`

Because AppleInfo is a relative path the folder will be created in your Documents folder.

> **Note**  If you would like to know more about any of these commands, please feel free to read the related man page.

7  Use `cp` to copy MacModels.txt into AppleInfo (don't forget to try tab completion):

client17:Documents cadmin$ `cp MacModels.txt AppleInfo`

8  Use `ls` to view the contents of AppleInfo:

client17:Documents cadmin$ `ls AppleInfo`

**Fix a Naming Error**

The list in MacModels.txt includes a couple of items that are not technically Macs. Let's rename the file and clean up the extra copies.

9  Remove (delete) the Comps.txt file and the MacModels.txt file in the AppleInfo folder:

client17:Documents cadmin$ `rm Comps.txt AppleInfo/`
`MacModels.txt`

This will delete both files while only executing the command once.

10  Move the MacModels.txt file into the AppleInfo folder using the mv command:

client17:Documents cadmin$ `mv MacModels.txt AppleInfo`

11  Change your working directory to AppleInfo using the cd command.

12  Rename the MacModels.txt file AppleHardware.txt using the mv command.

client17:AppleInfo cadmin$ `mv MacModels.txt`
`AppleHardware.txt`

It turns out that a move and a rename are virtually identical in terms of the operation in the file system. They both result in the creation of a directory entry and the deletion of a directory entry, with an optional copy of the file contents in between if we are moving a file from one volume to another. As a result, we use the same command to achieve both a move and a rename.

> **Note**  You could have accomplished both steps 10 and 12 in one command with $ `mv MacModels.txt AppleInfo/`
> `AppleHardware.txt`.

## Remove a Folder

It seems silly to have a single file contained in a folder, so now you will move the AppleHardware.txt file back to the Documents folder and remove the AppleInfo folder.

1   Change your working directory back to the Documents folder.

There are a few different ways to accomplish this:

- Use the absolute path /Users/cadmin/Documents.

- Use the home folder shortcut ~/Documents.

- Use the relative path (..).

The .. notation always refers to the parent directory of the current directory. So, because your current working directory is /Users/cadmin/Documents/AppleInfo, .. refers to /Users/ cadmin/Documents.

Occasionally, you will see the .. notation in the middle of a path instead of at the beginning, for example, /Users/cadmin/ Documents/../Desktop. It still has the same meaning, so in this example, it refers to Client Administrator's Desktop folder.

Similarly, a single . refers to the current directory or location in the path.

Each directory actually contains a reference to both itself and its parent. These are visible if you use `ls -a` (note the lowercase a instead of the uppercase A you used previously).

2  Move the AppleHardware.txt file to Documents and rename it AppleHardwareInfo.txt:

```
client17:Documents cadmin$ mv AppleInfo/AppleHardware.txt
AppleHardwareInfo.txt
```

Do not press the Return key until you get to the end of AppleHardwareInfo.txt.

Remember that the path AppleHardwareInfo.txt is relative to your current working directory, so this will move AppleInfo/AppleHardware.txt to the current working directory (Documents) and rename it AppleHardwareInfo.txt.

3  Use `rmdir` to remove the AppleInfo directory.

```
client17:Documents cadmin$ rmdir AppleInfo
```

`rmdir` succeeds because AppleInfo is empty. The man page for `rmdir` tells us that it is only capable of removing folders that are empty. If you wanted to remove a directory that still has files in it, you would want to use the `rm` command with the `r` option:

```
client17:Documents cadmin$ rm -r AppleInfo
```

## Create and Edit a Text File

Sometimes you want to create or edit a text file in the command-line environment. Mac OS X includes several different command-line text editors. Many people have strong opinions regarding which editor is the best. You are encouraged to try several different editors and decide on your personal CLEOC (Command-Line Editor Of Choice). In this exercise, you will be introduced to one of the included editors, `nano`, in order to create a file in your documents folder.

1   Use nano to create a new file named fruit.txt:

`client17:Documents cadmin$ nano fruit.txt`

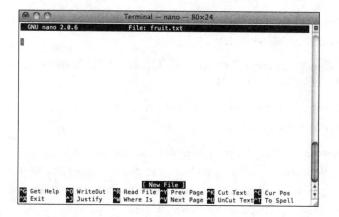

nano is a full-screen editor. It takes over your Terminal window and allows you to edit text in it.

2   Place the following words in the file on separate lines. Press the Return key at the end of each line.

`apple`

`pineapple`

`grapefruit`

`pear`

`banana`

`blueberry`

`strawberry`

Text editors were the predecessors to word processors (though some text editors came along after the invention of word processors). The concepts are very similar. Command-line editors generally don't have menus and controls that you can click, though, so you have to give them commands some other way. In nano's case, you use control characters to tell it what to do.

3   Tell nano you want to exit (quit) by typing Control-X (hold down the Control key and press and release X).

4  When nano asks, "Save modified buffer (ANSWERING 'No' WILL DESTROY CHANGES)?", type Y.

5  When nano asks "File Name to Write: fruit.txt," press the Return key.

nano saves your file and exits, returning you to the command prompt.

6  Log out.

> **Note**  You will use some of the files you created in this exercise later.

# 3.2 System Automation

As you have learned, one of the primary reasons for learning the command line is that it provides a powerful platform for system automation. In short, anything that you can do at the command line can be turned into an automated script. However, command-line scripting certainly isn't the only system automation technology built into Mac OS X. For automating tasks in the graphical environment, Mac OS X also offers two powerful solutions, Automator and AppleScript. This lesson will introduce you to Automator, AppleScript, and command-line scripting. Further, you will also learn how you can combine these technologies to automate any task in Mac OS X.

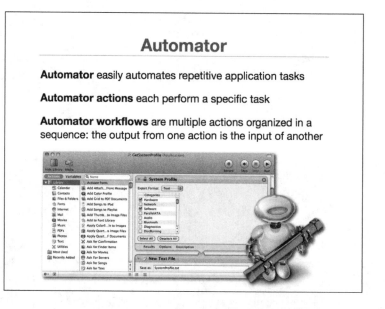

For detailed instructions, see "Using Automator and AppleScript" in Chapter 3 of *Apple Training Series: Mac OS X Support Essentials v10.6*.

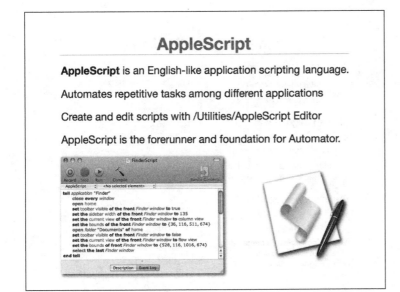

For detailed instructions, see "Using Automator and AppleScript" in Chapter 3 of *Apple Training Series: Mac OS X Support Essentials v10.6*.

For detailed instructions, see "Using Automator and AppleScript" in Chapter 3 of *Apple Training Series: Mac OS X Support Essentials v10.6*.

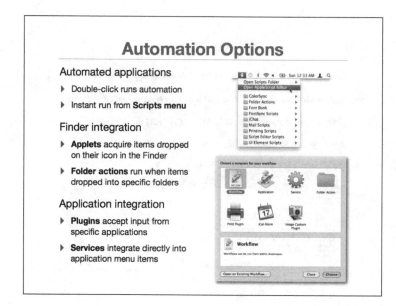

For detailed instructions, see "Using Automator and AppleScript" in Chapter 3 of *Apple Training Series: Mac OS X Support Essentials v10.6*.

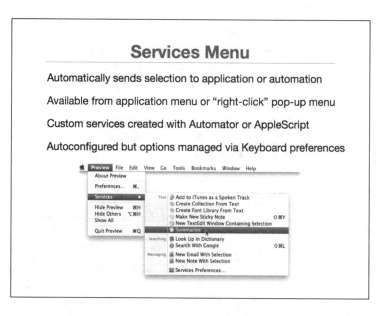

For detailed instructions, see "Combining Automation Techniques" in Chapter 3 of *Apple Training Series: Mac OS X Support Essentials v10.6*.

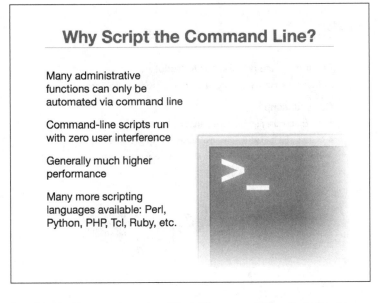

For detailed instructions, see "Basic Command-Line Scripting" in Chapter 3 of *Apple Training Series: Mac OS X Support Essentials v10.6*.

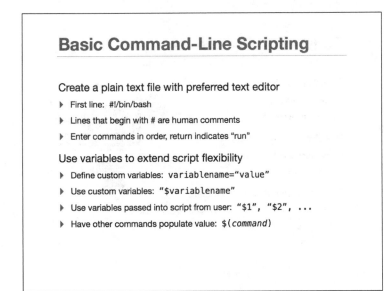

For detailed instructions, see "Basic Command-Line Scripting" in Chapter 3 of *Apple Training Series: Mac OS X Support Essentials v10.6*.

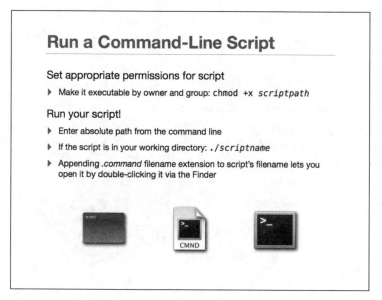

For detailed instructions, see "Basic Command-Line Scripting" in Chapter 3 of *Apple Training Series: Mac OS X Support Essentials v10.6*.

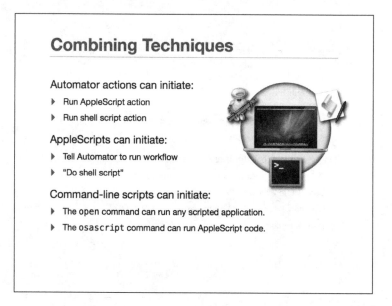

For detailed instructions, see "Combining Automation Techniques" in Chapter 3 of *Apple Training Series: Mac OS X Support Essentials v10.6*.

# Using Automator

## Objective

- Use Automator to automate a repetitive task

## Summary

You will use Automator to pull a System Profiler report and save it to the desktop. System Profiler is an included tool for retrieving information about your computer. You will save the Automator workflow as an application so that it can be double-clicked. Once you have the basics of a workflow down, you can then expand upon it. For example, you could have the Mail program mail the report to a particular email address or grab a screen capture to go with it. While this exercise will not take you that far (you don't have Mail configured, for example), you should begin to get a sense of what can be done with Automator.

## Start an Automator Application

You will create an Automator workflow application to generate the System Profiler report and manipulate it.

1  Log in as Client Administrator.

2  In the Finder, open the Applications folder.

3  Open Automator.

   Automator will open an Untitled (Workflow) window and open a template chooser sheet.

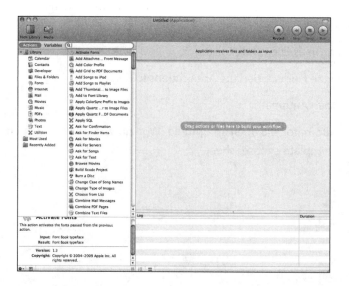

4   Click the Application icon in the template chooser and
    click Choose.

    Automator opens an Untitled (Application) window. The left
    side is a list of actions—steps that can be combined to build up
    a workflow—that are available. The right side is where you build
    your workflow. Note that at the top of the workflow, Automator
    has placed a note saying "Application receives files and folders
    as input."

5  Find the System Profile action and drag it to the workflow on the right side of the window. You can use the search field to filter the action list.

You can click Select All to select all types of profile information for the report or you can select individual types of reports.

If you run this, it will generate a profile. Unfortunately, it is not very useful yet because you have no way to see the report. Next you need to save it to a file.

6  Find the New Text File action and drag it to the workflow *after* the System Profile action.

7  In the Save as field enter `SystemProfile.txt`.

8  Check "Replacing existing files."

Be careful with this one. You may end up overwriting files on the user's desktop.

9   Leave the other options at their defaults.

This action will save the profile report to the desktop, but it would be nice to know when the report was generated.

10  Find the Rename Finder Items action in the list of available actions and drag it to your workflow *after* the New Text File action.

Automator will open a dialog sheet asking if you would like to add a Copy Finder Items action before the Rename Finder Items action in order to preserve the original files.

11  Click Don't Add. You just created the file. You don't need an additional copy of it.

12 In the new action, ensure Add Date or Time is selected in the pop-up menu. Then set the other pop-up menus as follows. Note the example at the bottom of the action.

- Date/Time:    Current
- Where:        After name
- Separator:    Underscore
- Format:       Hour Minute Second
- Separator:    Dash
- Select Use Leading Zeros.

This will rename the SystemProfile.txt file SystemProfile-*hh-mm-ss*. txt where *hh* is the hour, *mm* is the minute, and *ss* is the second.

13 Drag another Rename Finder Items action to the workflow after the one you just configured.

14 Click Don't Add.

15 In the new action, ensure Add Date or Time is selected in the pop-up menu. Then set the other pop-up menus as follows. Note the example at the bottom of the action.

- Date/Time:    Current
- Where:        After name
- Separator:    Underscore
- Format:       Year Month Day
- Separator:    Dash
- Select Use Leading Zeros.

This will rename the above file so that the final file name is SystemProfile-*hh-mm-ss-yyyy-mo-dd*.txt where *yyyy* is the year, *mo* is the month, and *dd* is the day. This naming convention allows you to run multiple reports on the same day without filename collisions occurring. However, if you manage to run the workflow more than once in the same second of the clock, you will still get an error.

16 Click the Run button on the toolbar. Your workflow is ready to run. This will test it.

Depending on how many items you selected in step 5, generating the profile may take a little time.

A file appears on your desktop.

17 Click the new file on the desktop and press the Space bar.

This will open the file using Quick Look, allowing you to view its contents without having to open an application.

18 Press the Space bar again to end Quick Look.

19 Switch back to Automator and save your application to your desktop as `GetSystemProfile`.

You now have a double-clickable application that you can email to your customers to generate a System Profiler report on their computers.

20 Quit Automator.

21 In the Finder, move the system profile report on the desktop to the Trash.

22 Double-click GetSystemProfile on your desktop.

GetSystemProfile launches briefly and places a new system profile report on your desktop.

23 Log out.

# Basic Command-Line Scripting

## Objectives

- Create a basic shell script

- Manipulate the input and output of a command

## Summary

The UNIX command-line environment provides a great deal of flexibility. Most commands are designed to be relatively small, special-purpose tools that can be chained together with other focused commands to accomplish larger tasks.

In this exercise, you will look at how to manipulate the input and output of a few commands as well as how to create a very simple shell script.

## Search an Input File and Create a New File with the Results

The command grep (short for Global Regular Expression Print) searches for patterns (regular expressions) in text and outputs lines that match. Sometimes it is useful to collect the output into another file. That's what you will do in this exercise.

1  Log in as Client Administrator.

2  Open Terminal, in /Applications/Utilities.

3  Change your working directory to your Documents folder.

4  Use ls to remind yourself what files you have in this folder.

   You are going to search for specific characters in AppleHardwareInfo.txt.

5 Use grep to look for the pattern "mac" in AppleHardwareInfo.txt:

client17:Documents cadmin$ grep mac AppleHardwareInfo.txt

Generally, grep commands are structured this way:

grep *options pattern file...*

You are given another prompt with no results displayed.

*Question 1  Why does grep not find any results?*

_____

_____

_____

6 Take a few minutes to skim through the man page for grep. In particular, look for the -i option.

7 Run grep again, this time with the case-insensitivity option, -i.

client17:Documents cadmin$ grep -i mac AppleHardwareInfo.txt

MacBook Pro

Mac Pro

MacBook

iMac

Mac Mini

That gives a good list, but it would be nice if it were sorted.

A pipe or pipeline takes the output of one command and sends it as input to another command. You designate a pipeline by including a pipe character (a vertical bar, Shift-\ on most keyboards) between the two commands. In this case, the first command will be the grep command above. The second command will be the sort command.

8 Take a little time to skim through the man page for sort.

9   Now sort the list by piping the output of grep to sort.

```
client17:Documents cadmin$ grep -i mac AppleHardwareInfo.
txt | sort
```

You see the same list in a slightly different order.

It would be nice to be able to have the sorted list stored in a file. You can take the output of any command and store it to a file using output redirection. This is accomplished by placing > or >> after the command and then specifying the file you would like the output to go to. The > form will replace the contents of the file with the output (creating the file if necessary). The >> form will append the output to the file, again creating the file if necessary.

10  Save the sorted list to the file Macs.txt.

```
client17:Documents cadmin$ grep -i mac AppleHardwareInfo.
txt | sort > Macs.txt
```

Do not press the Return key until you have typed Macs.txt.

11  Use ls to verify that Macs.txt was created.

12  Use less to verify that the contents of the file are what you expect.

## Create a Small Script to Sort the Text on the Clipboard

The Clipboard is the system that facilitates copy and paste in Mac OS X. Apple has provided a number of features to make inter-action between the graphical and command-line environments easier. One of the results of this effort is that you can move data between the two environments easily using the Clipboard. You will create a small shell script that takes the contents of the Clipboard, sorts it, and places it back on the Clipboard.

A shell script is simply a text file that contains a series of commands that are executed in order when the script is executed.

1   While still in Terminal, use nano to edit a new file.

```
client17:Documents cadmin$ nano sort_clipboard.sh
```

There are many different naming conventions for script naming. The filename extension is not required and is mostly informative to the user, though some applications will use this information, too. The system knows that a file is executable using another feature called its mode.

2  Type the following into the sort_clipboard.sh file using nano in the Terminal window:

```
#!/bin/bash
#
# Sorts the Clipboard contents
#
pbpaste | sort | pbcopy
exit 0
```

Lines that start with a # are comments. That is, they are ignored. In fact, any text between a # and the end of a line is ignored.

The first line, called a shebang, sharp bang, hashbang, hashpling, or a number of other names, is a special comment and an exception to the above rule. When it occurs as the first line of a script, it tells the operating system which command interpreter to use. In this case, it says to use the interpreter found at /bin/bash, BASH (Bourne Again SHell, a revision to the Bourne Shell (sh)).

pbpaste outputs the textual contents of the Clipboard. At lower levels, the service that provides the Clipboard is called the pasteboard, thus pbpaste instead of cbpaste or something else. This difference is historical and not very important unless you are a developer.

You already know what sort does. pbcopy is the reverse of pbpaste. It takes the text sent as input to it and places it on the Clipboard.

3   Double-check that you typed everything correctly.

4   Exit nano and save your work.

Your script is complete but cannot be run as a command yet. To the operating system, your script is nothing more than a document file. To change that, you need to change the file's mode (specifically, in this case, its permissions) to tell the system it is a runnable file.

5   Mark the file as executable.

```
client17:Documents cadmin$ chmod +x sort_clipboard.sh
```

chmod changes a file's mode, in this case making it executable. You will look at chmod in more detail in later chapters.

6   Run the script.

```
client17:Documents cadmin$ ./sort_clipboard.sh
```

You have to specify the path to the file with the leading ./ in order to execute it. The reason is that your Documents folder is not on your PATH. The PATH defines where the system should look when you give it a command. There are various folders where commands are generally kept. Your Documents folder is not among them. So, you have to specify where to find the command you want to run.

You are presented with a prompt and there is no other output. The script does not generate any output. It simply takes the contents of the Clipboard, sorts it, and puts it back on the Clipboard. To see it function, you will use TextEdit.

7   Switch to Finder and open TextEdit from the applications folder.

8   Choose File > Open and open the AppleHardwareInfo file in your Documents folder.

9   Select the entire contents of the file by pressing Command-A.

10  Copy the file by using either Command-C or Edit > Copy.

11  Switch to your Terminal window.

12  Run the sort_clipboard.sh command again. You can use the Up and Down Arrow keys to move back and forth through the "history" of commands you have run. When you get to a command you want to run again, simply press Return.

13  Switch back to TextEdit.

14  Open a new document window.

15  Paste from the Clipboard using either Command-V or Edit > Paste.

    The list is definitely sorted, but perhaps not in the order you expected.

    *Question 2  How did sort order the list?*

    _____

    _____

16  Switch back to Terminal.

17  Review the options for sort by looking at sort's man page. Pay particular attention to the -f option.

18  Open your script in your editor again.

    `client17:Documents cadmin$ nano sort_clipboard.sh`

19  Add the –f flag to the sort command. Remember that this is a command-line, keyboard-oriented environment. You will need to use the arrow keys rather than the mouse to position the cursor in the right place.

    `pbpaste | sort –f | pbcopy`

20 Exit nano and save your changes.

21 Run sort_clipboard.sh again.

22 Return to TextEdit and paste into a new document.

   The list should now be sorted in a more traditional order.

23 Log out. You do not need to save any of the untitled documents
   you created.

## Exercise 3.2.3
# Combining Automation Technologies (optional)

## Objectives

- Combine automation technologies
- Create a service that can be used in other applications

## Summary

In this exercise, you will combine two built-in, GUI-level automation technologies, AppleScript and Automator, with a simple command-line statement to automate a repetitive task, opening a file in a command-line editor. Command-line editors, as straight text editors, are sometimes easier to work with than editors that have word-processing features or that understand markup languages like HTML, XML, or YAML. You will create an Automator application that allows you to drop files on it. When you drop a file on the application, it will use an AppleScript to cause nano to open the dropped file in Terminal.

## Create an Automator Application

In this section you will open Automator and start an application workflow. You'll use an application so that you can drop files onto the icon when you are done.

1   Log in as Client Administrator.

2   In the Finder, open the Applications folder.

3   Open Automator.

4   Click the Application icon in the template chooser and click Choose.

Automator opens an Untitled (Application) window.

5 In the second column of the Actions library, find Run AppleScript and drag it to the area on the right that says "Drag actions or files here to build your workflow." You can also use the search field below the toolbar to search for it.

This will create a Run AppleScript step in the workflow on the right. Note that at the top it is connected to "Application receives files and folders as input."

In the text box in the Run AppleScript action, you will see that it is prepopulated with a minimal script. This box is actually an AppleScript editor and is where you will craft the AppleScript that will tell Terminal to open the dropped file in nano.

There is a small toolbar above the text editor with run, stop, and compile buttons on it. These will run this step of the workflow (for testing purposes), stop running it, and run the text through the AppleScript compiler to make sure it is syntactically correct. The compiler ensures that what you have typed is correct AppleScript, not that it does what you want it to do.

6   Switch to the finder and open AppleScript Editor from /Applications/Utilities.

AppleScript Editor is a tool for creating AppleScripts. AppleScript is a flexible language that can be extended by applications to allow you to control an application by running a script. Many applications provide a set of extensions to AppleScript called a dictionary. AppleScript Editor allows you to view these dictionaries so you can write scripts for a particular application. Terminal provides such a dictionary. In order to know what we can tell Terminal to do, we need to view its dictionary.

7   In AppleScript Editor's File menu, choose Open Dictionary.

An Open Dictionary dialog opens that shows a list of all installed applications that have dictionaries.

8   Find and select Terminal, then click Choose.

The scripting terminology (dictionary) for Terminal opens. In the browser below the toolbar, you can see a list of suites that Terminal makes available. The Standard Suite contains many basic commands like open, close, save, etc. The Terminal Suite describes script commands that are specific to Terminal.

Below the browser, you see a view that describes the various nouns (like windows and tabs) and verbs (like open and close) that AppleScript understands for the Terminal application.

9   Select the Terminal Suite.

The second pane of the browser now shows the commands (do script) and classes (application, settings set, and tab) that Terminal declares. The "do script" command is what we are looking for.

10  Select "do script" and read its description. Dictionaries describe what the application understands and how to construct it syntactically.

11  Now that we know the AppleScript command we want to use, switch back to Automator.

12  In the Run AppleScript editor, replace:

```
(* Your script goes here *)
```

with:

```
tell application "Terminal"
    do script "nano " & quoted form of POSIX path of (input as string)
    activate
end tell
```

There are four lines here. Note that there is a space after the word nano and before the quotation marks.

In AppleScript text enclosed in (* *) is a comment and is ignored, so you are replacing a placeholder comment with your script.

AppleScript is a very natural language: tell application "Terminal" does just what it sounds like. It sends the following commands (up to the end tell) to Terminal.

do script sends the text to Terminal and tells it to run it at the command prompt. The text we send says "Use nano to open this file." The file is passed as the input variable into the AppleScript. Unfortunately, it comes into the AppleScript in an older format that has to be converted to a POSIX (UNIX) path. You quote the whole thing (quoted form) to avoid nano taking any spaces in the filenames as separating additional filenames and to make sure special characters that are part of filenames remain so.

activate causes Terminal to launch if it isn't running and become the application that has focus.

13 Click the compile (hammer) icon in the Run AppleScript action's
toolbar. If you typed everything correctly, the purple text should
change to various colors including black, blue, and green.

Double-check your typing if a compiler error is reported.

14 Save your application as "Open in nano" on your Desktop. Make
sure you choose Application as the file format. An Automator
icon will appear on the desktop.

15  In Automator's toolbar, click Run.

A dialog sheet appears telling you that the application will not receive any input while running in Automator. Recall that Automator applications take files and folders as input, generally by dropping them on the application icon. In Automator, you are running the workflow without dropping anything on it. This makes it rather difficult to test it inside Automator.

The workaround for this situation is to add a "Get Specified Finder Items" step to the workflow immediately before the Run AppleScript item.

16  Because you will be running the workflow a few times inside Automator, go ahead and check the "Do not show this message again" checkbox to avoid seeing this dialog repeatedly. Then click OK.

Automator tells you that the Run AppleScript action encountered an error. This error is because it didn't know what file to open in nano.

17  Click OK.

**18** In the actions list, find the Get Specified Finder Items action and drag it into the workflow *before* the Run AppleScript action.

**19** In the Get Specified Finder Items action in the workflow, click the Add button.

**20** Select the fruit.txt file in your Documents folder and click Add.

**21** Do not save the Automator application.

You added the Get Specified Finder Items action for testing. If you were to save the application now, it would only ever open fruit.txt.

**22** Run the workflow again by clicking the Run button in Automator's toolbar.

Terminal opens and becomes the focused application. It opens two windows, and opens nano in the second one to edit fruit.txt.

**23** Switch to the Finder.

**24** Use Finder to select the AppleHardwareInfo text file in your Documents folder.

25 Drag AppleHardwareInfo to the "Open in nano" item on your
   desktop and drop it there.

   Terminal becomes the focused application, opens a new
   window, and opens nano in it to edit AppleHardwareInfo.txt.
   You now have three Terminal windows open, two of which have
   nano editing different files.

26 Quit Terminal, telling it to Terminate Processes in the dialog
   that opens.

## Create a Service

Services allow you to use the features of one application inside
another. For this service, you will use the same AppleScript as you
did in the Automator application above.

1  In Automator, choose New from the File menu.

2  In Automator's template chooser, select Service and click Choose.

   As above, a new workflow editor window opens, this time for
   a service.

3  In the workflow portion of the window, choose "text files"
   from the pop-up menu so that the top of the workflow reads
   "Service receives selected text files in any application."

4  Drag a Run AppleScript action into the workflow.

5  Copy and paste the AppleScript from the "Open in nano" workflow into the new Run AppleScript action. Make sure you replace
   the entire script with the entire script from "Open in nano."

6  Save the service and name it "Open in nano." This saves the
   workflow to ~/Library/Services.

7  Switch to the Finder, browse to your Documents folder, and
   select fruit.txt.

8  Choose Finder > Services > Open in nano.

Terminal opens with two windows as it did before. One of those windows contains nano editing fruit.txt.

Services also appear in the contextual menu (Control-click or right-click if you have a multi-button mouse) and in Finder's Action (gear) menu.

9  Log out. You can close the Terminal window. Don't save the Automator document named "Open in nano (Application)."

# 4

# File Systems

# 4.1 File System Management

The file system is the underlying technology that allows a system to access storage. Thus, understanding how to manage and troubleshoot file system technology is fundamental to supporting any operating system. In this lesson you will learn about the Mac OS X file system technology. You will practice common storage management techniques including gathering information, partitioning, and erasing. You will also learn troubleshooting techniques specific to Mac OS X file system technologies.

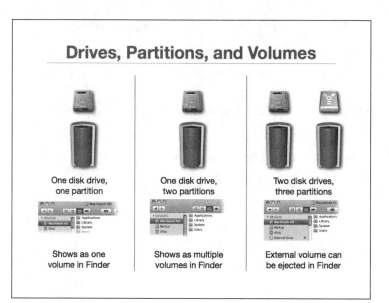

**Drives, Partitions, and Volumes**

One disk drive, one partition — Shows as one volume in Finder

One disk drive, two partitions — Shows as multiple volumes in Finder

Two disk drives, three partitions — External volume can be ejected in Finder

For detailed instructions, see "File System Components" in Chapter 4 of *Apple Training Series: Mac OS X Support Essentials v10.6.*

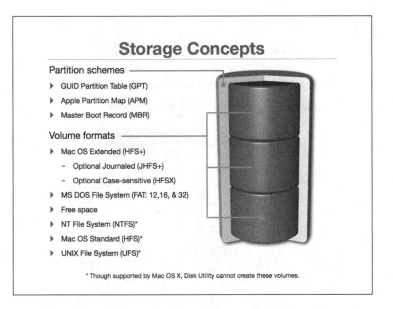

For detailed instructions, see "File System Components" in Chapter 4 of *Apple Training Series: Mac OS X Support Essentials v10.6.*

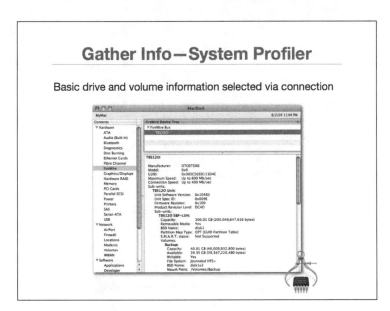

For detailed instructions, see "Gathering File System Information" in Chapter 4 of *Apple Training Series: Mac OS X Support Essentials v10.6.*

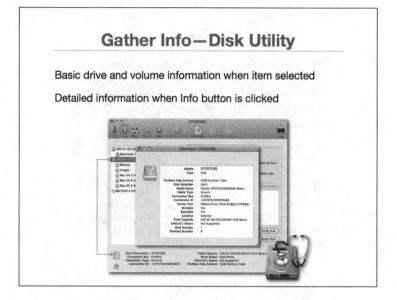

## Gather Info—Disk Utility

Basic drive and volume information when item selected

Detailed information when Info button is clicked

For detailed instructions, see "File System Management" in
Chapter 4 of *Apple Training Series: Mac OS X Support Essentials v10.6*.

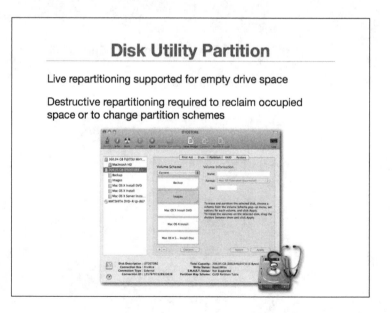

## Disk Utility Partition

Live repartitioning supported for empty drive space

Destructive repartitioning required to reclaim occupied
space or to change partition schemes

For detailed instructions, see "File System Management" in
Chapter 4 of *Apple Training Series: Mac OS X Support Essentials v10.6*.

## Disk Utility Erase Options

Method used to
erase full volume

Erases volume
free space

For detailed instructions, see "File System Management" in
Chapter 4 of *Apple Training Series: Mac OS X Support Essentials v10.6*.

## Secure Erase Items

Finder can perform 7-pass secure erase on trash items.

Alternatively, you can use the s rm command.

For detailed instructions, see "File System Management" in
Chapter 4 of *Apple Training Series: Mac OS X Support Essentials v10.6*.

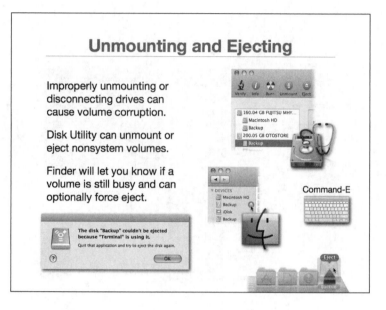

For detailed instructions, see "File System Management" in Chapter 4 of *Apple Training Series: Mac OS X Support Essentials v10.6.*

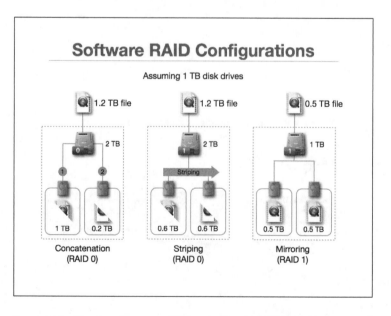

For detailed instructions, see "Using Software RAID" in Chapter 4 of *Apple Training Series: Mac OS X Support Essentials v10.6.*

## Managing Software RAID

Disk Utility is the primary tool for creating software RAID sets.

It's also used to verify RAID status and repair degraded mirrors.

For detailed instructions, see "Using Software RAID" in Chapter 4 of
*Apple Training Series: Mac OS X Support Essentials v10.6.*

## Optical Media via Finder

Finder disc burning

▸ Insert blank optical disc

▸ Choose File > Burn from menu

Finder allows you to create
burn folders to prepare items.

Items are aliased in local burn
folder to save space.

Burn folders can be temporary
or saved for later.

For detailed instructions, see "Using Optical Media" in Chapter 4 of
*Apple Training Series: Mac OS X Support Essentials v10.6.*

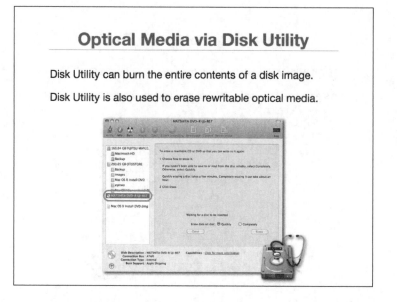

For detailed instructions, see "Using Optical Media" in Chapter 4 of *Apple Training Series: Mac OS X Support Essentials v10.6.*

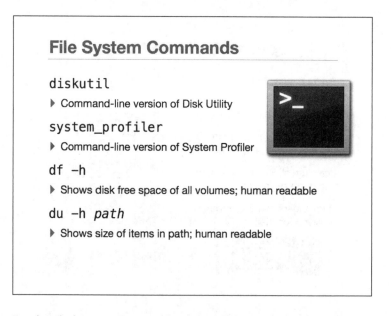

For detailed instructions, see "File System Management" in Chapter 4 of *Apple Training Series: Mac OS X Support Essentials v10.6.*

Exercise 4.1.1
# Using Disk Utility

## Objectives

- Use Disk Utility to view disk information
- Verify a disk image
- Partition a hard drive and disk image
- Understand the available partitioning schemes

## Summary

In this exercise, you will view disk information using Disk Utility and learn about the disk maintenance tools you will use frequently when supporting Mac OS X. Using a sample disk image, you will use Disk Utility to verify, repair, and partition a disk image. Finally, you will partition your internal hard drive using Disk Utility's live partitioning feature.

## View Disk Information Using Disk Utility

In this exercise you will open Disk Utility to view the various features provided for disk maintenance and repair. Your main objective is to see how you would gather disk information using the applications available on Mac OS X.

1   Log in as Client Administrator.

2   In the Finder, choose Go > Utilities.

3   Open Disk Utility.

On the left you see a list that includes all of the connected drives (internal and external devices), an entry for your optical drive and any media you have inserted, as well as disk images. The left flush entries represent physical devices. The indented entries represent volumes on those devices.

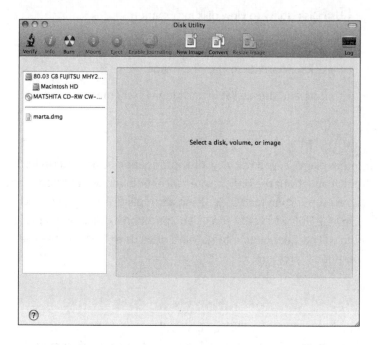

> **Note**  Screen shots may not exactly reflect what you see on the screen. Variables of system setup, hardware configuration, and software versions may cause things to display differently.

4   Select the entry in the list that represents your hard disk.

The disk entry includes the total size of the drive. Note that the Partition button is available when you select the disk device, but not when you select the volume indented below the disk.

## Use Disk Utility to Verify a Disk Image

In this exercise, you will use a sample disk image to experiment with verifying, repairing, and partitioning using Disk Utility. Using a disk image simulates using an actual disk.

> **Note**  You use a disk image in this exercise because it exactly mirrors the behavior of a disk drive; you can create and experiment with disk images at any time without any danger that you might erase a disk by accident.

1  In the Finder, go to /Users/Shared/StudentMaterials/Chapter4.

2  Open the Student_Image.dmg.

The Single_Partition volume will mount on the desktop.

3  Switch to Disk Utility and note the Single_Partition volume entry indented under the Student_Image.dmg entry.

4  Click the Student_Image.dmg entry in the device list.

The bottom of the screen displays details about the disk image, such as its total capacity (104.9 MB in this example), path to the dmg file, write status (Read/Write in this case), and connection bus (Disk Image).

> **Note**  With Mac OS X v10.6, the graphical interface changed
> from base 2 disk sizes (1,024 bytes per kilobyte) to base 10
> (1,000 bytes per kilobyte). As a result, a disk image that used
> to be 100 MB in size in v10.5 and before is now 104.9 MB in
> size. The difference will be larger for larger volumes.

5  Control-click Student_Image.dmg in the list to see a menu
of options.

This menu includes the operations you can perform on a
disk drive.

6   Close the menu by clicking in the Disk Utility window without holding down the Control key.

7   With the Student_Image.dmg entry still selected, click the First Aid button, if necessary.

8   With the Show Details checkbox enabled, click the Repair Disk button.

Disk Utility analyzes and attempts to repair the disk, if it finds any problems.

If you were to click Verify Disk, Disk Utility would only verify the disk, letting you know of any problems it finds. It would not attempt any repairs.

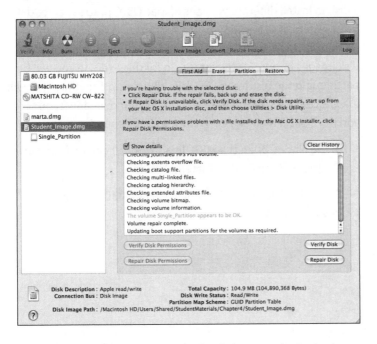

9   Eject the disk image by selecting the disk image device in the source list and clicking Eject in the toolbar.

## Use Disk Utility to Partition Using a New Partition Scheme

Most external storage systems (USB thumb drives, USB and FireWire hard drives, etc.) come preformatted, most of those for Windows. Many of them are partitioned using Master Boot Record (MBR). If you would like to boot your computer from one of these devices, you will need to repartition it.

In this exercise, you will use Disk Utility to partition a sample disk image that comes preformatted with the FAT file system and partitioned with a Master Boot Record partition scheme. Partitioning allows you to separate the disk into sections, or volumes. Each volume looks like a separate disk to the Finder. You might partition a disk to install different versions of Mac OS X, or to separate data from system files. Mac OS X v10.6 supports dynamic repartitioning on normal drives with Mac OS Extended volumes, but not with disk images or non-Mac volumes. So for this exercise you will be partitioning the disk image in Disk Utility using a method that will erase all data. If you use this method on your own drives, be sure you have backed up any essential files beforehand.

1  In the Finder, open the MBR_Image.dmg. It can be found in Chapter4 of the StudentMaterials folder.

2  Switch back to Disk Utility and select the MBR_Image.dmg device in the source list.

3  Click Partition and view the partitioning options available.

4  Choose 2 Partitions from the Volume Scheme pop-up menu.

This will give you two equally sized partitions. You can configure these partitions in several ways:

- Specify sizes for the partitions individually

- Drag the divider to set the partition size

- Rename the partitions

- Set the volume format individually for each volume

Because you chose 2 Partitions, by default each partition will be half the size of the total disk image. (In this example, the disk image is 102.4 MB and each of the partitions is about 51.2 MB by default. Your actual hard drive will probably be different.)

5 Click Options to choose a partition scheme.

If you are preparing a disk for use as a boot drive for a PowerPC-based Mac, choose Apple Partition Map. If you are preparing a boot drive to be used on an Intel-based Mac, choose GUID Partition Table. If the drive will be used for data only, the partition scheme is less important, but note that GUID Partition Table disks cannot be read by versions of Mac OS X earlier than 10.4. It is best practice to partition the disk according to the type of hardware that it will be used with most often.

If you need a disk that is DOS or Windows compatible, such as flash media to be used with a PC, choose Master Boot Record. (However, Boot Camp volumes are only supported when created by Boot Camp Assistant. We will discuss Boot Camp in a later chapter.) When preparing an external drive for booting, be sure to choose the right partition scheme for the Macs you will be booting with that drive.

6  Click GUID Partition Table and then click OK.

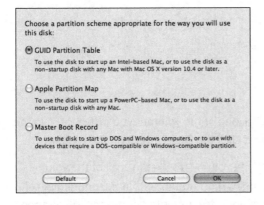

7  Name each volume by selecting it under the Volume Scheme pop-up menu and then entering a name in the Name text field. You can choose the names.

8  Select Mac OS Extended (Journaled) for the format for both volumes.

9  When you have made your selections, click Apply. A confirmation dialog will appear.

10 Click Partition to confirm that you want to destructively repartition this disk image.

Disk Utility then unmounts the disk image's volume, repartitions it as two volumes using GUID Partition Table, formats those volumes, and mounts those volumes. With default preferences, they will appear on the desktop. Note that the volume names will reflect those you chose in step 7.

11 In Disk Utility, click one of the volumes you just created in the list on the left and click the Eject button on the toolbar.

When you eject one volume from a drive, all of the volumes from the same disk will unmount, so that the entire disk can be removed. Both of your new mounted partitions will disappear from the desktop. However, the MBR_Image.dmg containing those volumes will remain in the source list of Disk Utility. If you were to click Unmount in the toolbar, rather than Eject, you could unmount just a single volume, leaving other volumes on the same device untouched.

The Finder conflates the concepts of unmounting and ejecting, calling it simply Eject in its menus.

In some contexts, if you eject only one volume of a multiply partitioned disk, the Finder will ask you if you want to eject the other partitions.

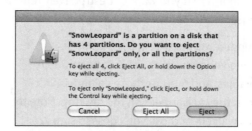

## Use Disk Utility to Partition Without Erasing

In this exercise, you will partition your internal hard drive. In earlier versions of Mac OS X, using Disk Utility to partition your hard drive meant erasing the drive first. As of Mac OS X v10.5 you can live-partition your hard drive without destroying the data. As always, it's a good idea to back up your data before partitioning.

1  If any applications other than Disk Utility are running, close them.

   Do not use any other applications while Disk Utility is working on the volume to repartition on the fly.

2  Select the disk device entry for your hard drive in Disk Utility, then click the Partition button.

3  Select your startup volume in the graphical depiction of the volume scheme and then click the plus sign at the bottom of the current Volume Scheme.

   The volume appears divided into two equally sized volumes.

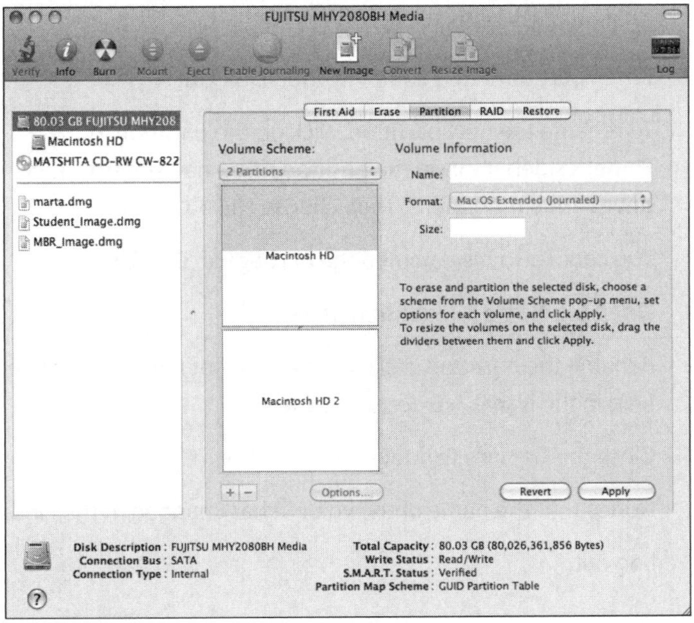

4   Click Apply.

Disk Utility opens a dialog asking you to confirm partitioning the disk. Note that the dialog indicates that no partitions will be erased.

Are you sure you want to partition the disk "Hitachi HTS543232L9SA02 Media"?

Partitioning this disk will change some of the partitions. No partitions will be erased.

This partition will be added:
    "Macintosh HD 2"

This partition will be resized:
    "Macintosh HD"

Cancel    Partition

5   Click the Partition button.

Disk Utility now partitions the drive. This can take a few minutes. Disk Utility has to move any data that is part of the first partition but resides on the disk in the space allocated to the second partition. It will also verify the file system before beginning its work.

6   When partitioning is complete, quit Disk Utility.

7   To rename the new partition, click on the partition in the Finder's sidebar (or on the desktop if you have internal hard drives appearing there), then choose File > Get Info.

You could also have named the partition in Disk Utility.

8   Open the Name & Extension pane.

9   Rename the partition Backup by typing that name into the text field in the Name & Extension pane.

10  Close the Get Info window.

Notice that the name of the volume has changed in the Finder.

11  Log out.

Exercise 4.1.2
# Viewing Disks and Volumes

## Objective

- View disk information using System Profiler, Disk Utility, and from the command line

## Summary

Mac OS X provides multiple ways to gather information about disks. Both the Disk Utility and System Profiler applications provide certain information about drives. These applications use a graphical user interface (GUI) to provide this information. Another method of gathering information and managing drives is by using the command-line interface (CLI) tools in the Terminal application. In this section, you will practice using both applications and command-line tools to gather information. Even if you rarely use the command line, you may encounter troubleshooting situations where you do not have access to graphical applications or the Finder. In this case, knowledge of command-line tools is essential.

## View Disk Information with System Profiler

System Profiler provides information about devices that are connected to your computer. In this exercise, you will view disk information with System Profiler.

1   Log in as Chris Johnson (chris).

2  In the Finder, choose Go > Utilities, then open System Profiler.

Another way to open System Profiler is to go to the Apple menu > About This Mac and click the More Info button.

System Profiler's window opens with the Hardware Overview displayed.

3  Click Serial-ATA on the left to display internal drives connected to your computer.

> **Note**  If you happen to be using a first-generation MacBook Air, you will want to select ATA. These computers use an ATA hard drive instead of a Serial ATA hard drive.

4   If necessary, select your hard drive and make a note of the
    following information:

    Hard Drive Device

    * Partition Map Type:

    Volume Macintosh HD

    * File System (Volume Format):

    * Capacity (Volume Size):

    * Available (Free Space):

    Volume Backup

    * File System (Volume Format):

    * Capacity (Volume Size):

    * Available (Free Space):

    The Hardware section of the source list on the left displays
    connection methods. System Profiler's information is bus-
    oriented, that is, connection-oriented. As you will see in a
    later chapter, System Profiler is especially useful when you are
    troubleshooting a suspected connection issue.

5   Quit System Profiler.

## View Disk Information with Disk Utility

Disk Utility is storage device–oriented, in that it provides both
information on disks connected to your computer and management
tools for those disks. In this exercise, you will gather information
about the disk drive on your computer using Disk Utility.

1   Open Disk Utility.

2   Click the entry for your hard drive in the source list on the left.

3   Click the Info button in the toolbar to view information about
    your hard disk.

Note that this window does not show information about space available or space used.

4  Close this information window.

5  In the source list, click the indented entry for Macintosh HD, and then click the Info button in the toolbar.

This info window displays information for the volume, including capacity, free space, and used space.

6  Use these two windows in Disk Utility to make a note of the
   following information:

   Hard Drive Device

   - Partition Map Scheme:

   Volume Macintosh HD

   - File System (Volume Format):

   - Capacity (Volume Size):

   - Available (Free Space):

   Volume Backup

   - File System (Volume Format):

   - Capacity (Volume Size):

   - Available (Free Space):

   The details for your computer are likely to be different from
   what you see pictured. Disk Utility refers to the Partition Map
   Scheme where System Profiler refers to the Partition Map Type.
   These are interchangeable terms.

7  Quit Disk Utility.

## View Disk Information from the Command Line

In the previous exercises, you used System Profiler and Disk Utility
tools to gather information about your internal drive. In this exercise,
you'll explore the command-line equivalents of those applications.
Familiarity with command-line tools is extremely helpful when GUI
applications are not accessible during troubleshooting.

1  Open the Terminal application from the Utilities folder.

2  At the command prompt, enter the `system_profiler` command.

   ```
   client17:~ chris$ system_profiler
   ```

   Be sure to type the underscore.

The `system_profiler` command shows all the information displayed by the System Profiler application. However, you may not want to display all the information System Profiler reports. The `-listDataTypes` option displays a list of the data types `system_profiler` understands.

3  Use the `SPSerialATADataType` option to have `system_profiler` display only the Serial-ATA information:

`client17:~ chris$ system_profiler SPSerialATADataType`

If you are using a first-generation MacBook Air, you will want to use `SPParallelATADataType` instead.

4  Take a moment to look through the results. They should appear similar to what you saw in System Profiler.

5  Run `system_profiler` again and save the output to a file in your Documents folder.

`client17:~ chris$ system_profiler SPSerialATADataType > ~/Documents/SerialATAInfo.txt`

Do not press return until after SerialATAInfo.txt.

6  Use du to view disk usage statistics.

`client17:~ chris$ du`

This command is useful if you want to focus on usage issues. However, the output from du may be difficult to interpret at first glance, because it includes hidden directories and shows sizes in terms of the number of blocks (generally 512 bytes) used. As in the previous example with `system_profiler`, you can modify the command to make it more useful.

7  Use a different set of options to du.

`client17:~ chris$ du -sh *`

These options and argument display usage in readable form for all directories in the current working directory (Chris's home folder). Notice that the sizes are now displayed in kilobytes and megabytes, and the entire contents of a folder are summarized rather than every subfolder.

```
client17:~ chris$ du -sh *
1.0M    Desktop
560K    Documents
1.5M    Downloads
2.4M    Library
1.5M    Movies
  0B    Music
4.0K    Pictures
  0B    Public
 16K    Sites
client17:~ chris$
```

In the Finder, Get Info will give you information such as capacity, free space, and space used for different items. In Terminal, you can use the df command to check for disk free space.

8   Enter the following command:

client17:~ chris$ **df -H**

The df command shows disk free space. If you leave off the H option, df will show the information in the same 512-byte blocks that du uses.

Notice the device identifiers disk0s3 and disk0s2. You may have noticed those in the System Profiler and Disk Utility information windows. They tell you the device special file (a file that forms a low-level interface to the volume or device) that is associated with the volume.

```
client17:~ chris$ df -H
Filesystem      Size   Used  Avail Capacity  Mounted on
/dev/disk0s2     40G   7.8G    32G    20%    /
devfs           110k   110k    0B    100%    /dev
map -hosts        0B     0B    0B    100%    /net
map auto_home     0B     0B    0B    100%    /home
/dev/disk0s3     40G   156M    40G     1%    /Volumes/Backup
client17:~ chris$
```

9   View the man page for diskutil.

client17:~ chris$ `man diskutil`

The command-line equivalent for many Disk Utility options is the diskutil command. All the commands in the Disk Utility application are available at the command line, and there are additional commands not available in the Disk Utility application. For example, you can initiate disk repair, partitioning, formatting volumes, and simple information gathering. Also, the hdiutil command, which is used for manipulating disk images, has many options with capabilities beyond what you will find in the Disk Utility application and the diskutil command.

The diskutil command has many options. Because there are so many options available, let's start by using the manual to review descriptions and syntax.

As you review the man page for diskutil, you'll see that you can mount and unmount drives, run permissions repair, and other useful commands.

10  Use diskutil to collect information about your boot drive.

client17:~ chris$ `diskutil info disk0`

The info option specifically asks for information about the size, capacity, space available, and space used for disk0. "disk0" will always refer to your boot drive, but is analogous to selecting the disk device in Disk Utility. To find out details on a particular volume, you need to either provide the device special file that corresponds to the volume (e.g., disk0s2) or the volume's mount point (/ for the startup volume, something inside /Volumes for most other volumes).

11  Using the command-line tools you have just tried, find the following information for your hard drive:

Hard Drive Device

- Partition Map Scheme:

Volume Macintosh HD

- File System (Volume Format):

- Capacity (Volume Size):

- Available (Free Space):

Volume Backup

- File System (Volume Format):

- Capacity (Volume Size):

- Available (Free Space):

*Question 1*  *How do your answers compare to those you found in the graphical interface?*

## View Where Volumes Are Mounted

You have seen that volumes appear in the Finder and, depending on your preferences, on the desktop. Mac OS X is placing references to your volumes in convenient places. These volumes are not actually being mounted on the desktop, but rather in a hidden location in the file system. In this exercise, you will look at what the system is doing behind the scenes.

1  Open MBR_Image.dmg found in Chapter4 of the StudentMaterials.

Notice that the two volumes appear on the desktop.

2  Back in Terminal, change your working directory to your desktop.

```
client17:~ chris$ cd ~/Desktop
```

3   Use ls to view the contents of your Desktop folder.

client17:~ chris$ `ls -A`

There is no reference to the volumes that were mounted.

4   Use cd to change your working directory to /Volumes.

5   Get a directory listing.

Here you find all the volumes that you mounted, including a reference to the boot volume. UNIX uses a single-rooted file system. Unlike some other file systems where every volume is separate (e.g., c:\, d:\, etc.), the UNIX file system is a single tree. New volumes are mounted so that they become new branches of the existing tree. /Volumes gives you a place to look to see all the volumes that are mounted. Advanced users can mount volumes outside this folder.

The Finder does not show you this folder by default. The most analogous thing that the Finder shows you is the Devices list in the sidebar. You can, however, go to this folder if you know it exists.

6   In the Finder, choose Go > Go to Folder.

A dialog drops down from the toolbar.

7   Enter /Volumes in the text field and click Go.

The Finder shows you the contents of the /Volumes folder. Notice that the Finder indicates that everything in /Volumes is an alias. The Go to Folder feature of the Finder can take you to any hidden folder.

8   Log out.

# Permissions and Troubleshooting

# 4.2

One of the fundamental security features of Mac OS X is file system permissions. Every single item in the file system has permissions associated with it that prevent unauthorized access to those items. Understanding file system permissions is necessary to manage secure sharing amongst users and to resolve authorization and permissions issues. In this lesson you will explore the permissions technologies used by Mac OS X. You will learn how to manage permissions from both the Finder and the command line. Finally, you will learn how to troubleshoot common permissions issues.

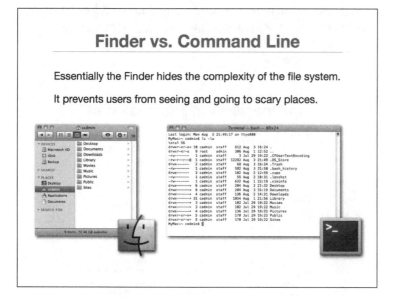

For detailed instructions, see "Managing Permissions via the Finder" in Chapter 4 of *Apple Training Series: Mac OS X Support Essentials v10.6.*

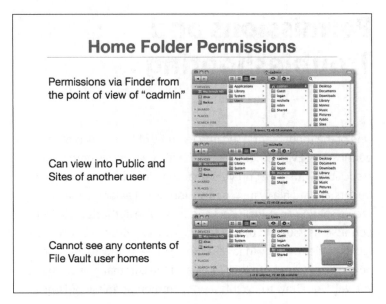

For detailed instructions, see "Understanding File System Permissions" in Chapter 4 of *Apple Training Series: Mac OS X Support Essentials v10.6*.

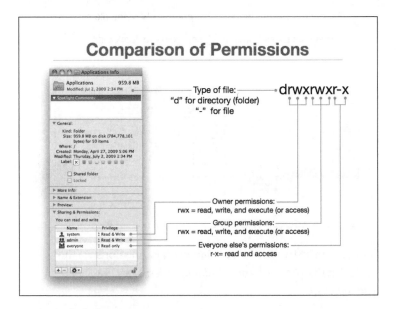

For detailed instructions, see "Understanding File System Permissions" in Chapter 4 of *Apple Training Series: Mac OS X Support Essentials v10.6*.

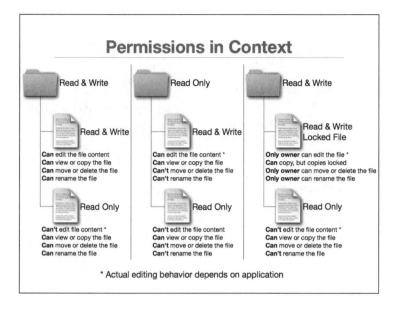

For detailed instructions, see "Understanding File System Permissions" in Chapter 4 of *Apple Training Series: Mac OS X Support Essentials v10.6*.

## Changing UNIX Permissions

### sudo chown *owner:group path*

▸ `sudo chown cadmin:staff /Users/Shared/ReadMe.rtf`

### Use –R option for folders

▸ `sudo chown –R cadmin /Users/cadmin`

### chmod *privilege path*

▸ `chmod g+w /Users/Shared/ReadMe.rtf`

| Who | Action | Permission |
|---|---|---|
| u (user/owner) |  | r (read) |
| g (group) | +, –, = | w (write) |
| o (others/everyone) |  | x (execute or access) |
| a (all=ugo) |  | t (sticky bit) |

For detailed instructions, see "Managing Permissions via Command Line" in Chapter 4 of *Apple Training Series: Mac OS X Support Essentials v10.6*.

## Access Control Lists (ACLs)

Extends standard UNIX permissions

Allows for any number of access control entries, hence the name "access control list"

Extremely flexible, thus often yields confusing results

Finder uses ACLs when adding additional users or groups

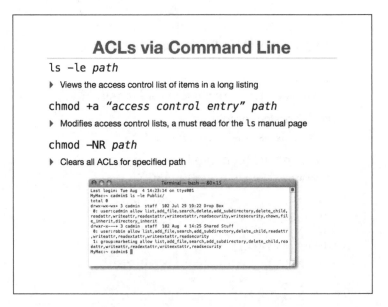

For detailed instructions, see "Understanding File System Permissions" in Chapter 4 of *Apple Training Series: Mac OS X Support Essentials v10.6.*

## ACLs via Command Line

`ls -le` *path*

▸ Views the access control list of items in a long listing

`chmod +a "access control entry" path`

▸ Modifies access control lists, a must read for the `ls` manual page

`chmod -NR` *path*

▸ Clears all ACLs for specified path

For detailed instructions, see "Managing Permissions via Command Line" in Chapter 4 of *Apple Training Series: Mac OS X Support Essentials v10.6.*

For detailed instructions, see "File System Troubleshooting" in Chapter 4 of *Apple Training Series: Mac OS X Support Essentials v10.6.*

For detailed instructions, see "File System Troubleshooting" in Chapter 4 of *Apple Training Series: Mac OS X Support Essentials v10.6.*

Exercise 4.2.1
# Fixing Permissions Issues with Disk Utility

## Objectives

- Understand how Disk Utility determines if permissions are correct
- Repair permissions using Disk Utility

## Summary

Disk Utility allows you to repair file and folder permissions for system files and Apple applications. The Apple installer creates receipts upon installation that Disk Utility uses for comparison. In this exercise, you will use Disk Utility to see how to fix permissions issues and you will review the location of installation receipts that are used by the Repair Disk Permissions command as well as which receipts are used for permission repair. It is important to know that only a subset of what has been installed on the system will be repaired and nothing in a user's home folder will be touched. The Password Reset Utility on the install disc can help with permission issues in the home folder.

## Identify Which Receipts Are Used for Permissions Repair

Anything installed by the Apple installer will generate a receipt. The information critical for permissions repair is maintained in a database. As of Mac OS X v10.6, that database is located in /var/db/receipts and consists of a bill of materials (bom) file and a property list (plist) file for each package. If you're having problems with an application that does not have an installation receipt in /var/db/receipts, Repair Permissions will not fix that problem. Even though you may see receipts for third-party applications, do not assume that these will be included in Repair Permissions. Repair Permissions also does not fix permissions issues on data files that you have created, such as items in your home folder.

1  Log in as Client Administrator.

2  Use Finder's Go to Folder command to navigate to /var/db/receipts.

This is where receipts are stored. As you can see, there are rather a lot of them installed by default. You can use Quick Look to view the plist files, but the bills of materials cannot be viewed this way.

Fortunately, there is relatively little information you need to access directly in this folder. Manipulating it directly is discouraged because Apple has provided command-line tools for viewing this information and manipulating it.

3  Open the Terminal application.

The tool that will tell you exactly which packages will be repaired is repair_packages. It lives in a slightly out-of-the-way place.

4  Tell repair_packages to tell you which receipt will be included when repairing permissions.

```
client17:~ chris$ /usr/libexec/repair_packages
--list-standard-pkgs
```

You see a list of package IDs. Each package has a package ID that uniquely identifies it. The package ID usually follows a reverse DNS–type naming scheme. These are the packages whose permissions are repaired by Disk Utility.

## Repair Permissions Using Disk Utility

In this exercise, you'll run an Automator application to alter expected permissions for a specific directory and then repair those permissions using Disk Utility. A common instance where permissions can routinely be altered is during the installation of software such as printer drivers. Because incorrect permissions on folders related to printing can interfere with a user's ability to print, Repair Permissions is often a quick fix for this issue.

1  In the Finder's sidebar, click the Applications folder.

2  Open the File menu, hold the Option key, and choose Show Inspector.

   The inspector is a Get Info window that updates dynamically to show info for any item selected in the Finder.

3  Open the Sharing & Permissions pane, if necessary.

   Note that the permissions for the Applications folder are Read & Write for administrators but Read Only for everyone. That means nonadministrative users cannot add to this directory by installing applications.

4    Using a new Finder window, double-click the ChangePerms
     icon in the Chapter4 folder of /Users/Shared/StudentMaterials.

     Notice that the inspector updates as your selection changes
     while you open the new window and navigate to the
     Automator application.

     ChangePerms is an Automator application that will run a script
     altering permissions on your computer.

     You may briefly see an indicator in the menu bar that the script
     has run. Because the script is short the menu bar indicator will
     disappear almost immediately.

5    Return to the inspector window for /Applications by clicking on
     the Finder window that is displaying /Applications. Verify that
     the write permissions for everyone have been added.

6    In the Finder, switch to the window you used to get to the
     student materials and choose Go > Utilities.

7    Open Disk Utility.

8    Select the icon for Macintosh HD in the source list.

9    Click the First Aid button, if necessary.

     This should be selected by default.

**10** Click Repair Disk Permissions.

Repairing permissions can take a few minutes. When it completes, note the output in Disk Utility and the change in the inspector window. You may have to click off Applications and go back to it for the inspector to update.

**11** Close the inspector window.

**12** Log out.

Exercise 4.2.2
# Understanding Permissions

## Objectives

- View and configure permissions using the Finder

- Understand how permissions on a folder affect files stored inside it

## Summary

A thorough understanding of ownership and permissions is essential to supporting and troubleshooting Mac OS X. Permissions control the access to files and folders by users and system services such as the printing system. The following exercises will give you a brief introduction to permissions in a user's home folder.

## View Permissions in the Finder

In this exercise, you will create some items to experiment with, set permissions, then log in as a different user to test the options.

1 Log in as Client Administrator.

2 Navigate to your home folder in the Finder, then choose New Folder from the File menu.

3 Name the new folder `Payroll Reports`, and be sure it is located in your home folder, along with the default Mac OS X folders.

4 Open TextEdit.

5 In TextEdit, choose File > Save to save the empty document that was created when you opened TextEdit. Name the new file `Company Org Chart`, then choose your home folder as the save location.

   You can click the disclosure button next to the Save As text field to have more options for choosing a save location.

6 In TextEdit, choose File > Save As, and name the new file `Secret Bonus List` and save it to the desktop.

7  Close the file.

8  Drag the Secret Bonus List.rtf file inside the Payroll Reports folder. This will move the file to the Payroll Reports folder.

9  Control-click (or right-click) the TextEdit icon in the Dock, then choose Keep in Dock from the Options menu of the pop-up menu that appears. You will be asked to create files in TextEdit throughout this chapter, so you might as well keep TextEdit in your Dock for easy access.

10  Quit TextEdit.

11  Use fast user switching to log in as Chris Johnson.

12  In the Finder, navigate to Client Administrator's home folder.

13  Click on the Desktop folder, then choose Get Info from the file menu. Open Sharing & Permissions if necessary.

With the exception of Public and Sites, which are designed for sharing, folders that Mac OS X creates by default in the home folder are protected from access by other users (the No Access permission).

*Question 2*  *What permissions do users other than the owner have for the Desktop folder?*

14 Close the Get Info window.

15 Open the Payroll Reports folder.

*Question 3  Can you see inside the folder? Can you open the Secret Bonus List file?*

This behavior may be contrary to what is expected by users. Be sure to guide your users to store their folders in the right place, based on the type of access they wish to allow for other users. While others cannot add or remove items stored in the Payroll Reports folder, they can open and read the contents. You can see the permissions explicitly when you select the folder, and choose File > Get Info.

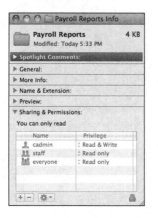

16 Open the Company Org Chart file.

*Question 4  Can you open the file? Save changes to the file? Why?*

17 Close the file without saving.

18 Navigate to the Users folder, and locate the user folder for Robin Banks (robin).

*Question 5  Can you open the folder?*

FileVault users present certain challenges when attempting to share files.

19 Log out of Chris's account.

20 At the login window, switch to Client Administrator.

21 Move the Payroll Reports folder and the Company Org Chart file to the Trash.

22 Log out.

Exercise 4.2.3
# Managing Permissions

## Objective
• Set permissions for folders and files

## Summary
While Mac OS X typically handles permissions for system services transparently, users may wish to modify the permissions for their own files as needed. In this exercise, you'll learn about how permissions work and how to view and set permissions for users' files and folders. As you have seen in previous exercises, permissions can be viewed and managed in the Finder and at the command line.

## View Default Permissions
In this exercise, you will create files and folders in various locations and test access by other users.

1   Log in as Client Administrator.

2   Open Client Administrator's home folder in the Finder.

    You of course have access to everything in your own home folder by default.

3   Open Chris Johnson's home folder.

You only have access to Chris's Public and Sites folders. These folders are preconfigured for sharing. Even though you are currently logged in as an administrator, you cannot see what is in Chris's other folders. The main thing that being an administrator gives you is the ability to elevate your privilege. Most of the time, an administrator is just another user.

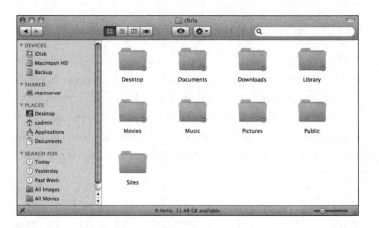

4   Open the Terminal application.

5   Get a long listing of your home folder that includes access control lists.

client17:~ cadmin$ `ls -le`

The l option provides a long listing. The e option shows extended security information (access control lists).

Files (and folders, but to UNIX everything is a file) that have an access control list have a plus sign (+) immediately following the file's mode (the sequence of various combinations of drwx- and a few other things you might see there). Any file that has an access control list gets at least one more line in the output of ls with the e option. Each additional line (the lines often wrap, but each starts with a number and a colon) represents a single access control entry.

In cadmin's home folder, all of the standard folders come preconfigured with an access control list:

```
0: group:everyone deny delete
```

everyone is a special group. Every user is a member of everyone. In other words, no one can delete the standard folders in a user's home folder. This is done to prevent a common class of user error.

Note the user (cadmin) and group (staff) for each file. With the exception of Public and Sites, the group and others (everyone, world) do not have permission on any of the standard folders.

If you have a Send Registration file, it looks a little bit different. It is owned by root and its mode starts with an l, indicating that it is a symbolic link (a form of alias or shortcut). The path after the -> indicates what the file is an alias to.

6  Change your working directory to Chris Johnson's home folder.

```
client17:~ cadmin$ cd ~chris
```

7  Get a long listing of Chris's home folder along with access control list information.

Things look much the same in Chris's home folder as they did in Client Administrator's. The major difference is that everything is owned by chris instead of cadmin.

8  Change your working directory back to Client Administrator's home folder.

```
client17:chris cadmin$ cd
```

The cd command with no argument automatically changes you back to your home folder.

9  Switch to the Finder and navigate back to Client Administrator's home folder.

10  Select the Documents folder and bring up the Get Info window.

11  Open the Sharing & Permissions pane, if necessary.

12 Change the everyone permission from No Access to Read & Write.

13 Switch back to Terminal and get another long listing with extended security information.

14 Compare the permissions (the file's mode) on the Documents folder against their previous setting.

Now everyone (others, world) has read, write, and execute (traversable) permission on Documents.

The Finder doesn't give explicit access to the execute permission. In the vast majority of cases, when a folder is readable or writable, you want it to be executable as well. This is what the Finder does. If the permission is anything besides No Access, the execute permission will be set.

Full read/write access on your Documents folder is a bit permissive.

15 Use `chmod` at the command line to remove write permission for everyone:

```
client17:~ cadmin$ chmod o-w Documents
```

chmod uses a series of symbols to allow you to set the permissions or mode on a file:

u   user

g   group

o   other

+   add a permission

-   remove a permission

r   read

w   write

x   execute

So, `o-w` means remove write permission from others (everyone).

16 Use `ls -le` to view the permissions again. Notice that the write permission on Documents has been removed.

17  Switch back to the Finder and notice that the Get Info window immediately updates to show Read Only access for everyone.

18  Use the Finder to return the permissions for everyone to No Access.

19  Close the Get Info window.

20  Create a new folder in your home folder. Name it Test.

21  Switch to Terminal and use `ls -le` to view the permissions on the new folder.

By default the folder is readable both by members of the group staff and by everyone.

22  Use `chmod` to remove read and execute permission from Test for members of the group and all others.

```
client17:~ cadmin$ chmod go-rx Test
```

23  Use the command line or the Finder to verify your change.

## Manage an Access Control List

While there are techniques for managing access control lists from the command line, it is easier by far to use the Finder. You will use the Finder to apply an access control list to your Test folder.

1  Switch to the Finder, if necessary, and bring up the Get Info window for your Test folder.

2  In the Sharing & Permissions pane, click the Add (+) button and select Chris Johnson from the Users & Groups list in the window that is presented. Then click Select.

Chris is added to the list.

3  Give Chris Read & Write permission.

4  Switch to Terminal and use `ls -le` to view what the Finder has done to Test.

Because a file can only have exactly one user associated with it (and that is Client Administrator because Client Administrator created this folder), the Finder used an access control list to allow the additional user (chris) access to the file.

## Examine a Drop Box

Drop box folders provide a convenient way for one user to send a file to another user. You will examine what happens when you use a drop box folder.

1   Use fast user switching to log in as Chris Johnson.

2   Open TextEdit and save an empty document, From Chris, on Chris's desktop.

3   Quit TextEdit.

4   In the Finder, navigate to Client Administrator's Public folder (/Users/cadmin/Public).

5   Drag From Chris from the desktop to the Drop Box folder in Client Administrator's Public folder.

A dialog appears telling you that you won't have permission to see the result.

6   Click OK.

7   Drag the same file to the Test folder in cadmin's home folder.

Note that this time it moved the file rather than copied it.

8   Log out as Chris Johnson.

9   At the login window, switch to Client Administrator.

10  In the Finder, open the Test folder.

11  Open From Chris.

The document opens because you have read access on it.

12  In the Terminal, view the permissions and ownership on the From Chris.rtf file in Test.

Chris owns the file. This is not surprising because Chris created the file and then moved it into this folder.

13  Make a change to the document and save it.

It saves successfully because you have write access to the folder that contains the file.

14  In the Terminal, view the permissions and ownership on the From Chris.rtf document now.

*Question 6   Has anything changed? If so, what and why?*

 

 

 

 

15  Change your working directory to ~/Public/Drop Box.

This is a good place to use tab completion or to drag from the Finder. cd would normally take the space in "Drop Box" as a separator between arguments, which would result in an error. To prevent that, you need to "escape" the space. That is, you need to tell the system that the space is part of the filename. Tab completion and dragging from the Finder will take care of that for you. If you want to type it, you need to put a backslash (\) in front of the space or place the whole path in quotation marks.

```
client17:Test cadmin$ cd ~/Public/Drop\ Box
```

**16** View the permissions and ownership on the From Chris.rtf document in the Drop Box folder.

The file is owned by chris as expected; however, the file has also picked up an access control list. This ACL is inherited from the Drop Box folder. ACE inheritance is optional and clearly was not set on the Test folder.

**17** Log out.

## Exercise 4.2.4
# Troubleshooting Permissions

## Objectives

- Verify the permissions on a folder that is inaccessible
- Correct the permissions to allow access to the folder

## Summary

You've had opportunities to practice hands-on setting and review-ing permissions issues. In this exercise, you will run a script that sets permissions in a location on the computer. Your task will be to determine the issue introduced by this and then resolve it. You will also see a technique for eliminating issues with access control lists.

## Troubleshooting Permissions

In this exercise, you'll run a script that modifies expected permis-sions in some way. Use either the Finder or the command line to investigate and fix this issue.

1   Log in as Client Administrator.

2   Open the Chapter4 folder in StudentMaterials, and locate the Automator application ChrisPublicPerms.

ChrisPublicPerms

3   Double-click the file.

You may briefly see a message in the menu bar indicating that the script has run.

4   Using fast user switching, log in as Mayta Mishtuk (mayta). If asked to correct her keychain password, go ahead and do so. Her old password is marta.

5  Drag the Project file from the desktop to Chris Johnson's Drop Box folder. If asked to authenticate, click Cancel.

*Question 7  Are you able to copy this file?*

*Question 8  Are the permissions for this folder set as you would expect? What tools can you use to find the answer?*

There are several ways to change the permissions on Chris's Public folder. For a little more practice with the command line, you will use chmod. You could also use the Finder or the Reset Password Utility on the install disc. You also will use chmod from the Client Administrator account in order to gain some exposure to sudo. sudo allows you to run commands as a different user. The most common usage is for an administrator to run commands as the superuser (also known as root or System Administrator).

6  Switch to the Client Administrator account.

7  Open the Terminal application. Open a new window.

8  Enter the following command:

client17:~ cadmin$ `chmod go+r /Users/chris/Public`

Note the syntax used in the above command: You are adding read permissions for the group and others, and specifying the directory to which you want these permissions applied.

You will see a message stating that this operation is not permitted. In order to change the permissions on folders owned by another user, you must perform this command as the root user. The command for performing commands as root is sudo, or "switch user do." Precede this command with sudo in order for it to work.

9  Enter the following command:

client17:~ cadmin$ `sudo chmod go+r /Users/chris/Public`

Enter cadmin's password when prompted. Note that it will not echo (display on the screen) as you type.

10  Check the permissions on Chris's Public folder.

*Question 9*  Were you able to change the permissions?

11  Switch back to Mayta's user account.

12  Copy the Project.rtf file from Mayta's desktop to Chris's drop box.

*Question 10*  Were you successful?

13  Log out Mayta.

## Eliminating ACLs

Sometimes you want to eliminate an access control list that a file or folder picked up. There are several ways to approach this. You will use one technique that will quickly eliminate all the ACLs on a particular object.

1  Switch to Client Administrator.

2  In a Terminal window, change your working directory to ~/Public/Drop Box.

3  Use `ls -le` to view the access control list on From Chris.rtf.

4  Enter the following command:

    client17:Drop Box cadmin$ `chmod -N "From Chris.rtf"`

The `-N` option to `chmod` eliminates the access control list on the file. Because you have permission to change permissions on the file, you can delete the ACL.

You may have to provide cadmin's password.

5  Use `ls -le` to view the access controls on From Chris.rtf.

The access control list is gone.

6  Log out.

# 5

# Data Management and Backup

# 5.1

# Mac OS X Volume Hierarchy

The average Mac OS X installation is well over 200,000 individual files. While this may seem like an overwhelming number of files, the system has been organized in a logical manner that makes things easy to find for both basic and advanced users. This lesson focuses on how Mac OS X is organized, and how an administrator can take advantage of this organization to control access to resources.

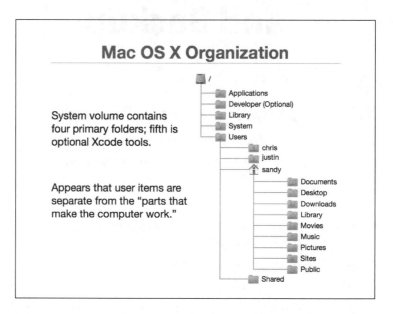

For detailed instructions, see "Mac OS X Volume Hierarchy" in Chapter 5 of *Apple Training Series: Mac OS X Support Essentials v10.6.*

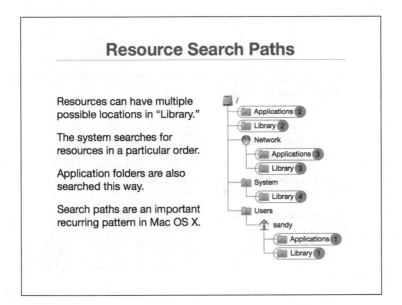

For detailed instructions, see "System Resource Hierarchy" in Chapter 5 of *Apple Training Series: Mac OS X Support Essentials v10.6*.

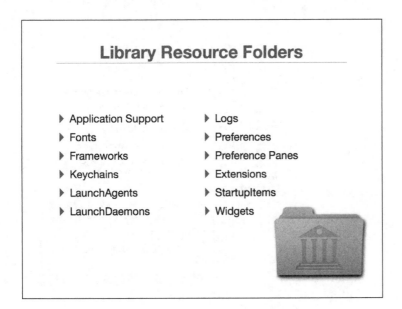

For detailed instructions, see "System Resource Types" in Chapter 5 of *Apple Training Series: Mac OS X Support Essentials v10.6*.

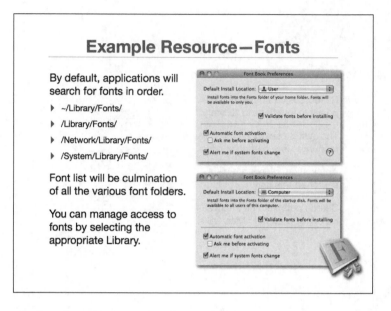

For detailed instructions, see "Managing Font Resources" in Chapter 5 of *Apple Training Series: Mac OS X Support Essentials v10.6.*

## Mac OS X Hidden Folders

Many UNIX items are hidden from user's Finder view.

Items are hidden by:

▸ Period at beginning of name

▸ Setting the hidden file flag:
  `chflags hidden path`

For detailed instructions, see "Managing Hidden Items" in Chapter 5 of *Apple Training Series: Mac OS X Support Essentials v10.6.*

## Exercise 5.1.1
# Configuring Time Machine (optional)

## Objective

- Set up Time Machine

## Summary

Time Machine provides an easy-to-use method for users to back up their computers. It saves space by ignoring files that have not changed. In this exercise, you will set up Time Machine to back up the Users folder on your computer. You will use the backup to restore "lost" data in a later exercise.

## Copy Some vCards to Address Book

1   Log in as Client Administrator.

2   Open the StudentMaterials folder in /Users/Shared.

3   Open the Chapter5 folder.

4   Drag the vCards folder to the Address Book in the Dock.

    A dialog sheet opens to confirm that you want to add the contacts to your address book.

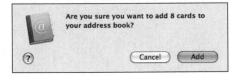

5   Click Add.

    This imports eight vCards into Address Book.

## Set Up Preferences for Time Machine

1  Open System Preferences.

2  Click Time Machine.

3  Turn on Time Machine by sliding the switch to ON.

4  Select Backup, and click Use for Backup.

A dialog slides down to confirm that you want to back up to another volume on your boot drive. Normally you would not want to do this because a failure of that one hard drive would likely result in loss of your data and your backups.

5   Click Use Selected Volume.

Another dialog informs you that FileVault home folders are only
backed up when the user is not logged in.

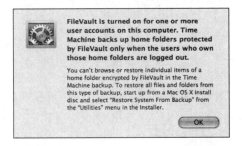

FileVault is turned on for one or more
user accounts on this computer. Time
Machine backs up home folders protected
by FileVault only when the users who own
those home folders are logged out.

You can't browse or restore individual items of a
home folder encrypted by FileVault in the Time
Machine backup. To restore all files and folders from
this type of backup, start up from a Mac OS X Install
disc and select "Restore System From Backup" from
the "Utilities" menu in the Installer.

OK

6   Click OK.

At this point Time Machine will wait two minutes, giving you
time to set what you want to back up before it starts backing up
for the first time.

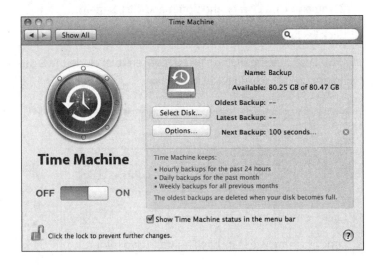

7  Click the Options button to reveal a dialog allowing you to exclude folders from backup.

8  Click the Add (+) button at the bottom of the dialog.

9  Select the Applications, Library, and System folders.

   Click Macintosh HD in the dialog's sidebar, then click Applications, Command-click Library, and Command-click System.

10 Click Exclude.

11 When you see the dialog "You've chosen to exclude the System Folder," click Exclude All System Files.

12 Click Done.

   Time Machine will start backing up in two minutes.

13 Close System Preferences.

14 Log out.

Exercise 5.1.2

# Understanding System Resource Locations

## Objectives

- Enable a font for just a single user
- Understand search paths for system resources, such as fonts

## Summary

System resources, such as fonts, sounds, application support files, and application preferences, are found at various locations in the file system. Where a resource is stored determines to whom it is made available. For example, a font located within the /Library/Fonts folder in a user's home folder is available to just that user, but a font located in /Library/Fonts is available to all users on that computer. In this exercise, you will remove a font from /Library/Fonts, where it was available to all users, and install it in a single user's Fonts directory.

## Remove a Font

You can use Font Book to watch what happens when you move a font to the Trash.

1 Verify that no users are logged in using fast user switching. If any users are logged in, log them out.

2 Log in as Chris Johnson (chris).

3 Open the Font Book application, which is located in /Applications.

4   Select Arial in the Font column and click the triangle to expand the list of font styles. Locate the Arial Regular typeface. It is listed as Regular indented under Arial.

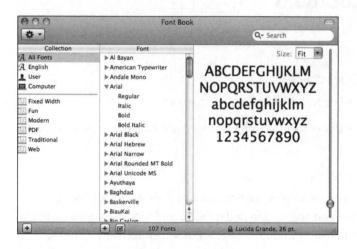

5   In the Finder, open the folder /Library/Fonts.

These fonts are available to all users on the system.

6   Locate the file Arial.ttf. It contains the Arial Regular font.

7   Drag Arial.ttf to the desktop. You should see a mouse cursor with a green badge with a plus sign on it attached to the pointer. This will be your backup copy of the Arial font.

8   Move the Arial.ttf file from /Library/Fonts to the Trash. You will have to authenticate as Client Administrator when prompted.

9  Click the Font Book window to make it the active application.

The Arial Regular font is no longer listed in the Font Book window. Font Book shows a real-time display of all the fonts in the system search path.

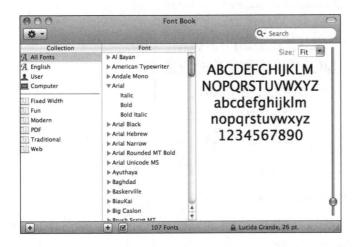

## Add a Font for Use by One User Only

You can use Font Book to install a font for just one user of the computer.

1  In Font Book, choose Font Book > Preferences.

2  Ensure that the Default Install Location is set to User.

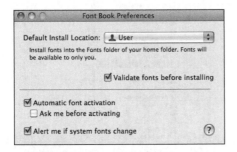

3  Close Font Book's preferences.

4   Switch to the Finder and double-click Arial.ttf on the desktop.

This will open Arial.ttf in Font Book, which will ask if you want to install the font.

5   Click Install Font.

The User collection should autoselect and Arial Regular should be listed there.

6   Quit Font Book.

7   Switch to the Finder and navigate to ~/Library/Fonts to confirm that Arial.ttf has been copied to your Fonts folder.

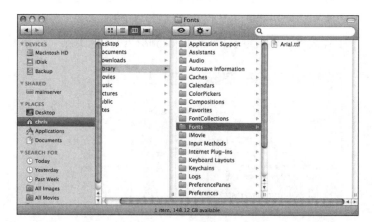

## Confirm that the Font Is Unavailable to Other Users

If you log in as a different user, you don't have access to the fonts in Chris's Fonts folder.

1   Use fast user switching to switch to Mayta Mishtuk's account (mayta).

2   Open Font Book and open the Arial font group.

You will notice that Arial Regular is not visible in Font Book for Mayta's account. At this time, you could add Arial to Mayta's user account, just as you added it to Chris's account earlier. You would have to copy the font file to somewhere Mayta can access.

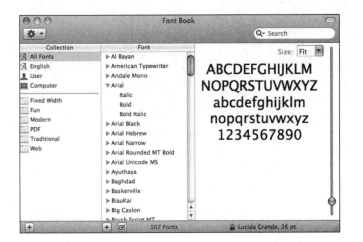

3   Quit Font Book.

## Clean Up and Validate Your Fonts

You have made a font change. Now you will undo the change.

1   Use fast user switching to switch back to the Chris Johnson account.

2   Drag the Arial font from the desktop to /Library/Fonts. Authenticate as Client Administrator when prompted. This will make Arial Regular available for all users again.

3   Navigate to ~/Library/Fonts and move Arial.ttf to the Trash.

4   Open the Font Book application.

5   Select the All Fonts collection and then select all the fonts (Command-A will select all).

6   Choose File > Validate Fonts.

This will cause Font Book to read and validate all of the font files, checking for any corruption.

7   Log out all logged-in users.

# File Metadata and Spotlight

# 5.2

Simply, metadata is information about an item in the file system. The most common form of metadata is an item's filename, and from there Mac OS X expands to allow for nearly limitless amounts of additional metadata to define an item. While most of this metadata is hidden from the user, you'll learn how to access and manipulate common forms of file system metadata. You'll also learn how the system maintains custom metadata even when saving files to third-party storage. Finally, you'll learn how to take advantage of Spotlight, Mac OS X's advanced metadata search engine.

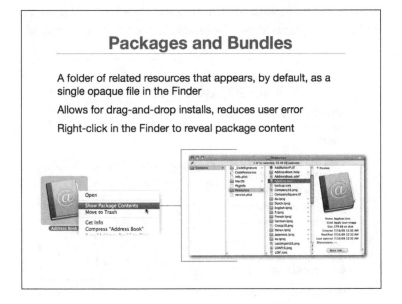

For detailed instructions, see "Bundles and Packages" in Chapter 5 of *Apple Training Series: Mac OS X Support Essentials v10.6*.

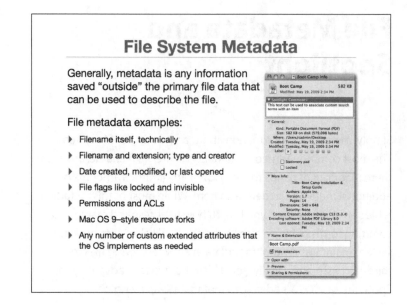

For detailed instructions, see "Understanding File System Metadata" in Chapter 5 of *Apple Training Series: Mac OS X Support Essentials v10.6.*

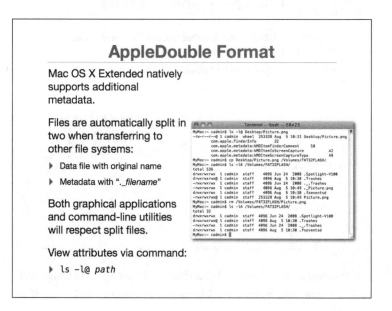

For detailed instructions, see "Metadata on non-Mac volumes" in Chapter 5 of *Apple Training Series: Mac OS X Support Essentials v10.6.*

## Managing Launch Services

Launch services determines which application to open based on filename extension.

Sets default application for a file by making a change to the file's metadata attributes

Sets default application for all files of that type for user

▸ ~/Library/Preferences/ com.apple.LaunchServices.plist

For detailed instructions, see "Managing Launch Services" in Chapter 5 of *Apple Training Series: Mac OS X Support Essentials v10.6.*

## Understanding Spotlight

Instantaneous drive data and metadata searches via index

Index initially created and then updated on the fly

Spotlight plugins allow for extensible indexing.

▸ Plugins located in various library Spotlight folders

Spotlight indexes stored at:

▸ /.Spotlight-V100

▸ /Volumes/volumename/.Spotlight-V100

▸ ~/Library/Mail/Envelope Index

For detailed instructions, see "Using Spotlight and Quick Look" in Chapter 5 of *Apple Training Series: Mac OS X Support Essentials v10.6.*

## Spotlight Security and Privacy

When users search through locally attached nonsystem volumes, they can choose to ignore ownership permissions.

Disable categories from searches

Specify exempt volumes in the privacy list—this also deletes the Spotlight index files—remove from list to rebuild index.

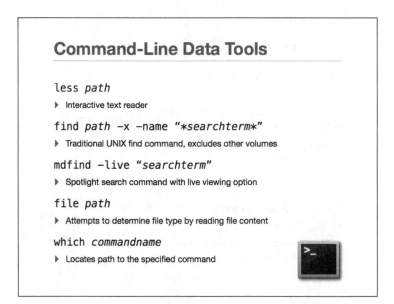

For detailed instructions, see "Spotlight Security" in Chapter 5 of *Apple Training Series: Mac OS X Support Essentials v10.6.*

## Command-Line Data Tools

`less path`
▶ Interactive text reader

`find path −x −name "*searchterm*"`
▶ Traditional UNIX find command, excludes other volumes

`mdfind −live "searchterm"`
▶ Spotlight search command with live viewing option

`file path`
▶ Attempts to determine file type by reading file content

`which commandname`
▶ Locates path to the specified command

For detailed instructions, see "Command-Line File Manipulation" in Chapter 3 of *Apple Training Series: Mac OS X Support Essentials v10.6.*

Exercise 5.2.1

# Viewing Package Contents (optional or walkthrough)

## Objectives

- View the contents of a package

- Understand how packages can be used to distribute localized languages in a single file

## Summary

In this exercise, you will use the Finder to view package contents. A package is made up of a collection of files an application uses to tell Installer what to install, how to install it, and how to verify that it was installed. These items reside in the Contents folder inside the package. You will look at an application and a document to see how packages can store multiple languages as resources.

## Examine the Contents of the Address Book Application Package

1   Log in as Chris Johnson. (As a walkthrough, the instructor can use the account they are using for presentations.)

2   Using the Finder, locate Address Book in the Applications folder.

3   Control-click Address Book and choose Show Package
    Contents. Change to column view if necessary.

    This command opens a new Finder window, in which the
    package contents are displayed.

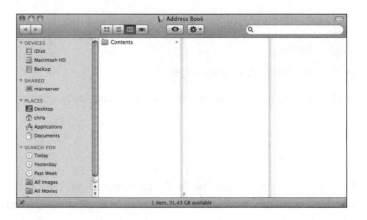

4   Open the Contents folder.

5   Select the Resources folder.

    Here you can see portions of the package structure and resources,
    including images (png, tiff, tif, etc.), scripting definitions (sdef),
    icons (icns), language projects (lproj, used for localizing an
    application to multiple languages), etc. Inside the lproj folders
    you'll see strings files and nib (NeXT Interface Builder) files (folders).
    These generally contain the user interface elements of the
    application, again localized to the appropriate language.

6   Select the AddressBook.help folder and navigate to the Contents/Resources/German.lproj folder within it.

7   Select the pgs folder and view some of the html files by selecting one and pressing the Space bar. You can use the arrow keys to move between other files.

*Question 1  What do you think these files are for?*

_____

_____

_____

8   Look at some of the same files in another language, possibly Japanese (Japanese.lproj), Korean (ko.lproj), or Russian (ru.lproj).

## Examine How Various Resources Are Used

1   Open Address Book.

As you would expect, the menus are in your environment's primary language, probably English.

2   Close (quit) Address Book.

3   Open System Preferences.

4   Click the Language & Text preferences icon.

5  Click the Language button and drag Français to the top of the language list. Do not close System Preferences.

6  Open Address Book again.

Notice that the menus have now changed to French.

7  Close Address Book.

8  Try another language if you like but make sure you do not quit System Preferences or it will be difficult to read the instructions in the Language & Text preferences pane.

9  Drag English to the top of the list of languages in the Language & Text preferences pane.

## Examine Contents of the Installation Instructions File

The Installation Instructions file can be located on any Mac OS X Install disc or in the student materials.

1   Locate the Installation Instructions file in the student materials in StudentMaterials/Chapter5. Switch to column view, if necessary.

Notice that the preview icon is a PDF but the kind is listed as an application. This file is an application that is masquerading as a document.

2   Control-click the Installation Instructions file and choose Show Package Contents.

3  Navigate to the Contents/Resources folder.

There are a number of folders for localizations. Some are denoted by the English name of the language, others by ISO codes for the country and/or language.

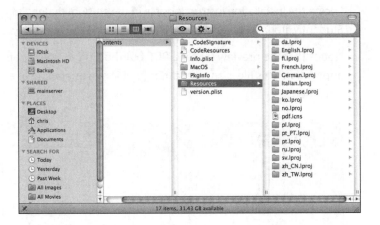

4  Close the Finder window.

5  Open the Installation Instructions file in Preview.

Preview displays the English instructions.

6  Log out.

Exercise 5.2.2
# Examining Launch Services

## Objectives

- Change the application used to open specific file types
- Examine a file using Quick Look

## Summary

In this exercise, you will examine how Launch Services keeps track of preferred applications for each user. It also provides a method to help ensure applications are not downloaded from questionable locations. You will download an application from the Pretendco.com website and examine how the system treats it. You will change preferences for opening text files and see where Mac OS X keeps track of these preferences.

1   Log in as Client Administrator.

2   Open Terminal.

3   Change your working directory to ~/Library/Preferences.

4   Run this command:

```
client17:Preferences cadmin$ ls -l > ~/Desktop/Prefs.txt
```

*Question 2  What does this command do?*

5   Open Safari.

6   Enter `mainserver.pretendco.com/Downloads` in the address bar and press Return.

7   When the webpage loads, click the Download Me link. When the download is complete, close (Command-Q) or hide (Command-H) Safari.

SubEthaEdit.app.zip is downloaded to your Downloads folder and uncompressed, leaving SubEthaEdit.app in your Downloads folder.

8   Drag the SubEthaEdit icon from the Downloads folder (you can drag it from the stack in your Dock) to the Applications folder.

9   Open SubEthaEdit.

The download was tagged with some additional metadata to indicate that it was downloaded from the Internet. The first time you open it, the system asks you to confirm that you in fact do want to open the application.

> **Note**  SubEthaEdit is a collaborative text editor from The Coding Monkeys. A free 30-day trial is available by downloading it from their website: http://codingmonkeys.de.

10  Click Open.

SubEthaEdit tells you about the 30-day trial.

11  Click OK.

12  Switch to Terminal.

13  In your previous Terminal window (or a new one with working
    directory ~/Library/Preferences), enter the following command:

    client17:Preferences cadmin$ `ls -l > ~/Desktop/2ndPrefs.txt`

14  Close Terminal.

15  Open the file Prefs.txt on the desktop. It opens in the TextEdit
    application.

16  Quit TextEdit.

17  Now Control-click the 2ndPrefs.txt file and choose Get Info
    from the contextual menu.

18  In the Get Info window, ensure that the "Open with" section
    is open.

19  Choose SubEthaEdit from the "Open with" pop-up menu.

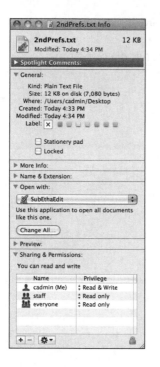

20  Click the Change All button, and click Continue in the dialog
    that opens.

*Question 3*  *What does clicking the Change All button do?*

_____

_____

_____

21  Close the Get Info window.

22  Open the 2ndPrefs.txt file by double-clicking it.

*Question 4*  *In which application does it open?*

_____

23  Double-click the Prefs.txt file.

It now opens in SubEthaEdit instead of TextEdit.

*Question 5*  *What is different in the two directory listings?*

_____

_____

_____

_____

_____

_____

_____

24  Quit SubEthaEdit.

25  In the Finder, navigate to the ~/Library/Preferences directory.

26  Click the com.apple.LaunchServices.plist file.

27  Press the Space bar to activate Quick Look.

Note the com.apple.LaunchServices.plist file is in Client Administrator's home folder. Each user can set his or her own Launch Services preferences.

```
                              com.apple.LaunchServices.plist
<?xml version="1.0" encoding="UTF-8"?>
<!DOCTYPE plist PUBLIC "-//Apple//DTD PLIST 1.0//EN" "http://www.apple.com/DTDs/PropertyList-1.0.dtd">
<plist version="1.0">
<dict>
        <key>LSHandlers</key>
        <array>
                <dict>
                        <key>LSHandlerContentType</key>
                        <string>public.plain-text</string>
                        <key>LSHandlerRoleAll</key>
                        <string>de.codingmonkeys.subethaedit</string>
                </dict>
        </array>
</dict>
</plist>
```

28  Control-click the 2ndPrefs.txt file and choose Get Info from the contextual menu.

29  Choose Console from the "Open with" pop-up menu.

30  Click the Change All button and then click Continue.

31  Repeat steps 25–27.

*Question 6  How has the com.apple.LaunchServices.plist file changed?*

32  Log out.

Exercise 5.2.3
# Using Spotlight

## Objective

• Understand searching with Spotlight

## Summary

Spotlight provides a fast, flexible search mechanism that is integrated with the system. By default, Spotlight only returns results for user visible files; however, the back-end indexing engine indexes much more than that. In this exercise, you will look at a way to see more than Spotlight normally wants to show you and to save the search for easy future reference.

## Search for Recently Modified Files

You will search for recently modified files, including ones you can't normally see, and then save the results as a Smart Folder.

1  Log in as Client Administrator.

2  From the Finder's File menu, choose New Smart Folder.

This creates a new window that is ready for your search criteria.

3   Click the Add (+) button next to the Save button.

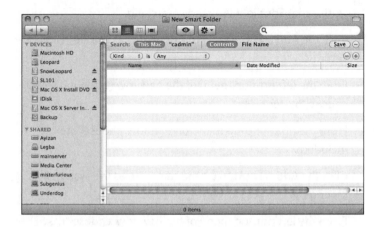

4   From the left pop-up menu (which has Kind selected),
    choose Other.

    A dialog slides down with a wide array of search criteria.

5   Find or use the search box to find "File invisible" and "System
    files" and check the In Menu box for both. This places those
    options in the pop-up menu you just used.

6   Click OK.

7   From the same (left) pop-up menu (with Kind selected), choose
    "File visibility."

8 From the right pop-up menu, choose Visible or Invisible.

Notice that Spotlight is already searching.

9 Click the Add (+) button on the same row as the file visibility settings.

10 From the left pop-up menu of the new row (with Kind selected), choose "System files."

11 From the right pop-up menu on that row, choose "are included."

12 Click the Add (+) button on the same line as the system files settings.

13 From the left pop-up menu of the new row, choose "Last modified date."

14 In the text field, enter 1.

What you have now is a live-updating list of all files (including folders) that have changed in the last day.

15  Click the Save button and name the search `Recently modified`, keeping the other defaults.

Specify a name and location for your Smart Folder

Save As: Recently modified

Where: Saved Searches

☑ Add To Sidebar

Cancel    Save

16  Scroll down the sidebar if necessary to see your Smart Folder in the Search For section of the Finder's sidebar.

17  Log out.

# 5.3 Archive and Backup

When it comes to supporting computer systems, your best insurance is a good backup. Arguably, those who still don't practice a backup routine have simply gotten lucky enough not to lose important data, but their day will come. In this lesson you will learn how to avoid data loss by taking advantage of archive and backup technologies built into Mac OS X. First you will explore Mac OS X's two primary archive technologies, zip archives and disk images. Then you will learn about Mac OS X's rather revolutionary personal backup technology, Time Machine.

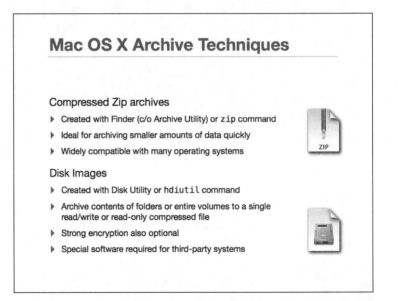

## Mac OS X Archive Techniques

### Compressed Zip archives

▸ Created with Finder (c/o Archive Utility) or `zip` command
▸ Ideal for archiving smaller amounts of data quickly
▸ Widely compatible with many operating systems

### Disk Images

▸ Created with Disk Utility or `hdiutil` command
▸ Archive contents of folders or entire volumes to a single read/write or read-only compressed file
▸ Strong encryption also optional
▸ Special software required for third-party systems

For detailed instructions, see "Using File Archives and Disk Images" in Chapter 5 of *Apple Training Series: Mac OS X Support Essentials v10.6.*

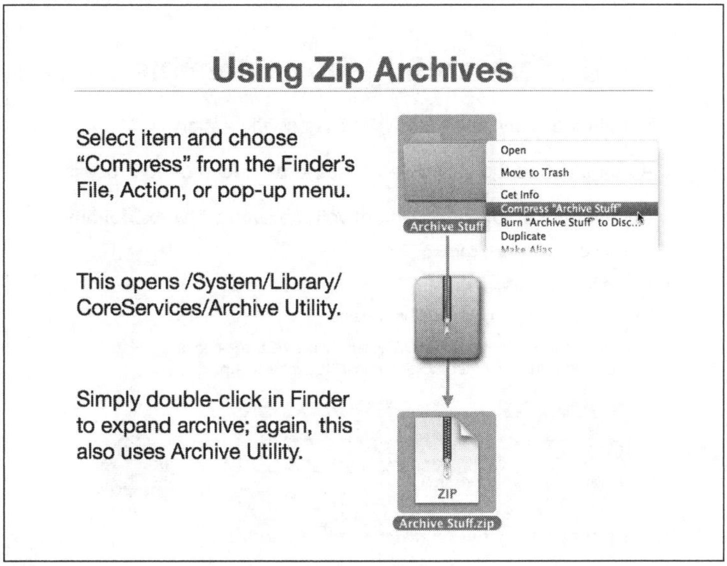

Using Zip Archives
Select item and choose "Compress" from the Finder's File, Action, or pop-up menu.
This opens /System/Library/CoreServices/Archive Utility.
Simply double-click in Finder to expand archive; again, this also uses Archive Utility.
Open
Move to Trash
Get Info
Compress "Archive Stuff"
Burn "Archive Stuff" to Disc...
Duplicate
Archive Stuff
ZIP
Archive Stuff.zip

For detailed instructions, see "Creating Zip Archives" in Chapter 5 of *Apple Training Series: Mac OS X Support Essentials v10.6.*

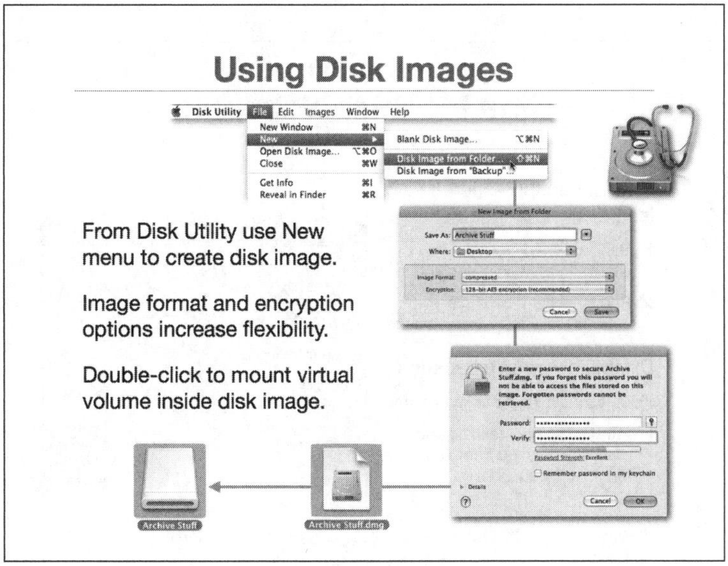

Using Disk Images
From Disk Utility use New menu to create disk image.
Image format and encryption options increase flexibility.
Double-click to mount virtual volume inside disk image.
Disk Utility
File
Edit
Images
Window
Help
New Window
New
Open Disk Image...
Close
Get Info
Reveal in Finder
Blank Disk Image...
Disk Image from Folder...
Disk Image from "Backup"...
Archive Stuff
Archive Stuff.dmg

For detailed instructions, see "Understanding Disk Images" in Chapter 5 of *Apple Training Series: Mac OS X Support Essentials v10.6.*

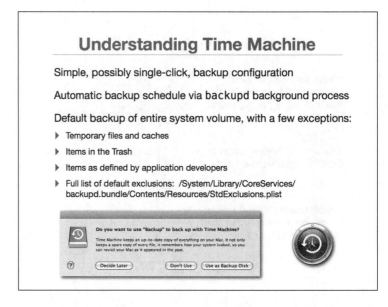

For detailed instructions, see "Understanding Time Machine Backups" in Chapter 5 of *Apple Training Series: Mac OS X Support Essentials v10.6.*

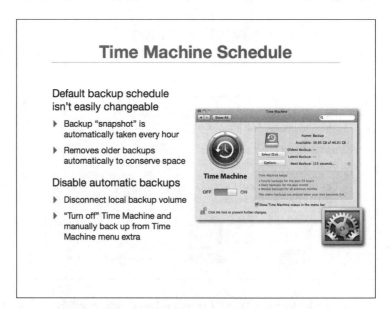

For detailed instructions, see "Configuring Time Machine" in Chapter 5 of *Apple Training Series: Mac OS X Support Essentials v10.6.*

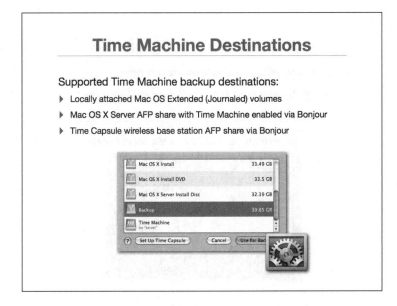

For detailed instructions, see "Configuring Time Machine" in Chapter 5 of *Apple Training Series: Mac OS X Support Essentials v10.6.*

## Time Machine Exclusions

Users can create custom exclusion list for volumes or files.

To exclude all system items, exclude the /System folder and you will be prompted to exclude hidden items as well.

Cannot easily exclude specific file types or user items

Exclude these items from backups:

| | |
|---|---|
| Mac OS X Server Install Disc | 6.74 GB |
| Test System | 7.1 GB |
| Test System 2 | 156 MB |
| Work Drive | 9.16 GB |
| /Applications | 1.09 GB |
| /Developer | 1.86 GB |
| /Library | 2.86 GB |
| System Files and Applications | 12.54 GB |

Calculating size of full backup...

☑ Back up while on battery power
☑ Notify after old backups are deleted

⑦                    Cancel    Do

For detailed instructions, see "Configuring Time Machine" in Chapter 5 of *Apple Training Series: Mac OS X Support Essentials v10.6.*

## Restore from Time Machine

Flashy restore feature encourages user adoption.

Leverages Spotlight and Quick Look to easily locate files

Some applications can directly access Time Machine restore.

Can also restore from install DVD and Migration Assistant

For detailed instructions, see "Restore from Time Machine" in Chapter 5 of *Apple Training Series: Mac OS X Support Essentials v10.6*.

## Time Machine Backup

Backup structure is readable via Finder.

Network backup destinations are inside a disk image.

Time Machine keeps "snapshots" of entire backup:

▶ First backup includes all items.

▶ Future incremental backups only include new and changed files.

▶ Time Machine uses hard links to simulate full backup for nonchanged items.

NOTE: Large files that change often are problematic for backups.

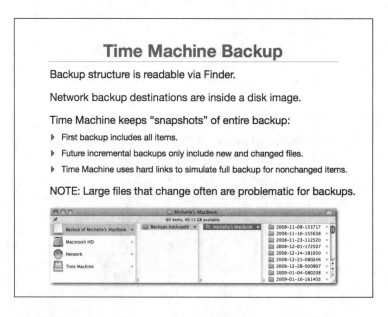

For detailed instructions, see "Manually Restoring from Time Machine" in Chapter 5 of *Apple Training Series: Mac OS X Support Essentials v10.6*.

## Exercise 5.3.1
# Creating Archives

## Objective

- Compress files using the Finder

## Summary

In many support environments, you will need to have your end users send you reporting information by collecting log files or other reports, such as from System Profiler. In this exercise, you will use the Search feature in the Finder to identify a group of files, move them into a folder, and then archive it. You might perform tasks like this in a number of different contexts, but most of the time, you will do this to reduce file clutter and compress files for transfer.

In this exercise, you will create an archive in the Finder. Archives are an effective way to move a group of files from one computer to another, regardless of the files you are copying or the computing platform.

## Copy Logs into a Folder and Archive It

You will create a folder on the desktop and copy some log files into it.

1  Log in as Client Administrator.

2  Create a new folder on the desktop. You can do this by clicking on your desktop and then pressing Command-Shift-N, choosing File > New Folder, or choosing New Folder from the contextual menu.

3  Name the folder Logs.

4  Open a new Finder window and browse to /Library/Logs.

5  Option-drag a copy of the files you find there to the Logs folder on your desktop. Holding down the Option key tells the Finder that you want to make a copy.

6  In the Finder window, browse to ~/Library/Logs.

7  Option-drag a copy of the files you find there to the Logs folder on your desktop.

8  Choose Go > Go to Folder.

9  Enter `/var/log` for the folder you want to go to.

10  Select all the files you find there and Option-drag a copy of them to the Logs folder on your desktop. Option-drag is probably not strictly necessary, but is good practice.

11  When prompted that you may need to enter administrator credentials, click Apply to All and then click Continue.

12  If prompted that a file already exists, click Apply to All, if available, and click Don't Replace.

Normally, you might want to place these files in a subfolder so that you preserve all the logging information. That isn't necessary for our present purposes.

13  If prompted, provide your administrator password.

The system will copy a substantial amount of log information to the Logs folder. These three locations, /Library/Logs, ~/Library/Logs for a particular user, and /var/log are the primary logging locations in Mac OS X.

14  Once the copy completes, select the Logs folder on the desktop.

15  From the contextual menu or the File menu, choose Get Info.

16  Unlock the Sharing & Permissions pane.

**17** In the action menu (denoted with a gear icon) in the Sharing & Permissions pane, choose "Apply to enclosed items."

This is necessary because some of the items you copied into Logs are not owned by you. You will change the ownership and permissions on the items in Logs so that you can create an archive.

Are you sure you want to apply the selected owner, group, and permissions to all the enclosed items?

You can't undo this.

Cancel    OK

**18** In the confirmation dialog, click OK.

**19** Close the Get Info window.

**20** Click on Logs on your desktop if necessary, and choose Compress "Logs" from the File menu or the contextual menu.

Logs.zip is created on your desktop. This zip file can be emailed to Macintosh or Windows users. As a support person, you could use this method to gather reporting information from computers that are not on your network.

**21** Move the Logs folder from your desktop to the Trash.

**22** Double-click the file Logs.zip to see how the Finder can automatically unzip files for you.

A folder named Logs appears on your desktop.

**23** Move the Logs folder from your desktop to the Trash again.

**24** Navigate to /System/Library/CoreServices and open Archive Utility.

Archive Utility is the utility that handles creation and extraction of archive files. It also presents some useful preferences.

25  Select Archive Utility > Preferences.

This is where you can set preferences for the Compress command.

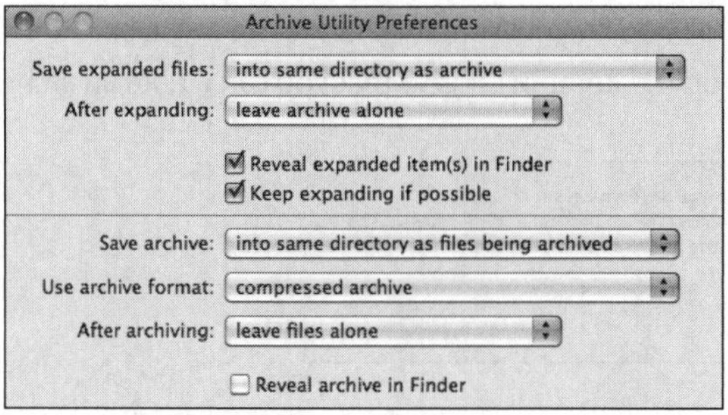

26  Change the "After expanding" preference to "move archive to Trash."

27  Double-click Logs.zip.

*Question 7  What happens?*

_____

_____

28  Once you have tested archiving and unarchiving using the Finder, move any folders or archives from the desktop to the Trash.

29  Log out.

Exercise 5.3.2
# Creating Disk Images (optional)

## Objective

- Create a disk image from a folder

## Summary

You will use Disk Utility to create a new disk image and copy files to the new volume. Disk Utility is the tool you will use most of the time to perform disk formatting and maintenance. A disk image is an extremely effective way to exactly reproduce a local file system. As an added bonus, you will encrypt the disk image in order to protect the contents.

## Create a Disk Image with Disk Utility

In addition to managing and repairing disk drives, you can use Disk Utility to create disk images. The following steps will guide you through using Disk Utility to create a disk image.

You will create a disk image from your home folder, something you might do if you wanted to move files from one computer to another or for backup. You might use disk images to back up particular folders in a number of situations, such as during computer migrations or for routine backups.

1  Log in as Chris Johnson.

2  In the Finder, choose Go > Utilities.

3  Open Disk Utility.

4  Choose File > New > Disk Image from Folder.

An Open dialog will appear.

5   Select your home folder.

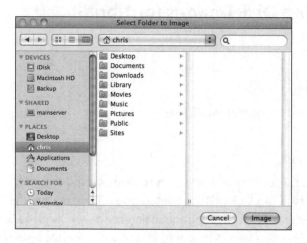

6   Click Image.

The New Image from Folder dialog will appear.

7   Set the image settings as follows:

Name:            ChrisHome

Where:           /Users/Shared (you might have to click the
                 disclosure button in order to select this
                 location)

Image Format:    compressed

Encryption:      128-bit AES encryption (recommended)

8   Click Save.

9   If prompted, authenticate as Client Administrator.

10  When asked to provide a password to secure ChrisHome.dmg,
    use chris.

    Normally you would want to use a much more secure password.
    Notice that the Password Assistant is available.

A Disk Utility Progress window appears.

When Disk Utility is finished, the image file ChrisHome.dmg
appears in Disk Utility.

You can use this method to quickly create backups of important
folders. As you saw, you do not need to encrypt every disk image.

Note that Disk Utility keeps the name of the disk image in its
volumes list, in the bottom section. You can double-click that
icon and mount the image later, as long as the disk image
remains in the same place where it was originally saved.

11  Quit Disk Utility.

**12** Double-click ChrisHome.dmg in /Users/Shared to open it.

The disk image opens without you having to provide the password because the password was stored on your keychain for you by default. You can change this behavior by unchecking the "Remember password in my keychain" checkbox when asked to set the password.

The chris volume will mount on the desktop. This is the volume contained within the ChrisHome.dmg. The filename does not have to reflect any volume name inside it.

A Finder window also opens to show you the contents of the image.

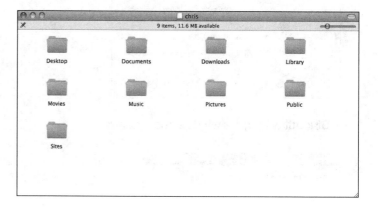

**13** Log out. This will unmount the disk image.

Exercise 5.3.3

# Restore a Backup Using Time Machine (optional)

## Objective

- Use Time Machine to locate and restore a file from a backup

## Summary

In this exercise, you will examine how to use the Time Machine interface to recover lost files from the backup. You will use Time Machine to recover an accidentally deleted entry in your address book and a deleted file from the Downloads folder.

## Restore a Contact Using Time Machine

Here you will delete a contact from your Address Book and then restore it using Time Machine.

1   Log in as Client Administrator.

2   Open System Preferences.

3   Click Time Machine to open Time Machine preferences.

4   Check "Show Time Machine status in the menu bar" if it is not selected.

5  Close System Preferences.

6  Find the Time Machine status menu bar item.

7  Choose Back Up Now from the Time Machine status menu bar item.

A backup will occur immediately. Wait for it to finish.

8  Open Address Book.

You are going to delete some data so that you have something that needs to be restored.

9  Select Rusty Hinjes.

10  Press the Delete key.

11  When asked if you are sure, click Delete.

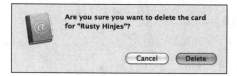

12  Close Address Book.

13  Move your "Open in nano" Automator application from the desktop to the Trash.

14  Choose Finder > Empty Trash. In the confirmation dialog, click Empty Trash.

15 Now imagine you are trying to call Rusty Hinjes. Open Address Book and search for his phone number.

16 With Address Book the active application, open Time Machine.

There are a couple of ways you can open Time Machine. You can click its dock icon or you can choose Enter Time Machine from Time Machine's menu bar item.

17 Navigate to an earlier time by clicking the up arrow to the lower right of the Address Book window. It points back in time.

Rusty Hinjes's entry will appear in the address book.

18 Restore Rusty Hinjes's entry by selecting his card and clicking Restore in the lower right of the screen.

Time Machine mode ends and you are returned to Address Book. Address Book asks if you are sure you want to add 1 card to your address book.

19 Click Add.

20 Switch to the Finder and use a window to view your desktop.

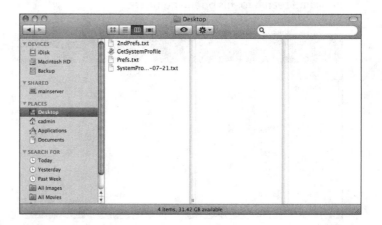

21 Open Time Machine.

22 Navigate back in time until "Open in nano" appears in the Desktop folder.

23 Select "Open in nano."

24 Click Restore.

You are returned to the Finder and "Open in nano" is now in the Desktop folder (and therefore on your desktop).

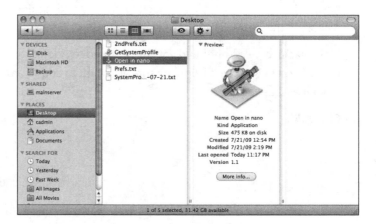

## View and Restore Directly from the Time Machine Backups

Time Machine stores its backups in the file system. This nice feature means that you can restore files by directly inspecting the backup and copying files out of it.

1  In the Finder, select the Backup volume in the sidebar.

2  Open the Backups.backupdb folder. Inside this folder, you will see a folder for your client. Open it.

In this folder you will see a series of folders, the names of which are date/time stamps. There is also an alias named Latest that always points to the latest backup.

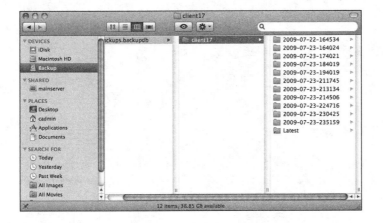

3  Browse through these folders: Latest/Macintosh HD/Users/ cadmin/Desktop.

4  Drag a copy of 2ndPrefs.txt to your desktop.

A dialog appears asking whether you want to replace the copy of 2ndPrefs.txt on your desktop with the one from the backup.

5  Click Keep Both.

The system copies 2ndPrefs.txt to your desktop and renames the 2ndPrefs.txt that was there to 2ndPrefs (original).txt

6  Log out.

# 6

# Applications
# and Boot Camp

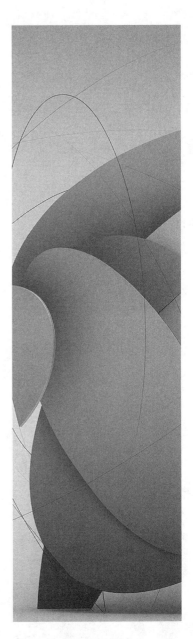

# 6.1 Application Environments

Ultimately, the primary job of the operating system is to serve as a platform for running user applications. Mac OS X excels by allowing users to run a wide range of applications both new and old. Further, Mac OS X v10.6 introduces several high-performance features that make applications even more responsive. In this lesson you will explore the various types of applications that can run on Mac OS X. This will provide a foundation for the ultimate goal of troubleshooting applications, wherein you will learn techniques for resolving a variety of application issues.

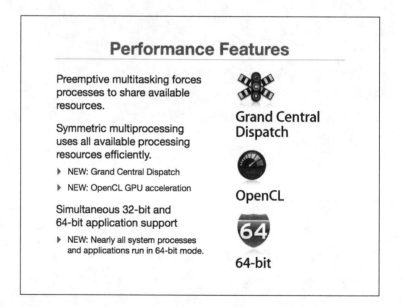

For detailed instructions, see "Understanding Applications and Processes" in Chapter 6 of *Apple Training Series: Mac OS X Support Essentials v10.6*.

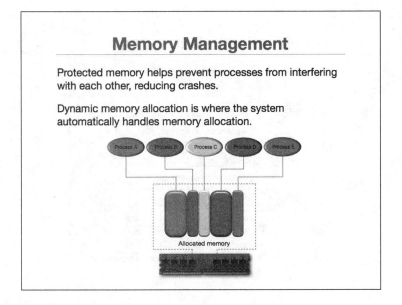

For detailed instructions, see "Understanding Applications and Processes" in Chapter 6 of *Apple Training Series: Mac OS X Support Essentials v10.6.*

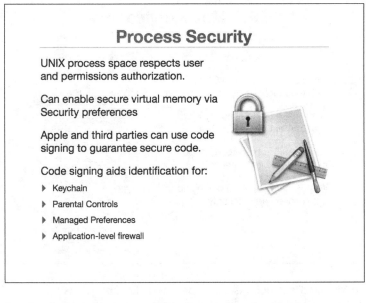

For detailed instructions, see "Understanding Applications and Processes" in Chapter 6 of *Apple Training Series: Mac OS X Support Essentials v10.6.*

## Mac OS X Architecture

**User Experience**

| Aqua | Dashboard | Spotlight | Accessibility |

**Application Frameworks**

| Cocoa | Carbon | Java |

**Graphics and Media**

| Core Animation | Core Image | Core Video | QuickTime |
| OpenGL | Quartz | Core Audio |

**Darwin**

For detailed instructions, see "Application Environments" in
Chapter 6 of *Apple Training Series: Mac OS X Support Essentials v10.6.*

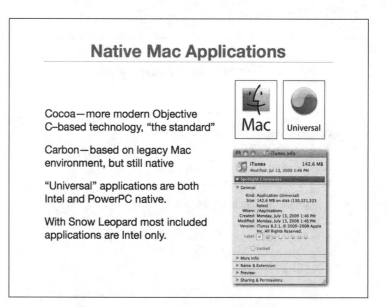

## Native Mac Applications

Cocoa—more modern Objective
C–based technology, "the standard"

Carbon—based on legacy Mac
environment, but still native

"Universal" applications are both
Intel and PowerPC native.

With Snow Leopard most included
applications are Intel only.

For detailed instructions, see "Application Environments" in
Chapter 6 of *Apple Training Series: Mac OS X Support Essentials v10.6.*

## 64-Bit Applications

Nearly all included system applications support 64-bit processing.

Major caveat: Older 32-bit application plug-ins are not supported in 64-bit mode.

System Preferences application automatically switches modes.

Other applications must be forced into 32-bit mode for compatibility with plug-ins.

For detailed instructions, see "64-bit vs. 32-bit Mode" in Chapter 6 of *Apple Training Series: Mac OS X Support Essentials v10.6.*

## Rosetta

Dynamically translates most PowerPC-based code

Not installed by default on Snow Leopard, but ...

Installed automatically by Software Update if needed

Rosetta does not support:

▶ Applications prior to Mac OS X

▶ Screen savers

▶ System Preferences panes

▶ Applications that require a G5

▶ Kernel extensions

For detailed instructions, see "Universal vs. Rosetta" in Chapter 6 of *Apple Training Series: Mac OS X Support Essentials v10.6.*

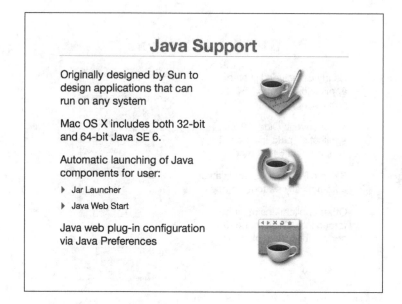

**Java Support**

Originally designed by Sun to design applications that can run on any system

Mac OS X includes both 32-bit and 64-bit Java SE 6.

Automatic launching of Java components for user:

▸ Jar Launcher

▸ Java Web Start

Java web plug-in configuration via Java Preferences

For detailed instructions, see "Application Environments" in Chapter 6 of *Apple Training Series: Mac OS X Support Essentials v10.6.*

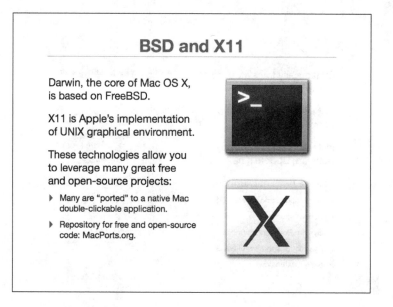

**BSD and X11**

Darwin, the core of Mac OS X, is based on FreeBSD.

X11 is Apple's implementation of UNIX graphical environment.

These technologies allow you to leverage many great free and open-source projects:

▸ Many are "ported" to a native Mac double-clickable application.

▸ Repository for free and open-source code: MacPorts.org.

For detailed instructions, see "Application Environments" in Chapter 6 of *Apple Training Series: Mac OS X Support Essentials v10.6.*

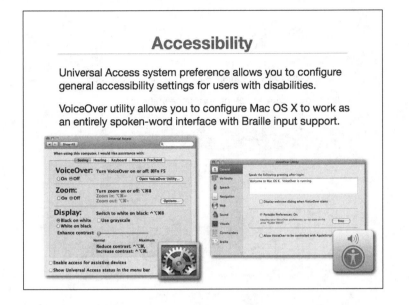

## Accessibility

Universal Access system preference allows you to configure general accessibility settings for users with disabilities.

VoiceOver utility allows you to configure Mac OS X to work as an entirely spoken-word interface with Braille input support.

For detailed instructions, see "Application Accessibility" in Chapter 6 of *Apple Training Series: Mac OS X Support Essentials v10.6*.

## System Profiler

Scans multiple locations in the system for any applications

Shows fundamental application information and version

Also shows Frameworks, or dynamic shared code libraries

For detailed instructions, see "Monitoring Applications and Processes" in Chapter 6 of *Apple Training Series: Mac OS X Support Essentials v10.6*.

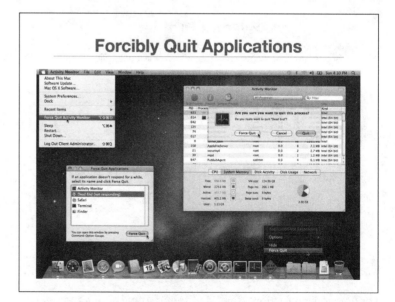

For detailed instructions, see "Monitoring Applications and Processes" in Chapter 6 of *Apple Training Series: Mac OS X Support Essentials v10.6.*

For detailed instructions, see "Forcibly Quit via Graphical Interface" in Chapter 6 of *Apple Training Series: Mac OS X Support Essentials v10.6.*

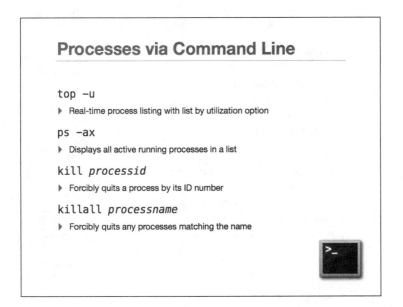

For detailed instructions, see "Problem Reports" in Chapter 6 of *Apple Training Series: Mac OS X Support Essentials v10.6.*

## Processes via Command Line

`top -u`

▸ Real-time process listing with list by utilization option

`ps -ax`

▸ Displays all active running processes in a list

`kill processid`

▸ Forcibly quits a process by its ID number

`killall processname`

▸ Forcibly quits any processes matching the name

For detailed instructions, see "Forcibly Quit via Command Line" in Chapter 6 of *Apple Training Series: Mac OS X Support Essentials v10.6.*

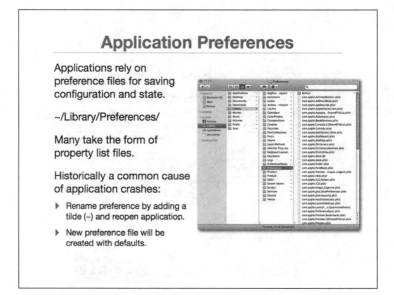

For detailed instructions, see "Preference Troubleshooting" in Chapter 6 of *Apple Training Series: Mac OS X Support Essentials v10.6*.

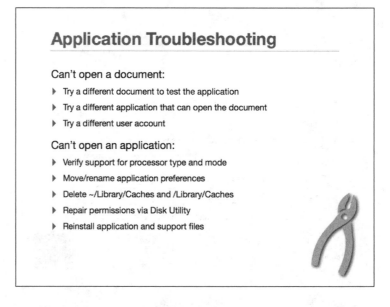

For detailed instructions, see "Application Troubleshooting" in Chapter 6 of *Apple Training Series: Mac OS X Support Essentials v10.6*.

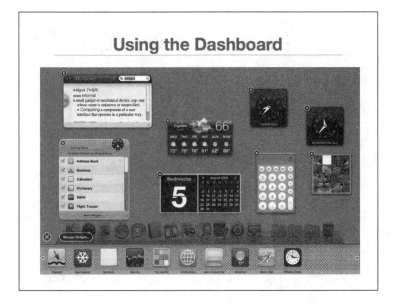

For detailed instructions, see "Managing Dashboard" in Chapter 6 of *Apple Training Series: Mac OS X Support Essentials v10.6.*

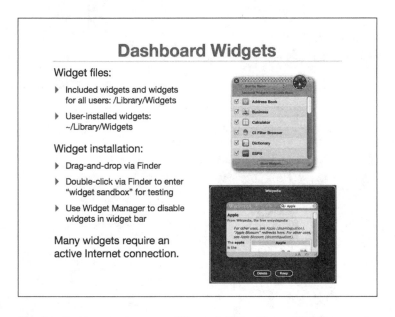

For detailed instructions, see "Managing Dashboard" in Chapter 6 of *Apple Training Series: Mac OS X Support Essentials v10.6.*

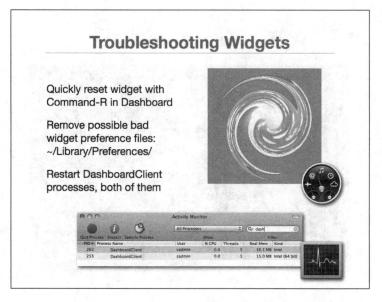

For detailed instructions, see "Troubleshooting Widgets" in Chapter 6 of *Apple Training Series: Mac OS X Support Essentials v10.6.*

Exercise 6.1.1
# Forcing Applications to Quit

## Objectives

- Identify different ways in the graphical user interface to force an application to quit
- Learn how to force applications to quit from the command line

## Summary

Troubleshooting applications is a normal part of any support professional's duties, and Mac OS X comes with the tools you will need to manage most issues you encounter. In this exercise, you will learn how to determine when an application has become unresponsive. You will learn different ways to force unresponsive applications to quit: from the Dock, using the keyboard shortcut, and using Activity Monitor. You will also learn the command-line equivalents of the graphical user interface tools, so that you can troubleshoot Mac OS X applications from Terminal. Even background processes without a user interface can have issues and stop running, so you'll learn how to manage processes as well.

## Force an Application to Quit via the Dock

In this exercise, you will launch an application that will become unresponsive. Just as you can use the Dock to quit an application, you can use the Dock to forcibly quit an application.

1  Log in as Chris Johnson.

2  In the Finder, open the Chapter6 folder of the student materials.

3  Open Dead End by double-clicking it.

Dead End is an application whose sole purpose is to become unresponsive, giving you an opportunity to practice different ways to force an application to quit.

Dead End opens a window that says Downloading the Internet.

4   Choose Dead End > Quit Dead End.

Dead End will become unresponsive. At some point you may see the wait cursor (looks like a colored pinwheel).

5   Control-click (or right-click) the Dead End icon in the dock, then choose Force Quit from the pop-up menu. Alternatively, you could press and hold the Dead End icon in the Dock, then choose Force Quit from the pop-up menu.

If Force Quit does not appear in the menu, repeat step 5 or hold down the Option key. When you hold down the Option key, Quit will change to Force Quit and you then select it to cause Dead End to force quit.

## Force an Application to Quit via the Force Quit Window

In this exercise, you'll use a keyboard shortcut and the Force Quit Applications window to force an application to quit. You will also monitor its behavior using the Terminal.

1   Open the Dead End application again, so you can try another method of forcibly quitting.

One way to open applications you've used recently is by going to the Apple menu and choosing Recent Items. By default, Mac OS X remembers the last ten applications you've used.

2   Choose Dead End > Quit Dead End.

3   Open Terminal.

Even though the wait cursor appears in Dead End, you can still click the desktop to make the Finder active. A single hung application should not affect the rest of the system.

4   Enter the following command:

```
client17:~ chris$ top -u
```

top is a tool for monitoring the process environment (number running, memory usage, etc.). The u option causes top to update every second with a list of processes sorted by their CPU usage over the last second.

You will notice that Dead End is using around 100 percent of the CPU. This number can be a little misleading. The total CPU percentage available is 100 percent multiplied by the number of cores on the system. Keep this window open and watch the Dead End process as you do the next steps.

5   Press Command-Option-Esc (or choose Force Quit from the Apple menu) to open the Force Quit Applications window.

6   Make sure you can see your Terminal window. Choose Dead End in the Force Quit Applications window, then click the Force Quit button. When asked to confirm, click Force Quit again.

7   Notice that with the next update, top no longer shows Dead End.

8   Close the Force Quit Applications window.

## Force an Application to Quit via Activity Monitor

There may be times when you need another method to force an application to quit. Activity Monitor not only forces applications to quit, but also allows you to review all processes running on the computer, gather information, and quit them when necessary.

1   Open Dead End.

2   Choose Dead End > Quit Dead End.

3   Click once on the desktop to make the Finder active.

4   In the Finder, choose Go > Utilities.

5   Double-click to open Activity Monitor.

Activity Monitor displays a list of all running processes. When you open this window, it shows processes that you will recognize as applications. It also shows other processes running in the background that do not have a graphical user interface.

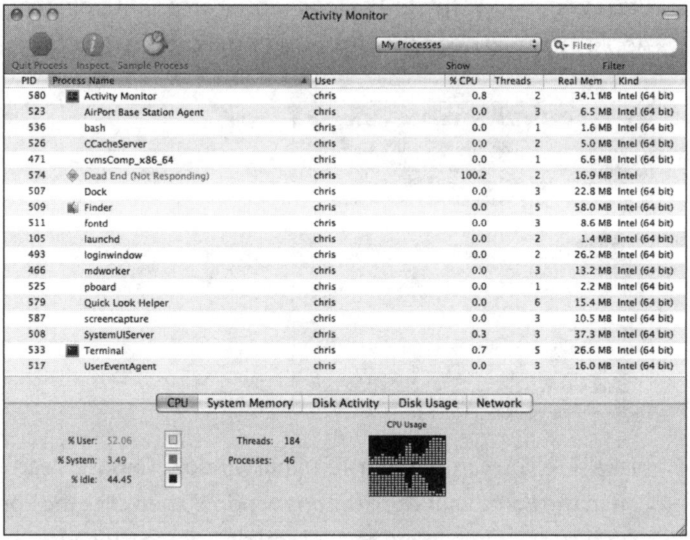

6   In Activity Monitor's window, click % CPU in the table header twice to get a top-down (most to least) list of processes in terms of their CPU usage. The triangle that appears next to % CPU should point downward.

7   Look for the Dead End process by name. It should be at the top.

The name of an unresponsive application will appear in red with a note to that effect. As you look at the Dead End process, notice how the CPU usage is close to 100 percent, just as you saw in top. You can see how an application can hijack your CPU, even though the application is not responding and appears to be doing nothing.

8   Choose Dead End in the process list, then click the Quit Process button on the toolbar.

9   When asked to confirm, click Force Quit.

You will note that Quit is the default option in the dialog that appears. However, since Dead End is not responding to its own Quit command, you will need to choose Force Quit in order to stop this process from running.

Dead End will disappear from the process list in the Activity Monitor window, from the Dock, and from top in the Terminal window.

10  Quit Activity Monitor.

## Force an Application to Quit via Command Line

In the previous steps, you used graphical user interface tools to force an application to quit. In this exercise, you will use command-line tools to locate an unresponsive application or process and force it to quit. Remember that most graphical user interface features of Mac OS X have a command-line equivalent. If you only have access to the command line, you'll want to be comfortable performing common commands.

1   Switch to your Terminal window and press Control-C to quit top.

2   Enter the following command:

`client17:~ chris$ ps`

The ps command shows a list of running processes and their
process IDs (PIDs). By default, ps shows only command-line
processes owned by you. The ax options will ask it to display
all processes.

3   Enter the following command:

`client17:~ chris$ ps ax`

You get a much longer listing.

Now you want to look for the process called Dock, and write
down the number under PID. This is the process ID for your
Dock. You could manually read through the process listing,
but on even moderately busy systems, there are often many
processes running, making such a technique error prone and
time consuming.

Instead, you could use grep to help you find the Dock process.

4   Enter the following command:

`client17:~ chris$ ps ax | grep Dock`

You will see five columns output. The first is the process ID and
the last is the command. Find the Dock command (hint: it is
not the grep command), and make a note of its PID. If you are
curious, you can look up what the other columns are telling you
in the man page for ps.

During the following steps, watch the Dock closely to see the
effects of your commands.

5   Enter the following command:

`client17:~ chris$ kill [Dock PID]`

The Dock will disappear, and then reappear.

When you quit the Dock process, the on-screen Dock disappears. However, the Dock is a child of a `launchd` process (you can see this in Activity Monitor using All Process, Hierarchically in the toolbar, if you are curious), which always checks for the presence of the Dock process. If `launchd` finds that the Dock process is not running, `launchd` automatically restarts the Dock.

6   At the command prompt, type the Up Arrow twice. This should select the `ps ax | grep` command. If not, use the Up and Down Arrows to scroll through your command history until you find it. Once you find it, press Return.

The shell remembers the commands you have and allows you to recall them by pressing the Up Arrow.

Find the Dock process, and compare the process ID to the one you noted previously.

When the Dock process is restarted, it is assigned a new process ID (PID). Be aware that as most processes start and stop, their IDs will change.

7   Quit the Terminal by using `killall`:

```
client17:~ chris$ killall Terminal
```

The `killall` command allows you to terminate a process by name rather than by process ID. There can be more than one process running with the same name, so you should be careful when using `killall`.

Terminal quits.

8   Log out.

Exercise 6.1.2
# Troubleshooting Preferences

## Objectives

- Restore preferences
- Fix corrupt preferences
- Switch users to troubleshoot preferences

## Summary

Most application preferences are created and stored for individual users in their personal Library folder. This compartmental approach can help when troubleshooting application issues. You'll learn how to set and restore a preference and see the effect of moving a preference file out of the ~/Library/Preferences folder.

## Restoring Preferences

You will observe how preferences work by modifying TextEdit's preferences, moving the preferences out of the Preferences folder, confirming that the preference settings revert to their original settings, and then restoring the original preference file.

1  Log in as Chris Johnson.

2  Open TextEdit.

3  In the window that appears, type some text.

4  Choose TextEdit > Preferences.

5   In the New Document preferences, click the button for Plain Text.

This changes TextEdit's default document format from Rich Text Format to plain text. This setting will be stored in the preference file (a property list or plist file) for TextEdit.

6   In the Font preferences, click the Change button for "Plain text font," and set the size to 14, instead of 10.

7   Close the Font panel.

Changing the font size for the plain text font will make the changes in preferences more visible.

8   Quit TextEdit. If prompted to save the file, click Don't Save.

9   Reopen TextEdit, and type some text to confirm that TextEdit is using the new preference of plain text.

You can see from the different window layout (no ruler, for example), font style, and size of the typed text that the plain text preference is working.

10  Quit TextEdit. When prompted to save the file, click Don't Save.

Another way to choose Don't Save in a dialog is to press Command-D.

11  In the Finder, open ~/Library/Preferences.

Another way to navigate to this folder is to press Command-Shift-G, which brings up the Go to Folder window. Type ~/L, then press Tab to automatically complete the path to the home Library folder. Then type /Preferences. When you have entered enough text that is unique to the name of the folder, Tab to autocomplete will work.

```
Go to the folder:

~/Library/Preferences/

                        Cancel        Go
```

12  Locate the com.apple.TextEdit.plist file and drag this file to the desktop. If your window is in column mode, you can double-click the two vertical bars (looks like a rotated equals sign) in the lower right of the column to make it widen to show you full filenames.

13  Open TextEdit again and type some text in the window.

You can see from the font style of the typed text that the preference has been reset to rich text. You can also look at TextEdit > Preferences to see this change.

14  Quit TextEdit. When prompted to save the file, click Save. Name the file test, and save it to the desktop.

15  Restore the preference file from the desktop by dragging it to ~/Library/Preferences. Replace the newer file when prompted.

16  Reopen TextEdit and type some text to see that the plain text settings are now restored.

You can see from the window, font style, and size of the typed text that the plain text preference is restored.

17  Quit TextEdit. If prompted to save the file, click Don't Save.

## Dealing with Corrupted Preferences

Mac OS X has some built-in features for dealing with corrupted preference files. You will explore what happens when a preference file becomes corrupt. Because a user's preferences are kept in his or her own home Library folder and are separate from other users' preferences, switching users can be helpful when troubleshooting.

1   Quit TextEdit, if it is running.

2   Open the Terminal application and make your working directory ~/Library/Preferences.

3   Open com.apple.TextEdit.plist in nano.

nano shows you a long line that starts with bplist00 and has a number of odd-looking characters in it. This is the binary encoding of a property list file. There are two other encodings that you might see, XML and OPENSTEP. The OPENSTEP format is rarely used anymore. The XML format is easier to edit by hand.

What you are going to do is corrupt the binary preference file. Look at the man pages for defaults and plutil for some tools capable of manipulating property lists correctly.

4   Somewhere in the string of characters that comes after bplist00, type a few random characters.

5   Exit nano and save the file, overwriting the original.

You have now corrupted the binary property list that contains TextEdit's preferences.

6   Use ls and grep to view TextEdit's preference files.

client17:Preferences chris$ `ls -l | grep TextEdit`

Take particular note of the size of the file (the number right before the date).

7   Open TextEdit.

8   TextEdit should revert to default preferences.

9   In your Terminal window, press the Up Arrow key and run the previous command again.

One of two things has happened. Either the system deleted your corrupt com.apple.TextEdit.plist or it ignored it. A good indicator that the system has dealt with a corrupt preference file is that the application inexplicably reverts to default preferences.

10  Back in TextEdit, choose TextEdit > Preferences.

11  Set the New Document preferences to plain text format and 14-point type for the plain text font.

12  Quit TextEdit.

13  In Terminal, use the Up Arrow to run the previous command again.

TextEdit has rewritten its preference file, removing the corruption you introduced.

14  Log out any logged-in users.

Exercise 6.1.3
# Launch Services and Quick Look

## Objectives

- Choose an application to open a file
- Troubleshoot a missing application
- Use Quick Look

## Summary

In a previous section you learned about Launch Services and how Mac OS X knows which applications should open files. In this exercise, you will learn different ways to choose applications to open files, either when you wish to make a one-time choice of a different application, or when the default application is not available. You will also use Mac OS X's Quick Look feature again, which lets you see the contents of common file types even when there is no application installed that is able to open that file.

## Choose an Application to Open a File

Typically, Mac OS X knows which application to use to open your files. However, there may be times where you want to choose a different application for opening a file. For example, you may receive a file created in an application you do not have installed. Or, you may want to open a file in a more lightweight application, such as opening a PDF file in Preview instead of Acrobat Professional. A default installation of Mac OS X contains many applications capable of opening the most common file formats.

1  Log in as Chris Johnson.

2  In the Chapter6 folder of the student materials, locate and open the file fw4.pdf.

   The file opens in Preview.

3   Quit Preview.

4   Locate the file again, and this time drag the file to Safari's icon in the Dock.

The file opens in Safari.

Safari is able to read and display PDF documents. If you know what kind of file you are trying to open, you can often find an application installed with Mac OS X that is capable of opening that type of file.

5   Quit Safari.

## Troubleshoot a Missing Application

In this exercise, you will open a file whose parent application is not installed on the computer. Microsoft Office 2004 and its applications, such as Word and Excel, are not installed on this computer. However, because Mac OS X automatically associates Word documents with TextEdit when Word is not installed, you will still be able to open a Word file.

1   Open the Applications folder, and note that Microsoft Office 2004 is not installed.

A quick way to open the Applications folder is to press Command-Shift-A in the Finder.

2   Open the Chapter6 folder and locate the Pet Sitter Notes.doc file.

In the Finder, choose Column view and then click the Pet Sitter Notes.doc file. Look for the Kind information, and verify that its native format is Microsoft Word.

3  Control-click the Pet Sitter Notes.doc file, then hover the mouse cursor over Open With in the pop-up menu.

A list of applications that claim they can open this type of document appears as a submenu of the contextual menu. TextEdit is annotated as the default application.

4  Click the desktop to dismiss the menu.

5  Double-click the Pet Sitter Notes.doc file to open it.

The file opens in TextEdit but retains the .doc extension.

TextEdit can open and save Word documents, so it is a great substitute when you need to open a Word file but do not have Word installed. TextEdit does not, however, understand the full range of Word formatting, so various aspects of the original document may be lost.

6  Quit TextEdit.

7  In the Finder, choose Go > Recent Folders > Chapter6.

The Go > Recent Folders command is a great shortcut for getting back to the last ten folders you've used.

8  In the Chapter6 folder, double-click the file edu.mit.Kerberos.

Mac OS X does not know what type of file this is. It does not have type or creator information and no installed application claims .Kerberos files.

9  Click Choose Application.

A window opens on the Applications folder, so that you can choose an application with which to attempt to open the file. In this case, the appropriate choice is TextEdit. TextEdit can open any plain text file. Notice that the default is Recommended Applications. You can choose All Applications and then try other applications besides the ones Mac OS X considers "recommended." Essentially, Mac OS X is guessing which applications are likely to be able to open the file.

10  Select TextEdit and then click Open.

The file opens in TextEdit. Notice that SubEthaEdit is also enabled as a recommended application. This file is a binary-format property list.

11  Quit TextEdit without saving.

## Use Quick Look to View the Contents of a File

Quick Look is an easy, built-in file preview feature. It allows you to view files without the overhead of opening a large application. Quick Look uses plug-ins that recognize various data types and have the ability to render the contents of a file in a read-only way to allow for quick preview.

1  Open the Chapter6 folder and double-click the Travel checklist.xls file.

The file opens in TextEdit. In Mac OS X v10.6, TextEdit claims a wide array of common file types. The creator application, Microsoft Excel, is not installed on this computer. If Excel were installed, the document would open in it rather than opening in TextEdit.

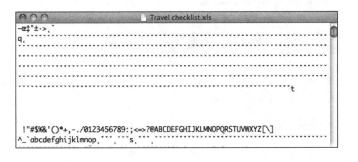

2  Quit TextEdit.

3  In the Chapter6 folder, click once to select the Travel checklist.xls file.

4   Click the Action button (looks like a gear) on the toolbar and
    choose Quick Look "Travel checklist.xls".

As you have already seen, you can use the Space bar to activate
Quick Look. It is also available in the contextual menu (which is
the same as the action menu) in the Finder's File menu. Quick
Look also has a button on the default Finder toolbar.

Look at the contents of the file. The Excel worksheet tabs at the
bottom are displayed as clickable buttons that will allow you to
look at each worksheet in this workbook.

5   Click the arrows for a full-screen view, then click the X to close
    the Quick Look preview.

6   Log out.

# Boot Camp

# 6.2

The move to Intel-based Macs means more than just faster computers, it also allows Macs to run other operating systems made for Intel-based computers. Most importantly, this allows you to run Microsoft Windows on Mac computers. The Boot Camp technology built into Mac OS X makes the process of installing Windows on your Mac as painless as possible. In this lesson you will explore Boot Camp and learn the steps required to configure Windows on your Mac.

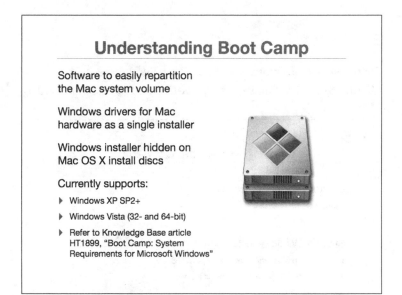

For detailed instructions, see "Understanding Boot Camp" in Chapter 6 of *Apple Training Series: Mac OS X Support Essentials v10.6*.

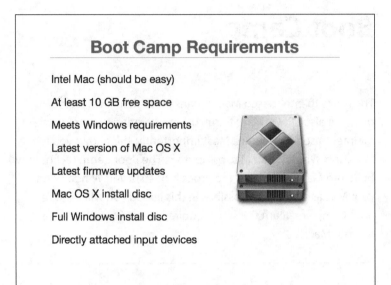

For detailed instructions, see "Boot Camp Requirements" in Chapter 6 of *Apple Training Series: Mac OS X Support Essentials v10.6*.

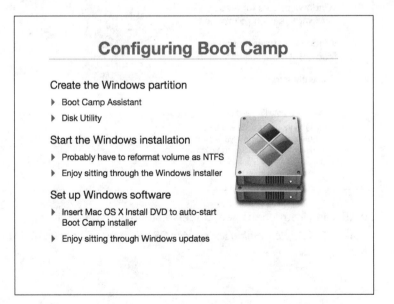

For detailed instructions, see "Configuring Boot Camp" in Chapter 6 of *Apple Training Series: Mac OS X Support Essentials v10.6*.

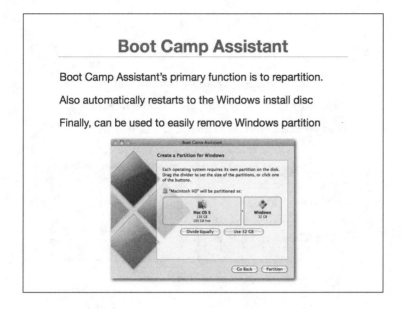

For detailed instructions, see "Boot Camp Assistant" in Chapter 6 of *Apple Training Series: Mac OS X Support Essentials v10.6.*

## Boot Camp Mac Drivers

Boot Camp's "magic" is the Windows drivers for Mac.

Only found on original media Mac OS X install discs

Includes all Mac-specific hardware drivers in one install

Also includes:

▸ Boot Camp Control Panel

▸ Apple Software Update for Windows

For detailed instructions, see "Install Boot Camp Drivers for Windows" in Chapter 6 of *Apple Training Series: Mac OS X Support Essentials v10.6.*

For detailed instructions, see "Switching Between Systems" in
Chapter 6 of *Apple Training Series: Mac OS X Support Essentials v10.6.*

**Note**  There are no exercises for this lesson.

# 7

# Network Configuration

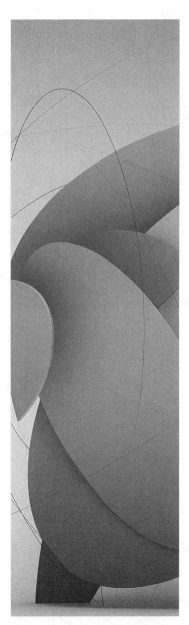

# 7.1

# Configuring Mac OS X Networking

It's important to have a basic understanding of general network technologies in order to effectively manage and troubleshoot Mac OS X networking. In the first part of this lesson you will learn the fundamentals behind TCP/IP networking. With that knowledge, you will then learn how to configure Mac OS X network locations, interfaces, and protocols. You will use both basic and advanced network configuration techniques, which cover the wide variety of network technologies available in Mac OS X.

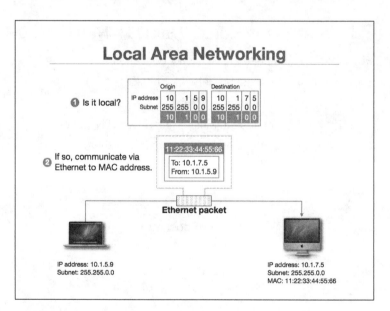

For detailed instructions, see "Networks In Action" in Chapter 7 of *Apple Training Series: Mac OS X Support Essentials v10.6.*

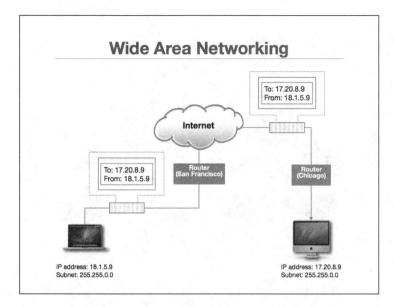

For detailed instructions, see "Networks in Action" in Chapter 7 of *Apple Training Series: Mac OS X Support Essentials v10.6.*

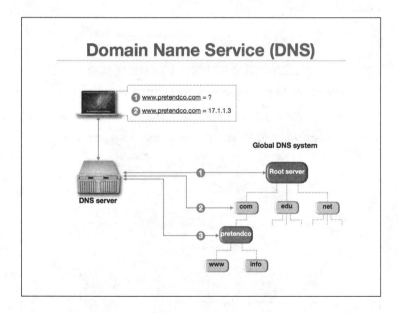

For detailed instructions, see "Domain Name System" in Chapter 7 of *Apple Training Series: Mac OS X Support Essentials v10.6.*

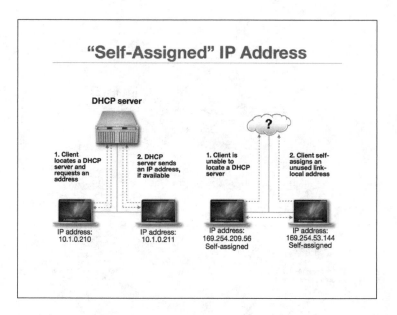

For detailed instructions, see "Dynamic Host Configuration Protocol" in Chapter 7 of *Apple Training Series: Mac OS X Support Essentials v10.6.*

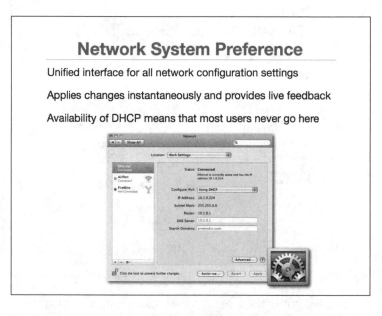

For detailed instructions, see "Basic Network Configuration" in Chapter 7 of *Apple Training Series: Mac OS X Support Essentials v10.6.*

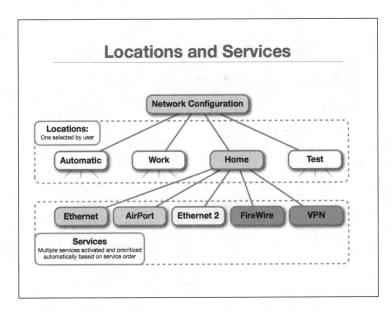

For detailed instructions, see "Using Network Locations" in
Chapter 7 of *Apple Training Series: Mac OS X Support Essentials v10.6.*

## Network Locations

Locations are used to define a
state for network configuration.

Use multiple locations to your
advantage for troubleshooting.

Users can switch network
locations from the Apple menu.

For detailed instructions, see "Using Network Locations" in
Chapter 7 of *Apple Training Series: Mac OS X Support Essentials v10.6.*

## Manual Ethernet Configuration

For detailed instructions, see "Using Hardware Network Interfaces" in Chapter 7 of *Apple Training Series: Mac OS X Support Essentials v10.6*.

## AirPort Configuration

Most users will manage AirPort via the menu bar.

Administrator options are in the Network preference.

For detailed instructions, see "Using Hardware Network Interfaces" in Chapter 7 of *Apple Training Series: Mac OS X Support Essentials v10.6*.

## Modems and PPP

For detailed instructions, see "Using Hardware Network Interfaces" in Chapter 7 of *Apple Training Series: Mac OS X Support Essentials v10.6.*

## Advanced DNS and WINS

For detailed instructions, see "Using Network Protocols" in Chapter 7 of *Apple Training Series: Mac OS X Support Essentials v10.6.*

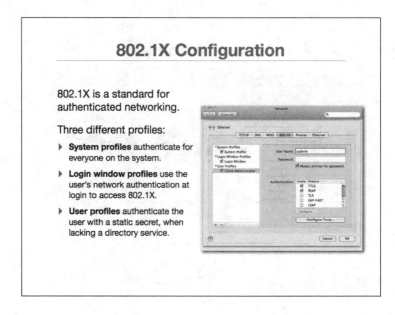

# 802.1X Configuration

802.1X is a standard for authenticated networking.

Three different profiles:

▶ **System profiles** authenticate for everyone on the system.

▶ **Login window profiles** use the user's network authentication at login to access 802.1X.

▶ **User profiles** authenticate the user with a static secret, when lacking a directory service.

For detailed instructions, see "Using Network Protocols" in Chapter 7 of *Apple Training Series: Mac OS X Support Essentials v10.6.*

# Proxies Configuration

For detailed instructions, see "Using Network Protocols" in Chapter 7 of *Apple Training Series: Mac OS X Support Essentials v10.6.*

For detailed instructions, see "Using Network Protocols" in Chapter 7 of *Apple Training Series: Mac OS X Support Essentials v10.6.*

For detailed instructions, see "Using Hardware Network Interfaces" in Chapter 7 of *Apple Training Series: Mac OS X Support Essentials v10.6.*

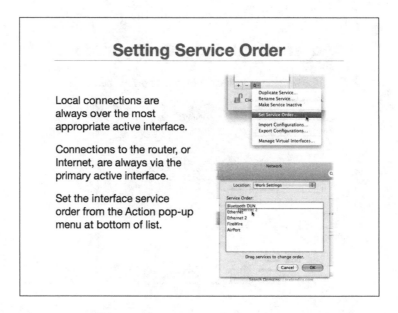

## Setting Service Order

Local connections are always over the most appropriate active interface.

Connections to the router, or Internet, are always via the primary active interface.

Set the interface service order from the Action pop-up menu at bottom of list.

For detailed instructions, see "Using Hardware Network Interfaces" in Chapter 7 of *Apple Training Series: Mac OS X Support Essentials v10.6.*

## Virtual Private Network

Mac OS X includes VPN for:

▸ L2TP over IPSec

▸ PPTP

▸ Cisco IPSec

You must add new interface.

For detailed instructions, see "Using Virtual Network Interfaces" in Chapter 7 of *Apple Training Series: Mac OS X Support Essentials v10.6.*

Exercise 7.1.1
# Monitoring Network Connections

## Objective
- View network connections using Network preferences

## Summary
In this exercise you will break your Ethernet connection to the network and observe how that change is reflected in the Network pane of System Preferences. The Network pane dynamically updates as network connectivity changes, so it is a valuable tool for trouble-shooting connectivity issues. This task demonstrates how to gather troubleshooting information from Network preferences.

## Use the Network Status Pane to Monitor Connectivity
The Network Status view of Network preferences shows the status of all active configured network interfaces. User-initiated connections like PPP and VPN are also listed. Users can view the Network Status pane to verify their active connections in order of priority.

1  Log in as Client Administrator.

2  Open System Preferences and click Network.

   Notice the status of your network connections on the left side of the window.

   The status indicator next to Ethernet is green and it says Connected underneath. On computers with more than one Ethernet interface, you may see Ethernet 1 or Ethernet 2 at the top of the list.

   On the right side of the window it says Status: Connected and "Ethernet is currently active" and has an IP address assigned to it.

> **Note**  If you have any other services active, make them
> inactive by selecting them in the service list and  choosing
> Make Service Inactive from the Action menu (the gear icon)
> at the bottom of the service list. When you have done this
> for all of the other services, click Apply.

3   Unplug the Ethernet connector from your computer and watch
    the status indicator next to your Ethernet listing.

> **Note**  Depending on your classroom configuration, it might
> be easier to unplug your computer from the switch. Either
> end of the Ethernet cable can be disconnected. Choose the
> end that is easiest for you to access for this exercise.

The Ethernet status indicator changes to red and the status text
on the right side of the window states Cable Unplugged.

If your Ethernet cable is plugged into an inactive port, such as a
broken or unpowered switch, you will see similar behavior.

Do not plug the cable back in yet.

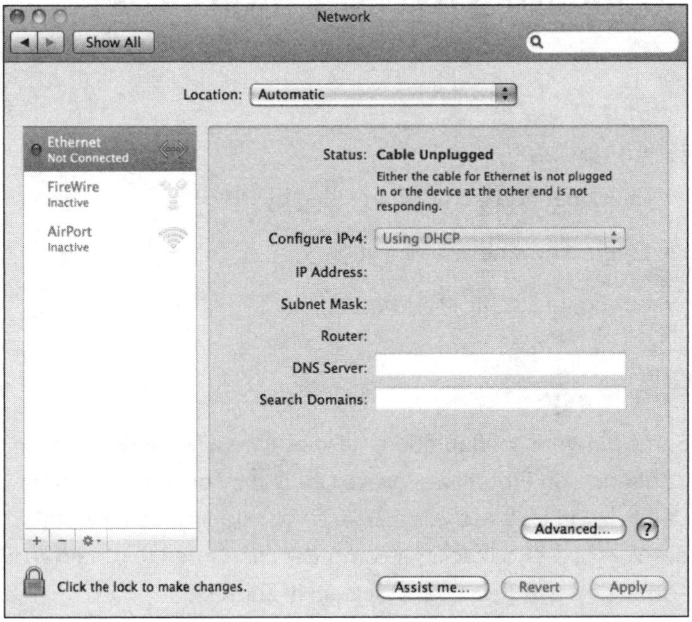

## Exercise 7.1.2
# Configuring Network Interfaces

### Objectives

- Check network settings provided by DHCP

- Create a new network location

- Configure a static IP address

### Summary

Some network configurations will not have a DHCP (Dynamic Host Configuration Protocol) server, or there may be times when the DHCP server fails. In these instances, to establish and maintain network access, a Mac OS X computer configured to obtain an IP address via DHCP will self-assign an IP address.

### Instructor Turns Off DHCP Service

At this point your instructor will turn off the DHCP service on the classroom server. Please inform the instructor you are ready for this to happen. Do not proceed until your instructor informs you that the DHCP service is off.

1  Tell your instructor that you are ready for DHCP to be turned off.

2  After your instructor has notified you that the DHCP service is turned off, plug the Ethernet cable back in to the computer.

   Pay attention to the Network status. It initially shows you connected using your old IP address, but shortly it changes to No IP Address and a status of Unknown State. After a longer delay, it switches back to Connected using your old DHCP address. This can take a minute or more.

The lease on your address is still valid, so it reverts to using your old address even though the DHCP service is no longer available. The computer will maintain this IP address until the lease expires. At that time, it will change to a self-assigned (link local) address. These are the 169.254.*x.y* addresses that you may have seen before. Rather than wait for that to happen (on average, it will take 30 minutes in this classroom), you will encourage it to self-assign an address.

3  Unlock Network preferences, if necessary.

4  After you see that Ethernet is active and that you have an IP address from the DHCP server (in the range of 10.1.0.200–10.1.0.250), click Advanced in the bottom right of the window.

5   Enter `testn` (where *n* is your student number) in the DHCP
    Client ID field.

6   Click Renew DHCP Lease.

7   If a dialog appears asking you to apply the change, click the
    Apply button.

8   Click OK.

9   When the Advanced dialog disappears, click Apply (if available).

    After a short delay, the Status field says Connected, with a
    self-assigned IP address.

## Attempt to Use the Network

Use the following steps to verify that your computer can still access other computers on the network.

1 From the Finder choose Go > Connect to Server.

2 Use the Connect to Server dialog to connect to `mainserver.local`.

3 Click Connect.

You are prompted to authenticate to mainserver. This proves that you have established a connection to mainserver.

4 Click Cancel.

Even though you have a self-assigned IP address, you can still communicate with other computers on your network. Bonjour allows you to look up .local names using mDNS (multicast DNS) and smooths the way for connecting to your local resources.

## Create a New Location with a Static IP Address

You will configure a new location called Static with a static IP address. The IP address you will use for your computer is 10.1.*n*.2, where *n* is your student number. For example, student 17 would use 10.1.17.2.

1  Open the Network pane of System Preferences, if necessary.

2  From the Location pop-up menu, choose Edit Locations.

3  Click the Add (+) button to create a new location.

4  Rename the Untitled location `Static`.

5    Click Done.

6    Switch to the new Static location, if it is not already selected.

7    Click Apply.

8    If necessary, select Ethernet from the Interfaces status on the left.

9    Choose Manually from the Configure IPv4 pop-up menu.

10   Enter the following information (replacing $n$ with your student number):

   - IP Address: 10.1.$n$.2/16

   - This will fill in the subnet mask (255.255.0.0) and router (10.1.0.1) when you tab out of the field.

   - DNS Server: 10.1.0.1

   - Search Domains: pretendco.com

You are using a shortcut to fill in the subnet mask and router information. 10.1.$n$.2/16 is CIDR (pronounced like *cider* and short for Classless Interdomain Routing) notation. It specifies an IP address and subnet mask by indicating the number of on bits (1s) in the subnet mask. In CIDR notation, a /16 subnet equates to a 255.255.0.0 subnet mask (binary 11111111 11111111 00000000 00000000). Once it has an address and the subnet mask, it can figure other things out.

It also assumes that the default gateway (router) will be the first usable address on the subnet. While common practice, this is not a given. Some network admins place the default router at the last usable address on the subnet. The gateway can be at any address on the subnet, so you may need to edit the router information to reflect the configuration of your network.

Addressing doesn't tell the computer anything about the DNS environment, so you still have to enter that information manually.

11 Inactivate any other services (interfaces) that may be part of the Static location.

12 Click Apply.

13 Quit System Preferences.

## Use Safari to Test Web Access

At this point you have correctly configured your computer to work on the classroom network. Now you will use Safari to verify that you can access the classroom website.

1  Open Safari.

2  In the Location bar, type

```
http://mainserver.pretendco.com
```

and press Return.

If Safari is trying to load a page that is not on your network, you don't need to wait for it to finish or time out. You should see the classroom server website when you are done.

3  Choose Safari > Empty Cache.

Browser caches can make testing websites rather challenging because it is often unclear whether what you see in the browser has been freshly downloaded from the server or retrieved from the cache.

4  Click Empty.

5  Quit Safari.

6  Log out.

Exercise 7.1.3
# Understanding Multiple Interfaces

## Objectives

- Determine current network configuration
- Understand how services and locations work

## Summary

Network services and locations offer easy-to-use ways to configure your access to the network and segregate one configuration from another. You will use two different services configured on the same physical interface to access the network and see how multiple services work together. You will use locations to set up these new services without affecting your existing network configuration.

## Create a New Location

Locations are useful organizing containers for your network settings. It is often a good practice to create a new location whenever you need to change your network settings. Once a location has been created, it is easy to switch between them using the Apple menu's Locations submenu.

1   Log in as Client Administrator.

2   Open Network preferences.

3   Authenticate to Network preferences, if necessary.

4   From the Locations pop-up menu, choose Edit Locations.

5  Select the Static location, and then choose Duplicate Location from the Action menu at the bottom of the location list.

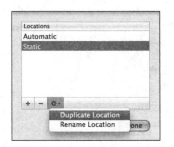

6  Rename the new location from Static Copy to Multi-homed.

7  Click Done.

8  Switch to the Multi-homed location, if necessary.

9  Click Apply.

10  Select Ethernet (or Ethernet 1 or Ethernet 2, whichever has the Ethernet cable plugged in to it, if you have a Mac with multiple Ethernet interfaces) in the list of services on the left.

11  From the Action menu, choose Rename Service.

12  Enter `With DNS` for the name and click Rename.

13  Click Apply.

14  Click the Add (+) button.

15  Choose Ethernet (or Ethernet 1 or Ethernet 2, whichever has the Ethernet cable plugged in) from the Interface pop-up menu.

16  Name the service `Without DNS`.

17  Click Create.

A service is a configuration assigned to an interface. An interface is a physical or virtual means of connecting the computer to other computers on a network.

18  Select the Without DNS service and configure it as follows:

- Configure IPv4: Manually

- IP Address: `10.1.n.3/16` (where *n* is your student number)

- DNS Server: Leave blank

- Search Domains: Leave blank

19  Click Apply.

Both services should have a green status indicator.

20 Open Safari.

21 Use the address bar to go to `http://mainserver.pretendco.com/`.

 Mainserver's main website loads.

22 In Network preferences, choose Set Service Order from the Action menu.

23 Drag Without DNS above With DNS and then click OK.

24 Click Apply.

25 Back in Safari, choose Safari > Empty Cache and then click Empty.

26 Reload the mainserver.pretendco.com page.

 You are presented with a page that tells you that Safari couldn't load the site "because your computer is not connected to the Internet." Specifically what it means is that it cannot find a name server to resolve the name.

 The Without DNS service now has priority over the With DNS service (it is higher on the list). Because Without DNS is not configured with any name servers, it cannot look up mainserver.pretendco.com and so fails with this error message.

27 Choose Locations > Static from the Apple menu.

28 Reload the page in Safari. This time it works because the Static location has DNS settings associated with its highest-priority (and only) service.

29 Log out.

Exercise 7.1.4

# Configuring Multiple Interfaces: VPN (optional)

## Objective

- Connect to classroom server using VPN

## Summary

Virtual private networks (VPNs) are commonly used to securely access a remote network. With a VPN connection you establish an encrypted tunnel over the public Internet to the remote network. The encryption protects your data while it is transmitted. Mac OS X v10.6 supports three types of VPN: Point to Point Tunneling Protocol (PPTP), Layer 2 Tunneling Protocol over IPSec (L2TP), and Cisco IPSec.

## Configure a VPN Service to Connect to the Classroom Server

In this exercise you will configure a VPN connection to the classroom server. A VPN can be used to provide secure remote connections to local network resources, or even to secure certain internal resources from the rest of the network clients. You will observe how Mac OS X handles multiple network connections and their priority in accessing network resources.

1   Log in as Client Administrator and open Network preferences.

2   If you are not on the Static location, select it and click Apply.

3   Click the Add (+) button at the bottom of the services list to add a new service.

4   Choose VPN from the Interface pop-up menu.

5  Choose L2TP over IPSec from the VPN Type pop-up menu and click Create.

Select the interface and enter a name for the new service.

Interface: VPN

VPN Type: L2TP over IPSec

Service Name: VPN (L2TP)

Cancel   Create

6  Select the VPN service from the service list.

7  For the Server Address type `mainserver.pretendco.com`.

8  For the Account Name enter `studentnumber`  (where *number* is your student number in words, i.e., studentseventeen).

9  Select the checkbox "Show VPN status in menu bar."

Network

Show All

Location:  Static

Ethernet
Connected

VPN (L2TP)
Not Connected

FireWire
Inactive

AirPort
Inactive

Status:  Not Connected

Configuration:  Default

Server Address:  mainserver.pretendco.com

Account Name:  student17

Authentication Settings...

Connect

Show VPN status in menu bar          Advanced...   (?)

Click the lock to prevent further changes.          Assist me...   Revert   Apply

10 Click Apply.

11 Click the Authentication Settings button and configure the settings as follows:

- Password: student

- Shared Secret: apple

12 Click OK.

13 At the bottom of the services list click the Action pop-up menu and select Set Service Order.

14 Drag VPN (L2TP) above Ethernet and click OK.

15 Click Apply to make the service order and new settings active.

Now you are ready to connect via VPN.

16 Click Connect.

Notice that the status order changes for VPN and Ethernet.

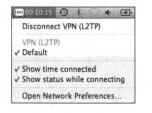

## Checking Your VPN Connectivity

Now that you are connected to the classroom network via VPN, you will access a network resource that was previously unreachable.

1   Open Safari.

2   Use the address bar to access `internal.pretendco.com`.

You have just opened an internal website. You will now verify that it was only accessible from a VPN connection.

3   From the VPN menu select Disconnect VPN (L2TP).

4   In Safari choose Safari > Empty Cache and click Empty in the resulting dialog.

5   Reload the internal website.

The website will not load, and you'll see an error page telling you that "the server where this page is located isn't responding."

6   Quit Safari and System Preferences.

7   Log out.

Exercise 7.1.5

# Configuring Multiple Interfaces: Ethernet and AirPort (optional)

## Objectives

- Connect to an AirPort network
- Configure Service Order for available network interfaces

## Summary

Wireless networking is a very common way to get on the Internet with a computer. Your classroom requires a wireless network and your computer needs an AirPort interface for you to perform this exercise. Ask your instructor whether to proceed.

## Configure Ethernet and AirPort

1   Log in as Client Administrator, and open Network preferences.

2   Make the AirPort service active using the Action menu.

3   Turn AirPort on if necessary and verify that "Show AirPort status in the menu bar" is checked. If asked to apply your settings, do so.

4  Click Apply if it is enabled.

5  Ask your instructor which network to join and what the password is, if any.

If the wireless network is unlocked, you may automatically be joined to the network.

If you did not automatically join the network, you can join a network using the Network Name pop-up menu. However, a more common way to join wireless networks is from the AirPort status menu bar item.

6  Click AirPort status in the menu bar.

Notice the number of networks you can potentially join. Networks with a lock icon next to their name require authentication. Next to the lock icon, there is a signal strength indicator (looks like a baseball diamond). The top line gives the overall status for AirPort. Generally this will be "on," but you may notice that periodically it says Looking for Networks.

Use the password provided by your instructor to join the network, if necessary.

7 Once the status indicator for AirPort in Network preferences goes green, open Safari.

The default webpage should fail to load.

8 In the Location bar, type `http://external.pretendco.com` and press Return.

The page should load as expected.

9 In System Preferences, click the Action pop-up menu at the bottom of services list.

10 Choose Set Service Order.

11 Drag AirPort above Ethernet and click OK.

12 Click Apply.

Notice that the AirPort service moves to the top of the services list.

13 Open a new window in Safari.

The default webpage should load from the Internet.

14 In the Location bar, type `http://mainserver.pretendco.com` and press Return.

The website does not load. You are presented with the error message "Safari can't find the server." This is because the DNS server that contains information about the name mainserver. pretendco.com is not available on the Internet.

15 Enter the IP address for mainserver (`10.1.0.1`) in the address bar and press Return.

The website should load. Your computer is still on the 10.1.0.0/16 network by way of the Ethernet service. Resources on that network are still available.

16 Quit Safari.

17 In Network preferences, choose Set Service Order again.

18 Drag Ethernet above AirPort and click OK.

19 Make the AirPort service inactive using the Action menu.

20 Click Apply.

21 Log out.

*Question 1*  *What happens with the domain name service when setting service priority?*

# 7.2 Network Troubleshooting

Once you understand how to configure Mac OS X networking, you can then learn how to troubleshoot network issues. Most networks are complex beasts, composed of many different components and systems, thus making troubleshooting potentially difficult. This lesson provides a methodology for network troubleshooting that helps you narrow your focus to one of three network concepts: local, network, or server. You can effectively troubleshoot many network issues by considering how each of these concepts could be the cause of your issue. Finally, in this lesson you will also explore the specific network troubleshooting tools included with Mac OS X.

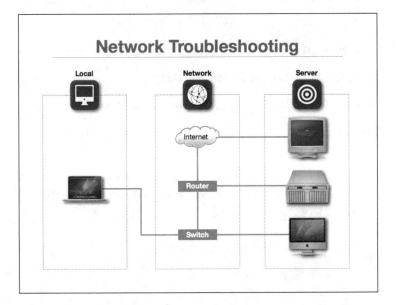

For detailed instructions, see "Network Troubleshooting" in Chapter 7 of *Apple Training Series: Mac OS X Support Essentials v10.6.*

## Network Preference Status

Local  Network  Server

For detailed instructions, see "Network Troubleshooting" in Chapter 7 of *Apple Training Series: Mac OS X Support Essentials v10.6*.

## Network Diagnostics

Local  Network  Server

For detailed instructions, see "Network Troubleshooting" in Chapter 7 of *Apple Training Series: Mac OS X Support Essentials v10.6*.

## Network Utility—Info

**Local**

**Network**

**Server**

Network Utility

| Info | Netstat | Ping | Lookup | Traceroute | Whois | Finger | Port Scan |

Select a network interface for information.

AirPort (en1)

**Interface Information**

Hardware Address: 00:22:41:f8:fc:38

IP Address: 172.16.0.208

Link Speed: 54 Mbit/s

Link Status: Active

Vendor: Apple

Model: Wireless Network Adapter
(802.11 a/b/g/n)

**Transfer Statistics**

Sent Packets: 393,475

Send Errors: 0

Recv Packets: 1,070,907

Recv Errors: 0

Collisions: 0

For detailed instructions, see "Network Troubleshooting" in Chapter 7 of *Apple Training Series: Mac OS X Support Essentials v10.6*.

## Network Utility—Ping

**Local**

**Network**

**Server**

Network Utility

| Info | Netstat | Ping | Lookup | Traceroute | Whois | Finger | Port Scan |

Enter the network address to ping.

10.1.0.1    (ex. 10.0.2.1 or www.example.com)

○ Send an unlimited number of pings
◉ Send only 10 pings                                         Stop

Ping has started…

PING 10.1.0.1 (10.1.0.1): 56 data bytes
64 bytes from 10.1.0.1: icmp_seq=0 ttl=64 time=0.388 ms
64 bytes from 10.1.0.1: icmp_seq=1 ttl=64 time=0.482 ms
64 bytes from 10.1.0.1: icmp_seq=2 ttl=64 time=0.359 ms
64 bytes from 10.1.0.1: icmp_seq=3 ttl=64 time=0.241 ms

For detailed instructions, see "Network Troubleshooting" in Chapter 7 of *Apple Training Series: Mac OS X Support Essentials v10.6*.

**Network Utility—Traceroute**

Local          Network          Server

Network Utility

Info | Netstat | Ping | Lookup | Traceroute | Whois | Finger | Port Scan

Enter the network address to trace an internet route to.

www.apple.com          (ex. 10.0.2.1 or www.example.com)

Trace

```
10  ae-83-88.ebr3.losangeles1.level3.net (4.69.146.20)  75.011 ms  74.006 ms
73.882 ms
11  ae-2.ebr3.sanjose1.level3.net (4.69.132.9)  84.586 ms  76.035 ms  73.790 ms
12  ae-93-93.csw4.sanjose1.level3.net (4.69.134.238)  86.454 ms  75.168 ms
74.672 ms
13  ae-31-99.car1.sanjose2.level3.net (4.68.18.203)  74.229 ms  73.966 ms  75.051
ms
14  * * *
15  * * *
```

For detailed instructions, see "Network Troubleshooting" in
Chapter 7 of *Apple Training Series: Mac OS X Support Essentials v10.6.*

**Network Utility—Lookup**

Local          Network          Server

Network Utility

Info | Netstat | Ping | Lookup | Traceroute | Whois | Finger | Port Scan

Enter an internet address to lookup.

mainserver          (ex. 10.0.2.1 or www.example.com)

Select the information to lookup:  Default Information

Lookup

```
Lookup has started...

; <<>> DiG 9.6.0-P1 <<>> mainserver +multiline +nocomments +nocmd +noquestion
+nostats +search
;; global options: +cmd
mainserver.pretendco.com. 10800 IN A 10.1.0.1
pretendco.com.        10800 IN NS mainserver.pretendco.com.
```

For detailed instructions, see "Network Troubleshooting" in
Chapter 7 of *Apple Training Series: Mac OS X Support Essentials v10.6.*

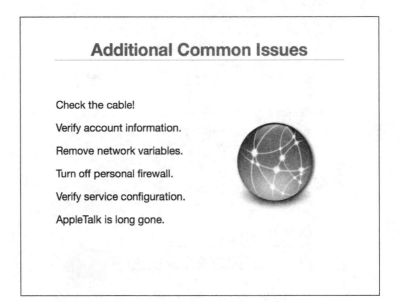

For detailed instructions, see "Network Troubleshooting" in
Chapter 7 of *Apple Training Series: Mac OS X Support Essentials v10.6*.

## Additional Common Issues

Check the cable!

Verify account information.

Remove network variables.

Turn off personal firewall.

Verify service configuration.

AppleTalk is long gone.

For detailed instructions, see "Network Troubleshooting" in
Chapter 7 of *Apple Training Series: Mac OS X Support Essentials v10.6*.

Exercise 7.2.1

# Network Troubleshooting

## Objectives

- Verify network settings

- Perform ping and port scan operations using Network Utility

## Summary

Network connectivity issues can be complex, but familiarity with the arsenal of tools included in Mac OS X will help you develop a solid plan of attack for their resolution. In this exercise you will run a script that simulates a networking error. You will troubleshoot with Network Utility and Network Diagnostics; when you have identified each of the problems you will document them and fix the errors. To verify your fix, you will view another website. Completing the tasks will acquaint you with the local subnet network, how DNS maps IP addresses to domain names, the plethora of tools included with Network Utility, and how to interpret the information these tools reveal about your network environment to resolve network communication problems.

## Break Your Network Settings

First, run a script that modifies your network settings.

1  Log in as cadmin. Make sure all other users are logged off, and no applications are running.

2  Make sure you are using the Static location (selectable under the Apple menu > Location), and you are not connected to a wireless network.

3  Open the NetworkChallenge application from /Users/Shared/StudentMaterials/Chapter7.

If NetworkChallenge displays an error message, follow its instructions before proceeding.

4  Open Safari.

5  In the Location bar, type `http://external.pretendco.com` and press Return.

The browser will attempt to contact the server. This process will time out after a delay. If the script ran correctly, you will get the error message "Safari can't connect to the proxy server."

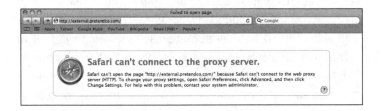

Before investigating the proxy problem in detail, let's take a quick look at the Network Diagnostics utility.

6  Quit Safari.

7  Open the Network pane of System Preferences.

8  Click the "Assist me" button at the bottom.

9  A dialog will open asking what you need assistance with; click the Diagnostics button.

Network Diagnostics scans your network settings and attempts to access the network. It will show green indicators for the Ethernet connection and Network Settings, but a red (failed) indicator for the ISP settings. After a minute the Internet and Server indicators will also turn red to indicate further failures.

10  Quit Network Diagnostics.

Network Diagnostics can help you resolve issues related to your network connection. For now, you will use more detailed troubleshooting techniques to diagnose your network problem.

First, you need to find out what proxy server Safari is attempting to use.

11  In the Network pane of System Preferences, select the active Ethernet service from the service list.

12  Click the Advanced button.

13  Click the Proxies button. You will see that there is a Web Proxy enabled.

14  Click on the Web Proxy entry in the protocol list (but do not click its checkbox; that would disable the proxy setting).

You see that your Mac is configured to use a web proxy on mainserver.pretendco.com port 90. The first step in troubleshooting this will be to figure out how to contact the proxy server.

15 Click Cancel to close the advanced settings dialog, but leave Network preferences open.

## Use Ping to Test the Connection to the Classroom Network

This exercise will walk you through the steps required to determine whether a computer is reachable using ping.

1 Open /Applications/Utilities/Network Utility.

2 Click the Ping button.

3 In the "Enter the network address to ping" field, type the domain name of the proxy server you are trying to reach (`mainserver.pretendco.com`).

4 Enter 5 in the "Send only" field and make sure it is selected.

5 Click Ping.

After a minute, it will report that it could not resolve mainserver.
pretendco.com. This error indicates that it was not able to use
DNS to look up ("resolve") the name mainserver.pretendco.com
and match it to an IP address to send the ping to. In this case,
we know that the name external.pretendco.com is valid on
the classroom network because we have used it before, so this
indicates that there is something wrong with DNS.

Unfortunately, this does not really tell us where the problem
lies, as it can be very hard to tell the difference between a DNS
problem and a complete network failure. If DNS resolution is
the only thing failing, it can mimic a complete failure because
almost all network access starts with (and depends on) a
DNS lookup. On the other hand, if the network is completely
disconnected, most attempts to use the network will fail at the
DNS step, so the only visible symptom will be DNS errors.

> **Note**  At this point you could use Network Utility's Lookup
> feature to test DNS lookups more directly, but it would
> not tell you anything you don't already know from the
> ping error.

One good way to distinguish between a DNS-only problem
and a complete network failure is to try to reach a server by its
numeric IP address. This bypasses the usual DNS lookup, and
hence will work even if DNS is broken.

6   In the "Enter the network address to ping" field, enter the numeric IP address of mainserver, 10.1.0.1.

7   Click Ping.

This time, ping reports the error "No route to host."

This error indicates that ping could not figure out how to send its test packets to the other computer. If the other computer is on the same subnet, it indicates that your computer could not find it. If the other computer is on a different subnet, it generally indicates that there was a problem finding a router to send the packets through.

In this case, since mainserver is on the same network segment as your computer, this indicates that something fairly fundamental is wrong with your network connection. You will need to verify your network connection and settings.

> **Note**  In a more complex network, where the computer you were trying to reach was not on the same network segment as your computer, this might be a good time to use Network Utility's Traceroute feature to find out more about the route your computer is using to try to reach the other computer. In this case, with the other computer on the same network segment, Traceroute will not tell us anything useful.

8   Switch to System Preferences, and verify that the Ethernet's status indicator is green. This indicates that your computer is seeing a valid connection to the classroom network. While this does not prove that there is nothing wrong with your Ethernet cable and connection, it is a very good indication that the physical connection is OK and you should proceed to checking your network settings.

## Verify Your Network Preferences

In a previous exercise you entered known good network settings. Now would be a great time to compare your current settings with the ones you entered earlier. Document the differences below.

| Good Network Settings | Current Network Settings |
|---|---|
| IP Address: | IP Address: |
| Subnet Mask: | Subnet Mask: |
| Router: | Router: |
| DNS Server: | DNS Server: |
| Search Domains: | Search Domains: |

*Question 2  What differences do you see?*

Networks rely on subnet information to define the network architecture—which hosts are local and which hosts are remote. The working network settings had a subnet mask of 255.255.0.0 (a /16 subnet); this allows for a greater number of IP addresses to be reached on a local network than the more restrictive 255.255.255.0 (a /24 subnet). The key difference in the network settings was the router and subnet mask information. Your current settings tell your computer that 10.1.0.1 is on a different subnet than your computer (since only 10.1.$n$.0–255 are on your subnet), and that in order to reach 10.1.0.1 packets need to be sent via the router at 10.1.$n$.1, which doesn't exist.

Subnet and router errors are uncommon on DHCP-configured computers, but easy to make on manually configured computers. They can also lead to somewhat mysterious symptoms, such as connections working properly to some computers, but not to others. When you are faced with a mysterious network problem, verifying the network settings is always a worthwhile step.

Let's see if these settings are all you need to fix to access those servers.

1  In Network preferences, enter the following information for the Static Location (replacing *n* with your student number):

   - IP Address: 10.1.*n*.2

   - Subnet Mask: 255.255.0.0

   - Router: 10.1.0.1

   - DNS Server: 10.1.0.1

   - Search Domains: pretendco.com

2  Click Apply.

3  Quit System Preferences.

4  Use Network Utility to send a ping to mainserver.pretendco. com again.

   It works, so you have reestablished your connection to the main classroom network by troubleshooting. Review the steps you used, and consider how this might work in your computing environment. Now you can try to access the originally requested server.

5   Use Network Utility to send a ping to external.pretendco.com again.

It also works, so now you have established that you have a good, working network between your computer and both the proxy server and your ultimate destination.

## Use Safari to Test Web Access

Different applications rely upon different network components to work properly. In the last step, you corrected your network settings. In this step, you will use Safari to test browsing with your current network settings.

1   Open Safari if it is not already running.

2   In the Location bar, type `http://external.pretendco.com` and press Return.

The site does not load, and still indicates that there is a problem connecting to the proxy server; but you just sent a ping to the address, and the ping worked. So you begin your next round of troubleshooting with the knowledge that there is basic connectivity to the server and a hint about proxy settings. This is a good starting point.

3   In the Location bar, type `http://mainserver.pretendco.com` and press Return.

This one does not load either.

*Question 3  Why didn't the websites load?*

4   Quit Safari.

## Determine the Open Ports on a System Connected to the Network

In this exercise you use Port Scan to determine the open ports on the proxy server.

1   Click the Port Scan button in Network Utility.

> **Note**  Many malicious network attacks start with or employ port scans, so your troubleshooting might be interpreted as an attack. Before you scan ports on a target computer, request permission of its owner or a network or server administrator if possible. As a general rule, only port-scan computers you have responsibility for. Many environments include automatic countermeasures. Simply scanning a server may get your computer or IP address blacklisted, preventing you from knowing if you have resolved the problem you are troubleshooting.

2   Enter the server address `mainserver.pretendco.com` in the IP address field.

3   Select the "Only test ports between…" option, and set the range to 1 through 1024.

4   Click Scan.

5   Watch the scan as it identifies the open ports.

A "well-known port" is a network port commonly associated with a particular service. For example, the well-known port for HTTP is TCP 80 and the well-known port for the Apple Filing Protocol is TCP 548. These well-known ports are commonly used in the industry and facilitate interoperability across different vendors' implementations of the same protocols. To test whether a computer has an HTTP (web) server, you would run a port scan on it and test whether or not TCP port 80 is open. Mail involves TCP ports 25, 110, and 143, among others. HTTPS (SSL secured web service) normally uses TCP port 443, so if HTTPS requests are not working, port 443 might be blocked or inactive.

For a listing of many "well-known" ports used by Apple products, see Apple Knowledge Base article #TS1629.

6   Recall that the proxy settings on your computer are set to use a proxy service on port 90 of mainserver.pretendco.com. Notice that port 90 is not one of the open TCP ports found by the port scan.

There are a number of things that might cause this problem: The proxy service on mainserver could have failed or been turned off, a firewall could be blocking access to it, or the setting on your computer could simply be incorrect.

In this case, the proxy settings are incorrect, mainserver is not running a web proxy, and a proxy is not needed on the classroom network.

7   Open the Network pane of System Preferences.

8   Select the Ethernet service and click Advanced.

9   Click the Proxies button.

10  Uncheck Web Proxy.

11  Review the other settings buttons across the top (TCP/IP, DNS, WINS, 802.1X, Ethernet) for any other anomalous settings. You should not see any.

12  Click OK.

13  Click Apply, and quit System Preferences.

14  Open Safari.

15  In the Safari location bar, type `http://mainserver.pretendco.com` and press Return.

The page loads successfully.

16  Now try the target website. In the Location bar, type `http://external.pretendco.com` and press Return.

This page finally loads. You are no longer trying to read your HTTP traffic through a nonexistent proxy server, and your basic network settings (IP address, subnet mask, router, and DNS information) match the network you are on.

A proxy server can do a few things, including:

- Caching your web content so it loads faster and keeps traffic across your routers down

- Filtering access to websites and other Internet sites your network administrator may wish to block through whitelists, blacklists, or content filtering

- Reducing information available to would-be attackers about the internal structure of your network

In many environments, proxies are configured transparently to the user. If an exhaustive check of other network parameters doesn't yield success, don't forget to check the proxy settings. Nice of Safari to suggest it.

17  Log out.

# 8

# Network Services

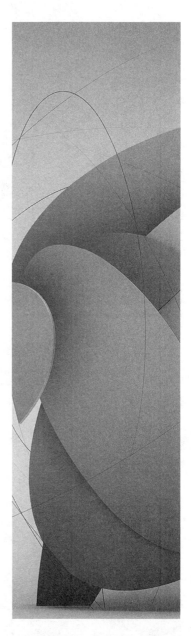

# 8.1  File-Sharing Services

While the previous chapter dealt with basic network functionality, all the real action is right here with network services. After all, the reason to establish a network connection is to share some service or resource. This lesson will first serve as an introduction to the network service client technologies built into Mac OS X. However, the primary focus of this lesson is on how Mac OS X can both access and share files via several standard file-sharing services. Further, you will also explore how Mac OS X can also share files through web sharing.

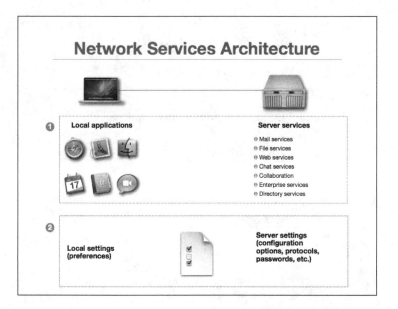

For detailed instructions, see "Understanding Network Services" in Chapter 8 of *Apple Training Series: Mac OS X Support Essentials v10.6.*

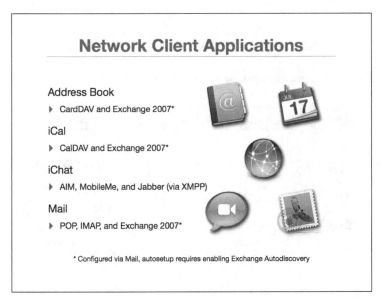

For detailed instructions, see "Using Network Applications" in Chapter 8 of *Apple Training Series: Mac OS X Support Essentials v10.6*.

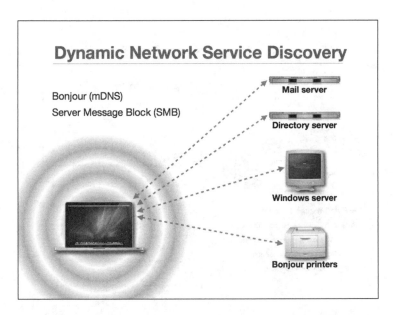

For detailed instructions, see "Understanding Network Services" in Chapter 8 of *Apple Training Series: Mac OS X Support Essentials v10.6*.

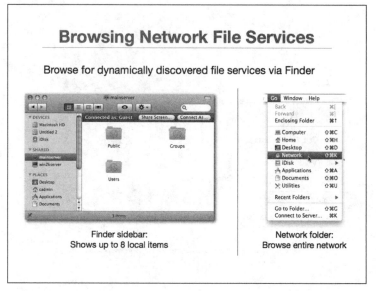

For detailed instructions, see "Using File-Sharing Services" in
Chapter 8 of *Apple Training Series: Mac OS X Support Essentials v10.6.*

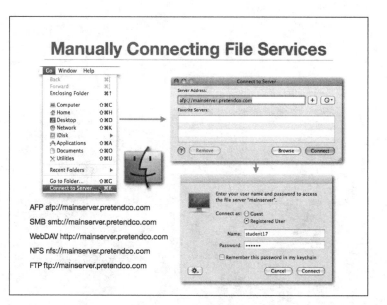

For detailed instructions, see "Using File-Sharing Services" in
Chapter 8 of *Apple Training Series: Mac OS X Support Essentials v10.6.*

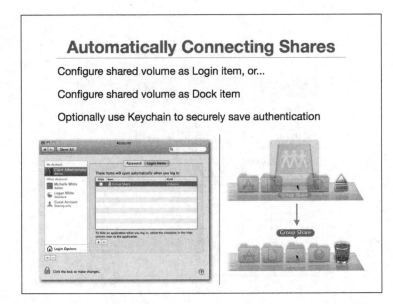

### Automatically Connecting Shares

Configure shared volume as Login item, or...

Configure shared volume as Dock item

Optionally use Keychain to securely save authentication

For detailed instructions, see "Using File-Sharing Services" in Chapter 8 of *Apple Training Series: Mac OS X Support Essentials v10.6.*

### Sharing Names

For sharing purposes the Mac can be identified via:

| Identifier | Example | Set by | Used by |
|---|---|---|---|
| IP address | 10.1.17.2 | Network preferences | Any network host |
| DNS hostname | client17.pretendco.com | Defined by DNS server | Any network host |
| Computer name | Client17 | Sharing preferences | Mac systems (via Bonjour) |
| Bonjour name | client17.local | Sharing preferences | Any Bonjour host |
| NetBIOS name | CLIENT17 | Network preferences | Any SMB host |

For detailed instructions, see "Host Network Identification" in Chapter 8 of *Apple Training Series: Mac OS X Support Essentials v10.6.*

## Enabling File Sharing

For detailed instructions, see "Using File-Sharing Services" in Chapter 8 of *Apple Training Series: Mac OS X Support Essentials v10.6.*

## Enabling FTP and SMB

By default File Sharing only enables the AFP service.

Click the Options button to manually enable FTP or SMB.

SMB sharing requires that you enter an SMB-specific sharing password per user.

For detailed instructions, see "Using File-Sharing Services" in Chapter 8 of *Apple Training Series: Mac OS X Support Essentials v10.6.*

For detailed instructions, see "Understanding Default File-Sharing Access" in Chapter 8 of *Apple Training Series: Mac OS X Support Essentials v10.6*.

For detailed instructions, see "Configuring Web Sharing" in Chapter 8 of *Apple Training Series: Mac OS X Support Essentials v10.6*.

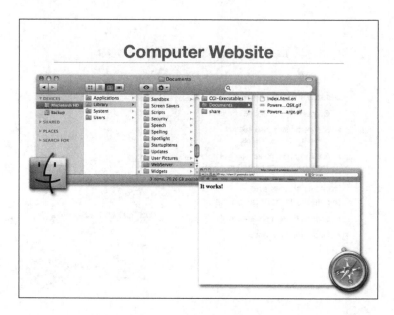

For detailed instructions, see "Configuring Web Sharing" in Chapter 8 of *Apple Training Series: Mac OS X Support Essentials v10.6*.

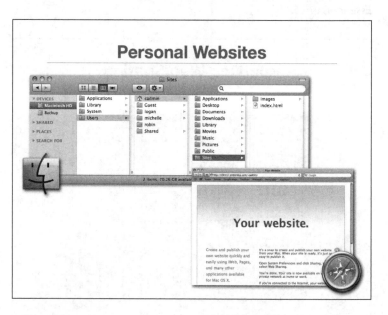

For detailed instructions, see "Configuring Web Sharing" in Chapter 8 of *Apple Training Series: Mac OS X Support Essentials v10.6*.

## Exercise 8.1.1

# Connecting to Shared Files

## Objective

- Connect to shared volumes using AFP and SMB

## Summary

Many protocols can be used to transfer files across networks and the Internet, but some of the most efficient are designed specifically to share file systems, such as AFP and SMB. In this exercise, you will use a Finder window and the Connect to Server command from the Finder's Go menu to connect to shared AFP and SMB volumes on another computer, copy a file from that volume to your desktop, and copy a file back to the mounted volume. You will then unmount the volume.

### Connect to an AFP Volume from the Sidebar

These steps will lead you through the process of using the sidebar to mount an AFP volume on the desktop.

1  Log in as Chris Johnson.

2  In a Finder window, select mainserver in the Shared section of the sidebar.

   Your computer contacts mainserver and attempts to log in as a guest.

3   Click the Connect As button.

4   When prompted to authenticate, enter student*n* (where *n* is your user number) and the password student, then press Return.

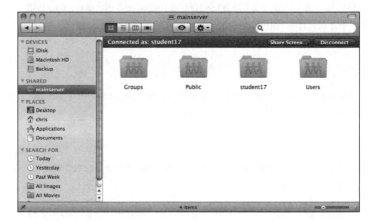

You are now connected to mainserver as your student account.

The Finder window shows all the folders to which you have access.

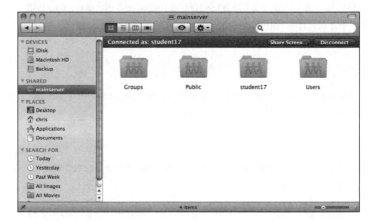

Now you will take a look at what you can see in the Users folder on the server.

5   Open Finder's preferences (Finder > Preferences or Command-,) and select "Connected servers," if it is not already selected.

This will show mounted server volumes on the desktop.

6   Close Finder's preferences window.

7   Open the Users folder.

Here you can see a number of users' home folders. The folder displays in the Finder and a new network volume icon appears on the desktop.

8   Open the folder named david.

You can see that server-hosted home folders carry the same permissions as local home folders.

9   Drag the Users desktop icon to the Trash.

The Trash icon turns into an eject icon as you drag to it, indicating that it won't delete the volume, but rather will eject it.

## Copy Files to a Network Volume

You will use the Finder to copy files to a mounted Apple Filing Protocol share point.

1   Connect to mainserver using the Finder's sidebar as you did in the previous steps. This time, mount the Public share point.

In the Public folder you see a file (copy.txt) and two folders (DropBox and SMB_DropBox) along with the StudentMaterials folder. Note the icon badge on the two folders indicating that they are write only.

2   Drag a copy of copy.txt to your desktop.

3   If necessary, give yourself (chris) read/write access to the copy using the Finder's Get Info window.

4  Rename the copy of copy.txt so that it looks like this:

`student.afp.n.txt`

(where *n* is your student number).

You can rename a file by selecting it and pressing Return or clicking on the filename and waiting a moment.

5  Drag the renamed file from your desktop onto the DropBox folder on the mounted Public volume.

The DropBox folder is a write-only folder, so you will see a dialog informing you that you will not be able to see the results of this action.

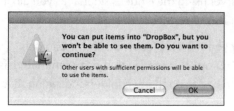

6  Click OK.

7  Disconnect from mainserver (unmount Public) by clicking the eject icon next to mainserver in the Shared section of the Finder's sidebar.

## Connect to an SMB Volume Using Connect to Server

These steps will lead you through the process of using Connect to Server (in the Finder) to mount an SMB volume on the desktop.

1  In the Finder, choose Go > Connect to Server.

2  In the Server Address field, enter `smb://mainserver.pretendco.com/Public` to connect using the SMB protocol.

Connect to Server understands a number of file-sharing protocols which you can specify with familiar URLs. Connect to Server defaults to AFP, so if you want to use a different protocol, you need to specify it in the URL, as you have done here.

3  Use the same credentials you used when connecting over AFP and select "Remember this password in my keychain." Click Connect.

The volume will mount and you will see the same files you saw when connecting using AFP. You have connected to the same folder on the server, so this is not surprising.

4  Drag a copy of copy.txt to your desktop.

5   If necessary, give yourself (chris) read/write access to the copy using the Finder's Get Info window.

6   Rename copy.txt as `student.smb.n.txt` where *n* is your student number.

7   Drag the renamed file to the SMB_DropBox folder.

You will see the same dialog telling you that you will not be able to see the results.

8   Click OK.

9   Log out.

Exercise 8.1.2
# Configuring File Sharing

## Objectives

- Enable file sharing using AFP and SMB

- Create a sharing-only user

- Set permissions for shared items

## Summary

After completing this exercise you will be able to configure a Mac to share files using AFP and SMB. For this exercise, you will work in pairs. Using System Preferences, you will configure your computers to share files using AFP and SMB. You will then verify that you can each connect to your partner's computer. You will also enable permissions for personal file sharing.

## Enable Fire Sharing

You will enable file sharing and check your computer's name in the Sharing pane of System Preferences.

1   Log in as Chris Johnson.

2   Open System Preferences and click the Sharing icon.

Your computer name should already be set to client*n*, where *n* is your student number.

3   Click the lock and authenticate as Client Administrator.

4   Click the File Sharing checkbox.

It should now say File Sharing: On.

Users with accounts can access your computer by connecting to it over the network.

5   Now that the service has started, read the information that states "Other users can access shared folders on this computer . . ."

6   Click Options.

7   Verify that "Share files and folders using AFP" is selected.

8   Select "Share files and folders using SMB (Windows)."

9   Select Client Administrator.

You will immediately be prompted to enter the account password. It is asking for Client Administrator's password.

10 Enter cadmin's password and click OK.

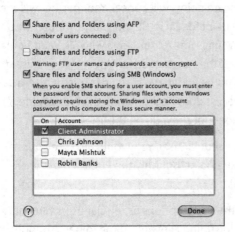

11 Click Done.

12 Quit System Preferences.

## Verify AFP File Sharing

This is the part where you will work with a partner. In this exercise, your partner will connect to your computer using AFP.

1 Have your partner choose Go > Connect to Server in the Finder on his or her computer.

2 In the Server Address field, your partner should enter your DNS name, client*n*.pretendco.com (where *n* is your student number). Your IP address would also work.

```
afp://clientn.pretendco.com
```

Connect to Server will default to AFP if not specified.

3  Have your partner connect as a guest.

A list of mountable share points will appear. Your partner will see a Public folder share point for each user on your computer who does not have a FileVault home folder. Users with FileVault home folders will be visible if they are logged in. Mayta is also omitted. If you recall, Mayta's home folder was created by restoring Marta's home folder. This process does not configure the Public folder for file sharing, so she does not show up on the list.

If you connected as a regular user, you would also see your home folder as a share point, but only the Public Folder share points of other users.

Administrators see the same options as regular users plus all mounted volumes (including FileVault home folders, though they don't have permission to see anything in the home folder).

If you connect as a FileVault user, you will see an option for your home folder. Once mounted, you will then have to open the sparsebundle disk image that contains your actual home folder. You will have to provide your password again to open this encrypted disk image.

Normal file system permissions apply, so just because you can mount the volume doesn't mean you have free access to it.

4   Choose Chris Johnson's Public Folder.

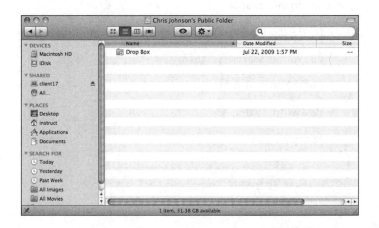

5   Have your partner attempt to create a folder in your Public folder.

*Question 1   What message did your partner receive at this attempt?*

*Question 2   Which users' Public folder share points did you not see?*

6   Disconnect from Chris's Public folder.

## Create a Sharing User and Modify Permissions

In this section of the exercise you will create a Sharing Only user and modify permissions on a folder in Chris Johnson's Public folder in order to make network collaboration easier.

1   Open System Preferences and click Accounts.

2   Click the lock and authenticate as Client Administrator.

3   Click the Add (+) button to create a new account with the
    following information.

    - New Account: Sharing Only

    - Full Name: Sharon  Schtuff

    - Short Name: sharon

    - Password: sharon

    - Verify: sharon

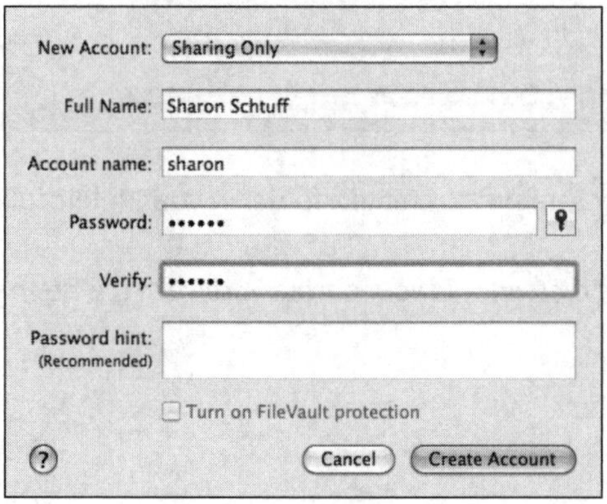

| | |
|---|---|
| New Account: | Sharing Only |
| Full Name: | Sharon Schtuff |
| Account name: | sharon |
| Password: | •••••• |
| Verify: | •••••• |
| Password hint: (Recommended) | |
| | ☐ Turn on FileVault protection |
| ? | Cancel    Create Account |

4   Click the Add (+) button again and create a group named
    Accounting.

    Groups can be used to organize users and set access controls.

5   Add Chris Johnson and Sharon Schtuff to the group by clicking the checkboxes next to their names.

6   Close System Preferences.

7   Open Chris Johnson's Public folder. (It is inside his home folder.)

8   Create a new folder called AccountingProjects.

9   Select the folder and press Command-I to open the Get Info window.

10  If necessary, open Sharing & Permissions.

11  Notice how the permissions are set.

12  If necessary, click the lock on the bottom right of the Info window and authenticate as Client Administrator.

You can now modify the default permissions for this folder. You should do this deliberately and carefully.

13 Click Staff (the group) and click the Remove (–) button to remove them from the AccountingProjects folder permissions.

This removes Staff from the group and sets the group permission to no access. However, as every file system object must have a group associated with it, if you use the command line, you will see that the group staff has been replaced with the group wheel. Wheel is a system group and by default, root is the only member.

14 Set "everyone's" privilege to No Access.

15 Click the Add (+) button to add Accounting to the AccountingProjects folder's permissions.

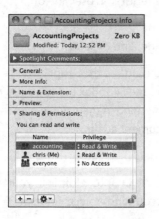

16 Select Accounting and click Select.

17 Set the accounting group's privilege to Read & Write.

18 Open Terminal and use `ls -le` to see what the Get Info window has done.

Notice that no group or everyone permissions have been granted and the group has been set to wheel. The Accounting group has been granted permission on the folder by way of an access control entry.

19 Close the Finder's information window.

## Verify Sharing Only Account and Permissions

You will now have your partner access your Public folder as Sharon Schtuff. They will place a document there that you can both access.

1 Have your partner eject any mounted AFP volumes.

2 Have your partner press Command-K.

   This is a shortcut to bring up the Connect to Server window.

3 In the Server Address field, your partner types `afp://clientn.local` where *n* is your student number. This is the Bonjour name of your computer. Of course, the usual domain name that you used above would work here, too.

4 Click Connect.

5 Have your partner connect as the registered user Sharon Schtuff (sharon).

6 Choose Chris Johnson's Public folder and click OK.

   Chris's Public folder opens and you can see the DropBox and AccountingProjects folders inside. The DropBox has write-only permissions, so once you put something in there you cannot see the result or retrieve that document again.

7 Open the AccountingProjects folder.

8 Copy PretendcoForecast.xls from the Chapter8 folder in your StudentMaterials folder to the AccountingProjects folder.

9  On your computer, open the AccountingProjects folder and select the PretendcoForecast.xls document.

10 Press the Space bar.

11 The document opens in Quick Look, even though you do not have Microsoft Excel installed.

12 On both computers, close all the open Finder windows and close the Quick Look window. (A great keyboard shortcut for this is Command-Option-W.)

13 Have your partner disconnect from your computer.

## Verify SMB File Sharing

Your partner will now connect to your computer to test SMB connectivity.

1  Have your partner choose Go > Connect to Server.

2  In the Server Address field, your partner types `smb://10.1.n.2` where *n* is your student number (not your partner's student number). Of course, you could also use the DNS name or the Bonjour name.

3  Click Connect.

4  Have your partner connect as the registered user Client Administrator and click Connect.

   Notice that in addition to the Public folder share points, there is the cadmin share point and any additional mounted volumes. This is the behavior of an administrator account under AFP as well.

5   Select cadmin and click OK.

Your partner now has access to your Client Administrator's entire home folder.

6   You and your partner should both eject any mounted network volumes and log out.

Exercise 8.1.3
# Configuring Web Sharing (optional)

## Objectives
- Enable Web Sharing
- Customize the default website files

## Summary

You can use the Apache web server software included with Mac OS X to host a website on your computer. Once enabled, webpages placed in the Sites folder in a home folder can be browsed at http://<computer name or address>/~username/. Pages placed in /Library/WebServer/Documents can be browsed at http://<computer name or address>/.

In this exercise, you will work in pairs. You will enable Web Sharing on your computer and your partner will connect to it from his or her computer. You will replace the default main website and Chris Johnson's personal website with web documents provided in the student materials.

## Turn on Web Sharing

First enable Web Sharing on your computer.

1  Log in as Chris Johnson.

2  Open the Sharing pane of System Preferences.

3  Click the lock and authenticate as Client Administrator.

4   Click the checkbox to start Web Sharing if it is not already enabled.

On the right are the URLs of your computer's website and your personal website. These are active links to your computer's default website and to the active user's website.

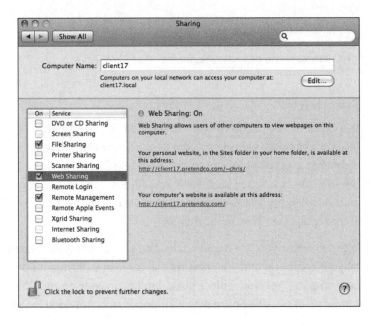

5   Click the second link to view the computer's website. Safari automatically opens and displays the default webpage.

In addition to clicking the link, you can access the computer's website by entering DNS names, the Bonjour name, or a static IP address in the browser's address bar (remember to use your student number for *n*):

`http://client`*`n`*`.pretendco.com`

`http://client`*`n`*

`http://client`*`n`*`.local`

`http://10.1.`*`n`*`.2`

You should see a webpage that says "It works!" This is the standard Apache web server initial page. This page is included in an Apache distribution so you can see that the server is working. Of course, it is assumed that you will replace this page with your own.

6   Try using the other address formats. All of them should work.

7   Display the personal webpage of the user Chris Johnson on your computer by entering the address of the page in one of the following formats:

`http://clientn.pretendco.com/~chris/`

`http://clientn/~chris/`

`http://clientn.local/~chris/`

`http://10.1.n.2/~chris/`

You should see a webpage that looks like the next screen shot. Note that the window title is Your Website.

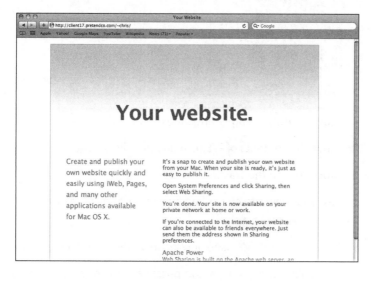

8   Try using the other address formats. All of them should work.

## Install New Web Documents

You will install two sets of web documents that were created for you. The first is Chris Johnson's personal home page. The second is a set of documents for the computer's main site.

1   Still logged in as Chris Johnson, use the Finder to navigate to Chapter8 of the student materials.

2   Copy chris.zip to ~/Sites.

    The Sites folder is where your personal web documents live.

3   Open chris.zip in your Sites folder by double-clicking it.

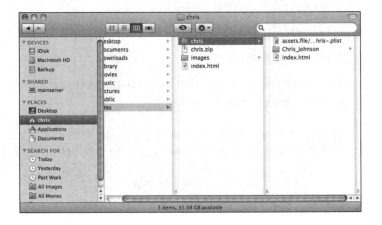

4   Move chris.zip, images, and index.html to the Trash.

5   Move the contents of ~/Sites/chris to ~/Sites.

6   Move chris to the Trash.

7   Test your new site by loading it in Safari: `http://client`*n*`.` `pretendco.com/~chris`.

8   Log out as Chris Johnson and log in as Client Administrator.

    The main website for the computer can only be modified by an administrator.

9   From Chapter8 of the student materials, copy pretendco.zip to your desktop.

10  Open pretendco.zip by double-clicking it.

11  Open the new pretendco folder on your desktop by double-clicking it.

    This will open a new Finder window.

12  Use a different Finder window to navigate to /Library/WebServer.

13  Rename the Documents folder OldDocuments.

14  Create a new Documents folder in /Library/WebServer.

15  Drag the contents of the pretendco folder on your desktop (they should be visible in another Finder window) to the Documents folder you created in /Library/WebServer.

16  Select both the Documents and the OldDocuments folders by clicking one and then Command-clicking the other.

17  Use File > Get Info (or Command-I) to open Get Info windows for both folders.

18  Make sure you can see the Sharing & Permissions pane for both folders.

    Notice that the permissions on these two folders differ. To allow other administrators of this computer to easily change the web documents, you want to give the admin group Read & Write privilege. To prevent others from changing the documents, you want everyone else to have Read only access.

19  Click the lock in the Sharing & Permissions pane of the new Documents folder and authenticate as Client Administrator.

20  Give the admin group Read & Write privilege.

**21** From the Action (gear) menu, choose "Apply to enclosed items."

This will apply the permissions above to all of the contents of /Library/WebServer/Documents. A dialog appears asking you to confirm.

> **Are you sure you want to apply the selected owner, group, and permissions to all the enclosed items?**
>
> You can't undo this.
>
> Cancel    OK

**22** Click OK.

**23** Close both Get Info windows.

**24** Test the update of the web documents by loading `http://clientn.pretendco.com` in Safari.

**25** Log out.

# Host Sharing Services and Security

Mac OS X network services go beyond simply sharing files, and in this lesson you will explore other methods of sharing resources between Macs. Specifically, the majority of this lesson focuses on how you can remotely control Macs via network screen sharing or remote command-line login. In this lesson you will also learn how you can secure your Mac's network resources using the built-in personal application firewall. Finally, you will learn some general network service troubleshooting techniques that will help you diagnose both file and host sharing issues.

## Enable Screen Sharing

For detailed instructions, see "Using Mac OS X Screen Sharing" in Chapter 8 of *Apple Training Series: Mac OS X Support Essentials v10.6*.

For detailed instructions, see "Using Mac OS X Screen Sharing" in Chapter 8 of *Apple Training Series: Mac OS X Support Essentials v10.6.*

## Screen Sharing via iChat

iChat also supports screen sharing without having to enable the service.

Works with any chat service that iChat can access

Automatically resolves network connections

Also starts voice chat session

For detailed instructions, see "Using iChat 5 Screen Sharing" in Chapter 8 of *Apple Training Series: Mac OS X Support Essentials v10.6.*

For detailed instructions, see "Understanding Remote Login" in Chapter 8 of *Apple Training Series: Mac OS X Support Essentials v10.6*.

For detailed instructions, see "Understanding Remote Login" in Chapter 8 of *Apple Training Series: Mac OS X Support Essentials v10.6*.

## Internet Sharing

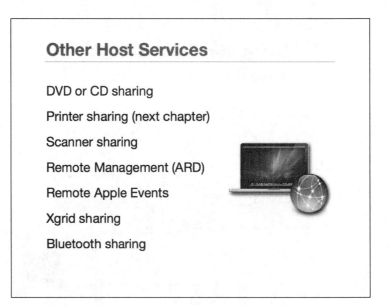

For detailed instructions, see "Sharing an Internet Connection" in Chapter 8 of *Apple Training Series: Mac OS X Support Essentials v10.6*.

## Other Host Services

DVD or CD sharing

Printer sharing (next chapter)

Scanner sharing

Remote Management (ARD)

Remote Apple Events

Xgrid sharing

Bluetooth sharing

For detailed instructions, see "Using Host Sharing Services" in Chapter 8 of *Apple Training Series: Mac OS X Support Essentials v10.6*.

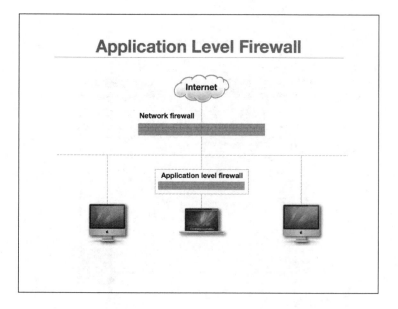

For detailed instructions, see "Securing Network Services" in Chapter 8 of *Apple Training Series: Mac OS X Support Essentials v10.6.*

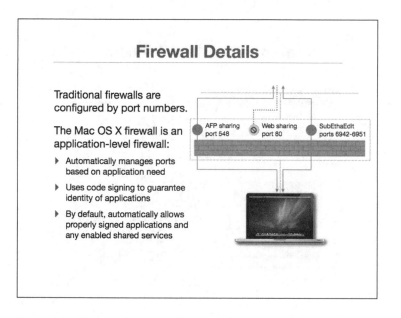

For detailed instructions, see "Securing Network Services" in Chapter 8 of *Apple Training Series: Mac OS X Support Essentials v10.6.*

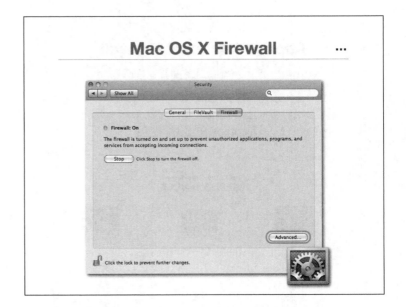

For detailed instructions, see "Securing Network Services" in
Chapter 8 of *Apple Training Series: Mac OS X Support Essentials v10.6*.

For detailed instructions, see "Securing Network Services" in
Chapter 8 of *Apple Training Series: Mac OS X Support Essentials v10.6*.

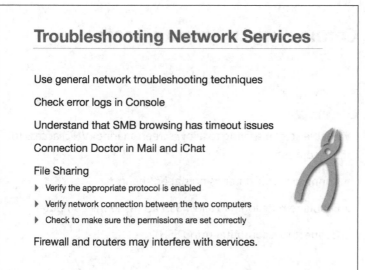

**Troubleshooting Network Services**

Use general network troubleshooting techniques

Check error logs in Console

Understand that SMB browsing has timeout issues

Connection Doctor in Mail and iChat

File Sharing

▶ Verify the appropriate protocol is enabled

▶ Verify network connection between the two computers

▶ Check to make sure the permissions are set correctly

Firewall and routers may interfere with services.

For detailed instructions, see "Troubleshooting Network Services" in Chapter 8 of *Apple Training Series: Mac OS X Support Essentials v10.6*.

**Exercise 8.2.1**

# Connecting to Remote Hosts

## Objectives

- Enable screen sharing to allow screen sharing (VNC) access to the computer
- Connect to computer using screen sharing
- Enable remote login to allow SSH access to the computer
- Connect to a computer using SSH

## Summary

Mac OS X provides two services that allow you to remote control the computer. Screen sharing (VNC, or Virtual Network Computing) allows you to remotely control the screen of a computer as though you were sitting in front of it. The remote computer's screen appears in a window on your local machine and your mouse movements, clicks, keystrokes, etc. are sent to the remote machine. Remote login (SSH, or Secure Shell) allows you to log into a remote machine at the command line. You can then execute commands on the remote machine as though you had a Terminal window open on that computer. In this exercise, you will enable both services and test their functionality.

## Enable Screen Sharing

You will log in as Client Administrator and enable screen sharing.

1   Log in as Client Administrator.

2   Open the Sharing pane of System Preferences.

3  Click the checkbox next to Remote Management, if it is not already selected.

4  Ensure that "All users" is selected for "Allow access for."

5  Click Options.

6  Ensure that all options are selected. An easy way to do this is to Option-click a checkbox until all of the checkboxes are selected.

7  Quit System Preferences.

## Remotely Control the Screen to Enable Remote Login

Your partner will control your screen by using screen sharing in order to enable remote login (SSH) access.

1  Ask your partner to use the Shared section of the Finder's sidebar to select your computer.

2   Your partner should click Share Screen and authenticate as Client Administrator and click Connect.

Screen sharing begins and your partner can see a window with a live, interactive picture of your desktop. If you move something on your desktop, they can see it. If they move something on your desktop, you can see it.

3   Have your partner open System Preferences on your computer and select the Sharing pane.

If using the Apple menu or the dock, they will want to use the one contained in the window, not the one at the edge of the screen.

4   Click the checkbox to enable Remote Login.

This enables the SSH service on your computer.

5   Your partner should choose Screen Sharing > Quit Screen Sharing from his or her menu.

6   Switch roles and repeat these steps.

## Use Terminal to Connect with SSH

You and your partner will connect to each other's computers using the Terminal. You will open a Terminal window and use the ssh command to connect. On Mac OS X, SSH services are advertised using Bonjour. Terminal knows how to browse for these services. Next you will use Terminal's New Remote Connection feature to establish an SSH connection to your computer. You and your partner can perform these steps at the same time.

1   Have your partner open the Terminal application.

2   Ask your partner to use ssh to connect to your computer as Chris Johnson:

    client18:~ cadmin$ `ssh chris@clientn`

    (where n is your student number).

    Here your partner is telling ssh that he or she wants to log into clientn as the user chris.

    ssh retains information about all of the computers you have used it to connect to. If this computer is not on that list (as it shouldn't be since you have not done this yet in this class), ssh will prompt you saying (the exact numbers below may vary):

    ```
    The authenticity of host 'client17' (10.1.17.2) can't be
    established.
    ```

    ```
    RSA key fingerprint is 99:5b:55:ee:fb:97:3f:30:c8:b4:5a:
    62:c7:82:f3:af.
    ```

    ```
    Are you sure you want to continue connecting (yes/no)?
    ```

3  Your partner should type yes and press Return.

Your partner has to enter the full word *yes*. ssh is trying to ensure that you connect to the computer you want to connect to. It has no special mechanism for ensuring the identity of the remote computer, so it has to ask the user. Ideally, this "RSA key fingerprint" is communicated to the user by the owner of the remote computer so that the user can confirm it.

4  Next ssh prompts your partner for Chris's password. He or she should enter it and press Return. No feedback will be displayed on the screen as you type.

Your partner is presented with a new prompt.

5  You should both notice that the prompt has changed, indicating that you are logged into a different computer as a different user:

```
client17:~ chris$
```

6  Ask your partner to change his or her working directory to ~/Public and then get a directory listing.

7  Your partner should see Chris's AccountingProjects folder.

8  Ask your partner to type Control-D, exit, or logout to log out of Chris's account.

9  Your partner should choose Shell > New Remote Connection from Terminal's menu.

10 Ask your partner to choose Secure Shell (ssh) from the Service list and your computer from the Server list.

11 Your partner should enter chris for the User and choose SSH Protocol 2 from the pop-up menu.

> **Note**  Version 1 of the SSH protocol has demonstrated security weaknesses. It is recommended that you always use version 2.

Below the text field and pop-up menu, you can see the command that Terminal is generating. You can use this command in the future to connect this way just by typing it at a prompt.

**12** Click Connect.

A new Terminal window opens.

**13** Continue connecting as above and provide Chris's password.

Your partner is now connected. ssh remembers each name you use to connect to a particular computer separately. Previously the DNS name was used. This time, the Bonjour name was used.

**14** Have your partner confirm that he or she can see the AccountingProjects folder.

**15** Have your partner log out of the remote connection, and quit the Terminal application.

**16** Log out.

Exercise 8.2.2

# Configuring the Personal Application Firewall (optional)

## Objective

- Enable and configure the Mac OS X personal application firewall

## Summary

A firewall blocks network traffic based on port numbers and proto-cols, or in the case of Mac OS X's firewall, it only allows ports based on application and service requests. Mac OS X's built-in firewall is also simple to configure from the GUI. In this exercise you will turn on the firewall and start a network-aware application. Then, you will view the firewall log. You will also configure the advanced Stealth option and attempt to ping another student's computer.

## Turn on the Firewall and Modify Its Settings

You will enable the firewall service.

1  Log in as Client Administrator.

2  Open System Preferences and click Security.

3  Click the Firewall button.

4  Click the lock and authenticate, if necessary.

5  Click Start to turn on the firewall service.

6  Click Advanced.

Notice that File Sharing, Remote Login, Remote Management, and Web Sharing (if you did optional Exercise 8.1.3) are already on the list as "Allow incoming connections." Mac OS X assumes that if you enable a service in the Sharing pane, you must want users to be able to connect to it, so it automatically allows those services through the firewall.

7   Click Cancel.

You did not make any changes to this dialog. It is always a good idea to cancel dialogs and other settings screens when you don't make any changes.

8   Close System Preferences.

## Test Firewall Settings

You will test a few features of the firewall service.

1   Open SubEthaEdit, which can be found in the Applications folder. Tell it not to check for updates and click through the demo period reminder.

SubEthaEdit has a feature that allows for online collaborative editing of a document hosted on a single computer. In order to provide this service, it needs to be able to open a port for incoming connections. It attempts to do that when the application is opened. The firewall service does not allow it by default and so it asks the user whether to allow this potential incoming connection.

2   Click Allow and authenticate as Client Administrator if necessary.

3   Open System Preferences again and open Security preferences.

4   Click Firewall, if necessary.

5   Click the lock and authenticate, if necessary.

6   Click Advanced.

Notice that SubEthaEdit has been added to the allow list.

7   Open the pop-up menu for the SubEthaEdit entry.

Notice that you can also block incoming connections here.

Also notice that "Automatically allow signed software to receive incoming connections" is selected by default. If SubEthaEdit were a signed application, you would not have been prompted to approve its incoming connections.

Leave SubEthaEdit set to allow incoming connections.

8   Uncheck "Automatically allow signed software to receive incoming connections."

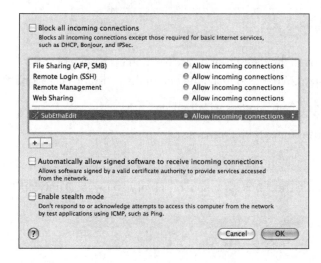

9   Click OK.

10  Quit System Preferences.

11  Open iTunes, which can be found in the Applications folder.

12  If it presents you with the iTunes Software License Agreement,
    click Agree.

    If this is the first time you have opened iTunes on this computer,
    the iTunes Setup Assistant will open.

13  Accept all the defaults and click Next on each pane of the
    assistant. When you reach the end of the assistant, click Done.

    iTunes's main window will open.

14  Choose iTunes > Preferences.

15  Click the Sharing icon.

16  Click the checkbox for "Share my library on my local network."

**17** Click OK.

**18** In the copyright reminder dialog, click OK.

The system opens a dialog to ask if you want iTunes to be allowed to accept incoming connections. Most Apple applications are signed, but if you tell the firewall not to trust signed applications, even Apple applications will require your approval to accept incoming connections.

**19** Click Allow.

**20** iTunes has also detected that the firewall is not configured to allow it through. You just corrected that, so you could click Ignore, but you will need System Preferences shortly anyway, so click Open Firewall Preferences.

If iTunes does not present this dialog, open System Preferences now.

**21** In the Firewall pane of the Security pane of System Preferences, click Advanced.

**22** Open Console from the Utilities folder.

**23** If the source list sidebar is not shown, click the Show Log List button in the toolbar to enable it.

**24** In the files section of the source list on the left, select /private/var/log. This is one of the standard log locations on the system.

25 Click the disclosure triangle next to it and select appfirewall.log.

26 This is the log file that the firewall service logs to. If you scroll through it you may notice various allow and deny messages.

27 Ask your partner to open Network Utility from /Applications/ Utilities.

28 Your partner should click the Ping button and then ping your client:

`clientn.pretendco.com`

(where *n* is your student number).

Your partner should see successful pings. Nothing related to the pings appears in the appfirewall.log file.

29 On your computer, select "Enable stealth mode" in the advanced settings of the firewall.

30 Click OK and switch back to Console.

31 Ask your partner to repeat the steps to ping your computers.

Now your partner gets "Request timeout" messages and you see at least one "Deny ICMP" message in the appfirewall.log file.

> **Note**  While Stealth mode is an excellent security feature, it interferes with network troubleshooting. If a machine does not respond to a ping, in addition to checking cables, you should check firewall settings as well.

32 On your computer stop the firewall service.

*Question 3  Why would you have a firewall enabled on your computer if you already have a network firewall?*

33 Log out.

# Directory Services

# 8.3

Directory services provide your Mac with the information it needs to identify and authenticate resources such as users, groups, and computers. Primarily, directory services are used to provide unified user identification, authentication, and management across network hosts and resources. Mac OS X implements directory services through technology known as Open Directory. In this lesson you will explore general directory service concepts and understand how Open Directory makes these resources available to your Mac. This lesson covers both configuration and troubleshooting of your Mac's Open Directory system.

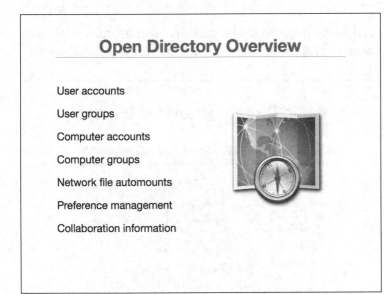

## Open Directory Overview

User accounts

User groups

Computer accounts

Computer groups

Network file automounts

Preference management

Collaboration information

For detailed instructions, see "Understanding Directory Services" in Chapter 8 of *Apple Training Series: Mac OS X Support Essentials v10.6*.

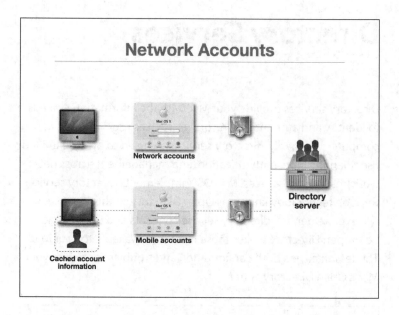

For detailed instructions, see "Understanding Directory Services" in Chapter 8 of *Apple Training Series: Mac OS X Support Essentials v10.6*.

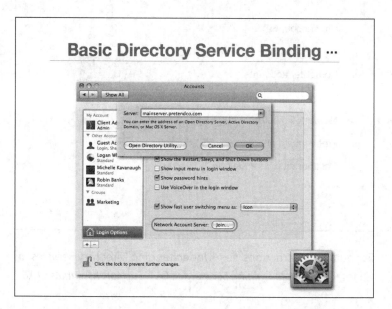

For detailed instructions, see "Configuring Network Directory Services" in Chapter 8 of *Apple Training Series: Mac OS X Support Essentials v10.6*.

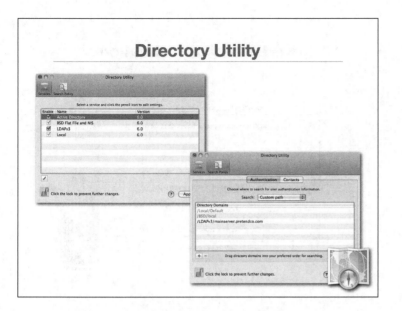

For detailed instructions, see "Configuring Network Directory Services" in Chapter 8 of *Apple Training Series: Mac OS X Support Essentials v10.6.*

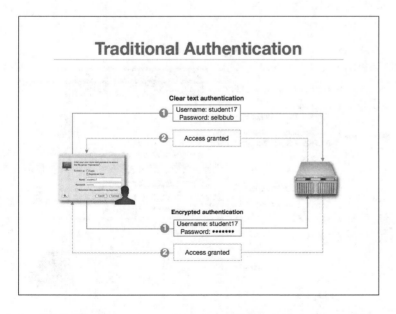

For detailed instructions, see "Managing Network Authentication" in Chapter 8 of *Apple Training Series: Mac OS X Support Essentials v10.6.*

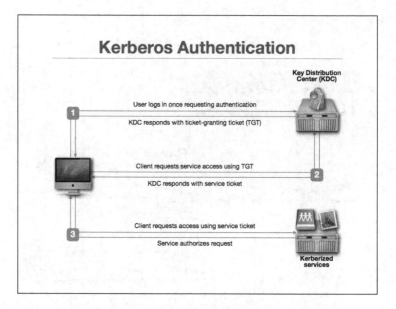

For detailed instructions, see "Understanding Kerberos Authentication" in Chapter 8 of *Apple Training Series: Mac OS X Support Essentials v10.6*.

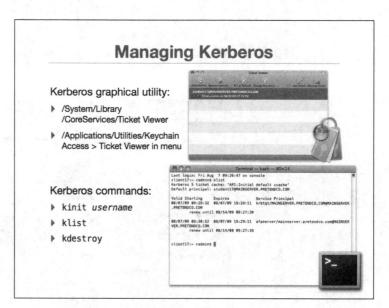

For detailed instructions, see "Verifying Kerberos Authentication" in Chapter 8 of *Apple Training Series: Mac OS X Support Essentials v10.6*.

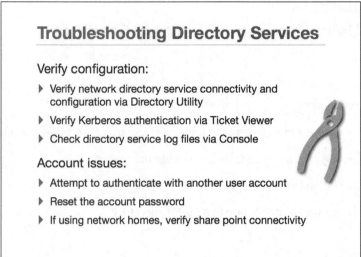

## Troubleshooting Directory Services

Verify configuration:

▶ Verify network directory service connectivity and configuration via Directory Utility

▶ Verify Kerberos authentication via Ticket Viewer

▶ Check directory service log files via Console

Account issues:

▶ Attempt to authenticate with another user account

▶ Reset the account password

▶ If using network homes, verify share point connectivity

For detailed instructions, see "Troubleshooting Directory Services" in Chapter 8 of *Apple Training Series: Mac OS X Support Essentials v10.6.*

Exercise 8.3.1

# Using Network Directory Services

## Objectives

- Connect to an Open Directory server using Accounts preferences
- Log in to a computer using a network account
- Understand single sign-on
- Remove a connection to an LDAP directory

## Summary

In a networked environment, a Macintosh computer might need to access an Open Directory server to retrieve system information, such as user accounts or resource locations. If DHCP is not configured to provide the location of the Open Directory server or your client computer isn't configured to use the information provided by DHCP, then you will need to use Accounts preferences or Directory Utility to manually specify the address of the server. In this exercise you will use Accounts preferences to configure your computer to retrieve user account information from the main classroom server. You will then log in using an account on the server. After you have tested the user account, you will reconfigure your computer to no longer use the classroom directory server.

## Bind Your Computer to the Classroom Directory Server

In order for your computer to use the information contained in the classroom directory server, you need to configure your client with information about the server, a process known as binding. Simple binding takes place in Accounts preferences in System Preferences.

1   Log in as Client Administrator.

2   In a Finder window, click your home folder in the sidebar.

3   Command-click the name of the folder in the Finder window's title bar.

    This shows the path to the folder being displayed. Notice that the Users folder is in a folder named mainserver.pretendco.com that is in a folder named Servers. This shows you that the home folder has been mounted from mainserver.pretendco.com.

4   Open System Preferences.

5   If you did the optional VPN exercise in the previous chapter, use Network preferences to Remove (–) the L2TP VPN settings. Don't forget to click Apply.

6   Open Accounts preferences.

7   Click the lock to authenticate if necessary.

8   Click Login Options.

9   Next to Network Account Server, click Join.

10  A dialog slides down asking for the name of your directory server.

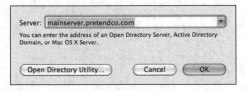

11  Enter `mainserver.pretendco.com`.

    After a moment, the dialog changes, telling you that the server offers VPN services.

Mac OS X has the ability to set up various services, including VPN, for your account if they are configured for your server account. This feature is beyond the scope of this class, so we will not explore it here. If you would like more information on automatic configuration, please see the Network Services chapter of the reference guide.

**The server "mainserver.pretendco.com" offers VPN services.**

You can join the server to use network accounts from this computer, and optionally set up your applications to use the offered services.

( Only Join )          ( Back )   ( Set Up Services )

12 Click Only Join.

13 If you are asked for administrator credentials, authenticate as Client Administrator.

Your computer communicates with the server and configures itself. The Network Account Server section has now changed to reflect being bound to the classroom server.

**14** Log out.

Notice that the login window has changed. It now provides an Other option. You may need to scroll to see the Other option.

## Test the Connection

Now that you have established a binding to the mainserver, you should be able to log in to your computer using a user account stored on the main classroom server.

**1** Click Other to log in.

**2** Provide your network credentials:

Name: `studentn` (where *n* is your student number)

Password: `student`

The login will take slightly longer than usual, because you are logging in to a network user account defined by the network account server binding you set in Accounts preferences. Your login is being authenticated by mainserver.pretendco.com and is connecting to a home folder shared from that server. The user account information is being communicated using LDAP, the Lightweight Directory Access Protocol; the authentication is being performed by Kerberos; and the home folder is being mounted using AFP.

3   Open System Preferences and click Accounts.

You did not create this account using System Preferences. It still shows up in Accounts preferences as long as you are logged in to it. Notice that it is indicated as being a network account.

4   Click Show All.

5   Click Desktop & Screen Saver.

6   Select a new background image.

7   Press Command-Shift-3 to take a screen shot.

A file named Screen shot <date time stamp> appears on the desktop.

8   Quit System Preferences.

## Examine Single Sign-On

When logging in to your network user account, the server authenticates your account using a technology called Kerberos. You will examine the behind-the-scenes activity when you go to a password-protected website. Single sign-on permits access to protected resources such as file servers and websites without having to reenter your password. One distinct advantage of Kerberos over other authentication methods is that during the authentication process, the user's password is not transmitted across the network, not even in encrypted form.

1   Open Keychain Access in the Utilities folder.

2   Choose Keychain Access > Ticket Viewer (Command-Option-K).

The Ticket Viewer application opens.

3   Notice that you have a ticket from MAINSERVER.PRETENDCO.COM already and that it expires in approximately 10 hours. This is your ticket-granting ticket, which you acquired as you logged in.

4   Open Safari.

5   Type https://mainserver.pretendco.com/protected/ into the address bar.

6   When Safari says it can't verify the identity of the website, click Continue.

The page loads. This page uses Kerberos for authentication.

7   Switch to Ticket Viewer.

8   Notice that nothing has changed in Ticket Viewer.

9   Open the Terminal application.

10  At the prompt, use the klist command to view your Kerberos tickets.

    client17:~ student17$ klist

    You should see your ticket-granting ticket (krbtgt) and an HTTP ticket. You may also see an AFP (afpserver) ticket, depending on how the server is configured.

11  Log out.

12  Log in as Chris Johnson.

13  Open Safari.

14  Type https://mainserver.pretendco.com/protected/ into the address bar.

    When Safari says it can't verify the identity of the website, click Continue.

    You are presented with an error page.

15  Open Keychain Access.

16  Open Ticket Viewer.

    You do not have any tickets.

    *Question 4  Why do you not have any tickets?*

## Log In to Your Network User Account on a Different Computer

After a classmate has finished configuring his or her computer to use network user accounts, change computers with the classmate, so that each of you can use the other's computer to access your own networked user account.

1   Switch places with any classmate.

2   On your classmate's computer, log in as studentn (where n is your student number).

    Even though you are working on a different computer, you should be able to log in with your network user account. After you are logged in, the desktop picture should be the one you selected earlier when you first logged in on your own computer. On your desktop, you should see the screen shot you created earlier.

3   Log out.

4   Return to your own computer.

## Remove the LDAP Binding

Currently, your computer is bound to the main directory server. If your computer no longer needs to retrieve data from a directory service, it is easy to unbind the server. In most cases, unless you need to be bound to a directory service, you should remove bindings to avoid potential security issues.

1   Log in as Chris Johnson.

2   Open the Accounts pane of System Preferences.

3   Click the lock and authenticate as Client Administrator.

4   Click Login Options.

5   Click the Edit button located next to Network Account Server.

6   Select mainserver.pretendco.com.

7   Click the Remove (–) button.

8  In the confirmation dialog, click Stop Using Server.

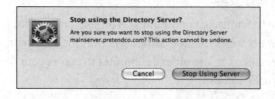

9  Click Done.

You can no longer log in to your computer using network-based user accounts and home folders, although you can still connect to services on mainserver with those account names. You can now only log in to this computer with a local account.

10 Log out.

# 9

# Peripherals and Printing

# 9.1 Managing Peripherals

While Apple may have pioneered "plug-and-play" technology with the original Mac operating system, there may still come a time where you will need to troubleshoot a peripheral issue. Generally speaking, a peripheral is any hardware device that adds functionality to your Mac. In this lesson you will first explore the general peripheral technologies supported by Mac OS X. You will then learn about how the different types of software in Mac OS X are designed to interact with peripherals. This understanding is necessary given the eventual goal of learning how to troubleshoot peripheral issues that may arise on Mac systems.

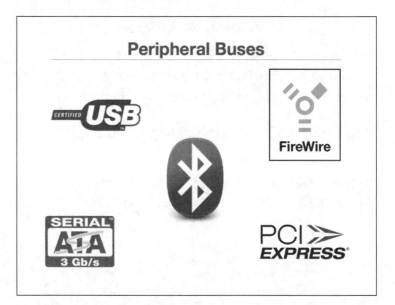

For detailed instructions, see "Understanding Peripherals" in Chapter 9 of *Apple Training Series: Mac OS X Support Essentials v10.6*.

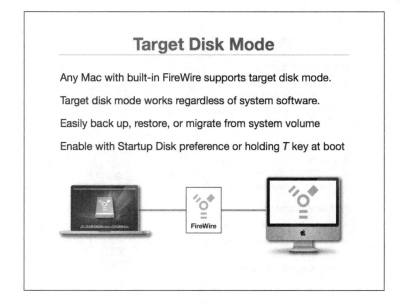

For detailed instructions, see "Understanding Peripherals" in Chapter 9 of *Apple Training Series: Mac OS X Support Essentials v10.6.*

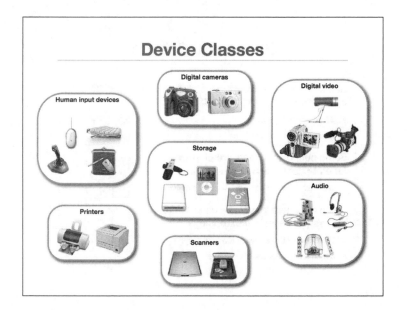

For detailed instructions, see "Peripheral Device Classes" in Chapter 9 of *Apple Training Series: Mac OS X Support Essentials v10.6.*

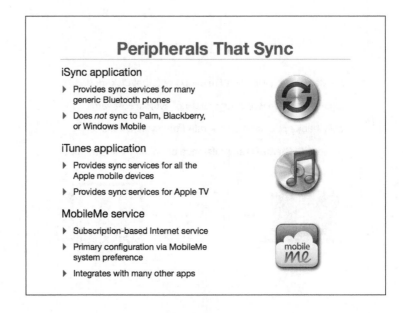

For detailed instructions, see "Peripherals That Synchronize" in Chapter 9 of *Apple Training Series: Mac OS X Support Essentials v10.6*.

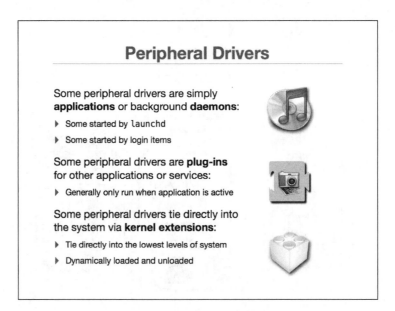

For detailed instructions, see "Troubleshooting Peripherals" in Chapter 9 of *Apple Training Series: Mac OS X Support Essentials v10.6*.

## Viewing Extensions

Only shows extensions currently loaded by the system

For detailed instructions, see "Inspecting Loaded Extensions" in Chapter 9 of *Apple Training Series: Mac OS X Support Essentials v10.6.*

## Inspecting Peripherals

Peripherals appear regardless of functioning software drivers

For detailed instructions, see "Troubleshooting Peripherals" in Chapter 9 of *Apple Training Series: Mac OS X Support Essentials v10.6.*

## Troubleshooting Peripherals

Use System Profiler to verify the device

Check the physical connections and power

Try a different port on the Mac

Unplug other peripherals and hubs

Try a known-good Mac OS X computer

Restart or shut down

Check for Apple software and driver updates

For detailed instructions, see "Troubleshooting Peripherals" in Chapter 9 of *Apple Training Series: Mac OS X Support Essentials v10.6*.

Exercise 9.1.1
# Managing Peripherals

## Objectives

- Use System Profiler to gather information about what devices are connected to a computer

- Use target disk mode to connect to other computers and external drives

## Summary

This exercise introduces you to peripheral connection buses, basic device configuration, and device troubleshooting.

## Discovering USB Devices with System Profiler

In an earlier exercise you used System Profiler to view information about your hard drive. Because it is bus-oriented, System Profiler is extremely useful when troubleshooting peripheral issues. In this exercise, you will use System Profiler to identify devices on a particular bus. Most Macs have several USB ports and use USB internally for several devices. Your instructor may choose to do this exercise as a demonstration if the equipment in the room doesn't provide USB devices.

1  Log in as Client Administrator.

2  Open System Profiler from the Utilities folder.

A System Profiler window opens with the Hardware Overview
displayed. The Contents list on the left displays all the reports
that System Profiler can generate.

3   Under the Hardware list, click USB to view devices connected to
the USB bus.

USB is a very common peripheral bus. It is often used for
keyboards, mice, trackpads, printers, scanners, storage devices,
and digital cameras.

In this example, System Profiler indicates that there are four USB buses, three of which have devices connected to them.

If a device is connected to a hub, it is listed beneath the hub and indented. This example shows a hub with a Bluetooth USB Host Controller connected. This hub and Bluetooth controller are actually internal devices.

4    Locate and select the mouse or another external USB device in the USB report for your computer.

If you do not have a mouse or other external device, your instructor may choose to demonstrate these steps.

Details about the device are displayed in the lower-right-side pane.

5    While viewing the USB information, unplug the mouse from your computer, plug it into a different USB port, then choose Refresh from the View menu.

System Profiler only polls for devices when it is opened and when you choose View > Refresh.

6    Locate the mouse in the report to see if it has changed places.

*Question 1*  *What do you think it would mean if the mouse (or other device) did not appear in the list?*

_____

_____

_____

_____

7    In the Hardware list on the left, click Disc Burning to view information about the optical drive.

*Question 2  List the CD media formats your computer can burn.*

---

---

---

*Question 3  Can your computer burn DVDs? Single or dual layer?*

---

---

---

8   Quit System Profiler.

## Use System Profiler at the Command Line

The command-line equivalent of System Profiler is system_profiler. This tool can return a full report at the command line, or you can specify which information you would like it to return. In this exercise, you'll see how to generate a report on a single connection type using system_profiler at the command line.

1   Open Terminal from the Utilities folder.

2   View the man page for system_profiler:

client17:~ cadmin$ man system_profiler

One of the options documented in the man page is –listDataTypes. This option is useful when you want to display results only for the bus you wish to troubleshoot. In this example you will display only devices connected by USB.

3   At the command prompt, type:

client17:~ cadmin$ system_profiler –listDataTypes

4   In the results, locate the entry for USB (SPUSBDataType).

5   Run system_profiler again with the above argument.

    client17:~ cadmin$ `system_profiler SPUSBDataType`

    System Profiler returns results for only the USB connections.

    You can limit the information displayed by the system_profiler command to just what you need for specific troubleshooting situations.

6   Quit Terminal.

## Connecting to a Computer in FireWire Target Disk Mode

You can use FireWire to connect your computer to another Mac and have one of the computers appear as an external hard disk on the other computer. This is referred to as target disk mode, sometimes abbreviated TDM. FireWire target disk mode allows a Macintosh computer with a FireWire port (the target computer) to be used as an external hard disk connected to another computer (the host). Once a target computer is started up as a FireWire hard disk and is available to the host computer, you can copy files to or from that volume just as you would with any other external volume.

Why would you want to use target disk mode? You can use it to back up data, to troubleshoot startup problems, and to run Disk Utility to repair a disk. Remember that because the user may elect to ignore ownership and permissions on a device connected in this manner, target disk mode can pose a security risk. Setting a firmware password will prevent the user from changing how the computer boots. As a result, with a firmware password in place, the user will have to provide it in order to start the computer in target disk mode.

In this exercise, you will partner with a classmate to use target disk mode. Pick one computer as the host computer and one as the target computer.

1   On the target computer, select the Macintosh HD icon in the Finder's sidebar or on the desktop if you have hard disks appearing there, then choose File > Get Info.

2   In the Name & Extension field, delete Macintosh HD and type
    `Target HD` to rename the volume, then close the Get Info window.

Renaming the hard drive makes it easier to distinguish between
the drives on the host computer. Target disk mode would work
the same with any name.

3   Shut down the target computer.

4   Connect the two computers with a FireWire cable.

5   Hold down the T key on the target computer while you press
    the power button. Keep holding the T key until you see a
    FireWire logo on the screen.

6   When you see the FireWire logo on the screen, release the
    T key. The Target HD and Backup volumes appear on the
    desktop of the host computer as external FireWire drives.

7   If a dialog appears asking if you wish to use Target HD as a Time
    Machine device, click Cancel.

8   Open System Profiler, then click FireWire in the list on the left.

9   Look for the entry for the drive connected via target disk mode. Review the information about the drive in the list.

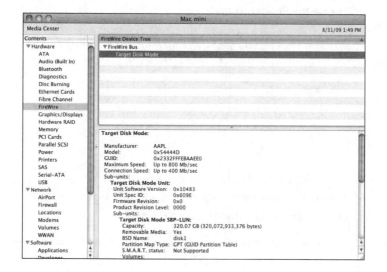

10 Quit System Profiler.

## Transfer Data in Target Disk Mode

Once the computers are connected using target disk mode, you can transfer data between them.

1   On the desktop, click Target HD, then choose File > Get Info.

2   In the Info window, open the Sharing & Permissions pane, if necessary. Look at the bottom of the window to see whether "Ignore ownership on this volume" is checked. Select it if it is not selected (you may need to click the lock and authenticate to do this).

Ignored ownership means that the normal permissions restrictions on data are gone, so you can freely browse the contents of home folders on the target booted disk. Effectively, the system treats you as though you own everything on the volume. The only exception to this is FileVault-encrypted accounts, like the one for Robin Banks. Because her home folder is contained in an encrypted disk image, you will still need that password in order to be able to see its contents.

3   On the Target HD, go to the home folder for Chris Johnson, and navigate to the Public/DropBox folder.

4   Locate the Project.rtf file.

*Question 4   Can you drag it to your desktop?*

5   When the copy is finished, return to the Info window and deselect "Ignore ownership on this volume" (you may need to click the lock and authenticate to do this).

6   Navigate to the root of Target HD and then back to Chris's drop box.

*Question 5   Can you see what is in Chris's drop box now? Why or why not?*

7   Eject the target volume.

8   Press and hold the power button to shut down the target computer, then unplug the cable when it has powered off.

9   Restart the target computer normally.

10   When the target computer restarts, log in as Client Administrator and rename the Target HD hard drive to Macintosh HD using the Name & Extension pane of the Finder's Get Info window for the volume.

11   Log out.

## Exercise 9.1.2
# Using Bluetooth (optional)

## Objective

- Enable Bluetooth connections and use Bluetooth to transfer data

## Summary

Bluetooth is a short-range wireless technology. It commonly provides what are called personal area networks (PANs). As a modern interface technology, it is quite flexible and can fit many use cases. In this exercise you will explore some of the basic features provided by Mac OS X for working with Bluetooth devices. Most, but not all, Mac computers come with Bluetooth preinstalled. If your classroom's equipment does not provide Bluetooth, your instructor may do this exercise as a demonstration or you may skip this exercise.

## Connect Computers via Bluetooth

In this exercise, you will set up a connection via Bluetooth to another computer. If you have Bluetooth-equipped computers in the classroom, you will pair up with another student to do this exercise. Select one computer to initiate the connection, and one to act as the receiving device.

1  Log in as Chris Johnson.

2  Click the Bluetooth icon in the menu bar, then choose Open Bluetooth Preferences.

If you do not see the Bluetooth icon in the menu bar, you can also open System Preferences and select Bluetooth. If the Bluetooth icon is not in the menu bar and there are no Bluetooth preferences in System Preferences, either you do not have Bluetooth installed or the system is having trouble recognizing the Bluetooth hardware.

```
  *   ◇  ◀  ◁►  Thu 1:42 PM  C
 Bluetooth: On
 Turn Bluetooth Off
 ✓ Discoverable

 Send File...
 Browse Device...

 Set Up Bluetooth Device...
 Open Bluetooth Preferences...
```

3  Click the Set Up New Device button, then click Continue.

The computer begins browsing for nearby Bluetooth devices that are discoverable.

```
●○○                          Bluetooth
 ◀ ▶   Show All                                          Q

  *      "client17" is the name Bluetooth devices use to connect to this computer.

         ☑ On          ☑ Discoverable

        ┌─────────────────────────────────────────────┐
        │                                             │
        │                                             │
        │                 No Devices                  │
        │                                             │
        │            ( Set Up New Device... )          │
        │                                             │
        └─────────────────────────────────────────────┘

 ☑ Show Bluetooth status in the menu bar   ( File Sharing Setup... ) ( Advanced... ) (?)
```

4  When your partner's computer's name appears in the list, select it and then click Continue.

This will attempt to pair your computer with your partner's. Pairing establishes mutual authentication and encryption between the two computers.

Mac OS X generates a passcode and displays it on your computer. It then contacts the other computer with a pairing request. The other computer asks that you enter the same passcode. When you do, the two computers are mutually authenticated and can communicate over Bluetooth.

5   Your partner should enter the passcode that is displayed on
    your screen.

    Once the passcode has been entered, the two computers
    configure themselves for the Bluetooth pair. Your computer tells
    you that it is done.

    Mac OS X gives you a little time to complete pairing. If you take
    too long, it will tell you that it failed to pair the computers. Click
    Go Back and start step 4 again.

6   Click Quit.

    Both computers now show the other computer in the list of
    known Bluetooth devices.

## Send a File via Bluetooth

Now that you have made a Bluetooth connection, you will use that connection to transfer a file between devices.

1   On the computer that will receive the file, open the Sharing pane of System Preferences.

2   Click the lock to authenticate, if necessary.

3   Select Bluetooth Sharing in the list of services.

4   Review the options. They should be set as follows:

When receiving items: Ask What to Do

Require pairing: Not selected

Folder for accepted items: Downloads

When other devices browse: Ask What to Do

Require pairing: Selected

Folder others can browse: Public

5   Click the checkbox to enable Bluetooth Sharing.

6  On the computer that will send the file, click the Bluetooth icon in the menu bar and then choose Send File.

7  Use TextEdit to create a file named My Document.rtf in your Documents folder.

8  In the Select File to Send dialog, navigate to Chris's Documents folder, select My Document.rtf, and then click Send.

You are now asked where to send it.

9  When asked to Select Bluetooth Device, select the computer you paired with and click Send.

The computer now tries to send the file. A progress meter is displayed on the sending computer and the receiving computer alerts the user to the incoming file and asks them to accept or decline it.

10 On the receiving computer, click the Accept button in the Incoming File Transfer dialog that appears.

On the sending computer, the status window disappears when the transfer is complete.

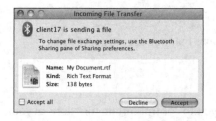

11 On the receiving computer, click Show in the Incoming File Transfer dialog. Notice that it has changed to reflect the fact that the file has been transferred.

A Finder window opens to the Downloads folder with My Document.rtf selected.

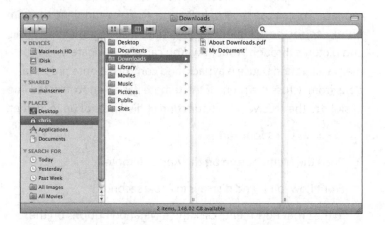

12 Log out of both computers.

## Exercise 9.1.3

# Using the Apple Remote (optional)

## Objective

- Use the Apple Remote and manage security settings

## Summary

The Apple Remote allows you to control certain functions of your computer (e.g., Front Row) from a short distance away using an infrared signal. Many Macs include an IR receiver that enables this control. While convenient, a Mac will by default respond to any Apple Remote. If you have two computers set up near one another and you activate the Apple Remote, they may both go into Front Row, for example. You will explore the Apple Remote and set up pairing so that your computer only responds to your remote. If your classroom does not have Apple Remotes or your computers don't have IR sensors, your instructor may do this exercise as a demonstration or you may skip this exercise.

## Using the Apple Remote

The infrared Apple Remote is an option for many Macintosh models. You can use the Apple Remote to wake and sleep the computer, control the volume, and play content such as movies, music, and pictures through Front Row. You can also navigate lists and menus, start and pause playback, and control Keynote presentations from across the room. If the remote has an unobstructed line of sight to the receiver, it can function at distances of up to 30 feet.

1  Log in as Chris Johnson.

2  Press the Menu button on the Apple Remote.

   Front Row loads and displays in a few seconds.

3  In the Front Row menu, click the navigation buttons on the remote to move through the different items you can play.

Arranged around the Play/Pause button is a ring of buttons that allows you to navigate the menu. Use + for up, – for down and the Next and Previous buttons for right and left, respectively.

If you have an Internet connection, you can browse for movie trailers in the Movies section.

4   Press the Menu button until you leave Front Row.

You may need to press Menu repeatedly until you get back to the main menu and then press it one more time.

Besides playing iLife content, you can use the Apple Remote to control the volume, put your Mac to sleep, wake it up, and more.

5   To increase the volume on your Mac, press the (+) button on the Apple Remote. To decrease the volume, press the (–) button.

Your Apple Remote can select a different boot option for your Mac.

6   Restart your Mac and hold down the Menu button on the Apple Remote while it is starting.

7   When the Startup Manager appears, release the Menu button.

8   Use the Apple Remote to click between the boot options, if there are any.

If the Target HD computer were still connected via target disk mode, it would be available as one of the boot options.

9   Select Macintosh HD and then click the Play button to start up from the internal hard drive.

10  After the Macintosh starts up, log in as Chris Johnson.

11  Once the desktop appears, press and hold the Play/Pause button on the remote until the Sleep symbol appears.

**12** Once the computer goes to sleep, press any button on the Apple Remote to wake it up.

**13** Log out.

## Securing the Apple Remote

Because any Apple Remote can work with your computer, you may want to pair your Macintosh with your specific remote, to keep other remotes from controlling your computer.

**1** Log in as Client Administrator.

**2** Open the Security pane of System Preferences.

**3** Click General.

Here you can pair your remote or disable the infrared receiver.

**4** Click the lock to authenticate as Client Administrator, if necessary.

**5** Click Pair.

A dialog slides down telling you how to pair your computer to your remote.

6   Press and hold the Menu and Next buttons at the same time until the paired remote graphic appears on the screen.

7   When the pairing symbol appears, release the buttons on the remote.

8   Try to use a classmate's Apple Remote to control your computer.

    Your classmate's remote doesn't work on your computer.

9   Select "Disable remote control infrared receiver."

10  Try to control your computer using your Apple Remote.

    It no longer works because the receiver has been disabled.

11  Uncheck "Disable remote control infrared receiver."

12  Unpair your computer and your Apple Remote by clicking Unpair.

13  Quit System Preferences.

14  Log out.

## Troubleshoot the Apple Remote

In this optional exercise, you will determine whether the Apple Remote's infrared connection is working. A digital camera or DV camera with an LCD display can be used to see if your Apple Remote is emitting a signal. You can use the built-in iSight camera on your MacBook or iMac computer. Infrared beams are invisible to the human eye, but most digital and video cameras use charge-coupled device (CCD) chips or image sensors that are sensitive to infrared light.

This exercise uses a built-in iSight camera to test the infrared signal on the Apple Remote. If you do not have a Mac with a built-in iSight camera, you can use a digital camera, or your instructor can do this exercise as a demonstration.

1  Log in as Chris Johnson.

2  Open Photo Booth. It is in the Applications folder and probably in your dock.

    Photo Booth turns on the built-in iSight camera and displays a window showing you what it sees.

3  Point the Apple Remote at the built-in iSight camera and press the Next button.

    A light flashing the remote indicates the remote is sending a signal. If you did not see a light, you would try other troubleshooting steps. For instructions on replacing the remote's battery, see Apple Knowledge Base article #HT1306, "How to replace the Apple Remote battery."

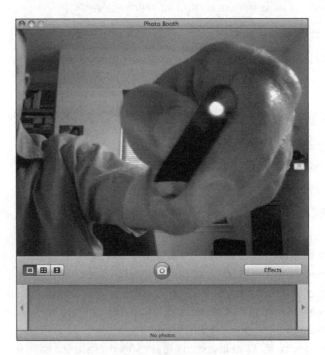

4  Log out.

# Managing Printing and Faxing

# 9.2

Printing may seem like a trivial task to most users, and that's certainly by design, but this belies the underlying complexity required to support the wide variety of printing and faxing options available in Mac OS X. With every revision of Mac OS X, Apple provides more printing functionality and refinement to the underlying CUPS architecture. In this lesson you will explore this printing architecture from both administrative and troubleshooting perspectives.

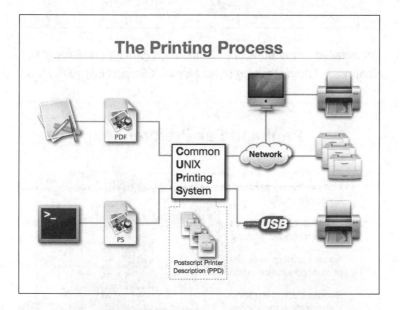

For detailed instructions, see "Configuring Printing and Faxing" in Chapter 9 of *Apple Training Series: Mac OS X Support Essentials v10.6*.

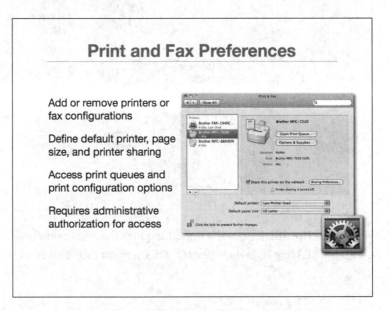

## Automatic Printer Configuration

Locally connected printers are automatically configured.

Print dialog allows you to add Bonjour or shared printers.

Software Update automatically downloads most drivers.

Administrator account is required to configure printers.

For detailed instructions, see "Configuring Printing and Faxing" in Chapter 9 of *Apple Training Series: Mac OS X Support Essentials v10.6.*

## Print and Fax Preferences

Add or remove printers or fax configurations

Define default printer, page size, and printer sharing

Access print queues and print configuration options

Requires administrative authorization for access

For detailed instructions, see "Configuring Printing and Faxing" in Chapter 9 of *Apple Training Series: Mac OS X Support Essentials v10.6.*

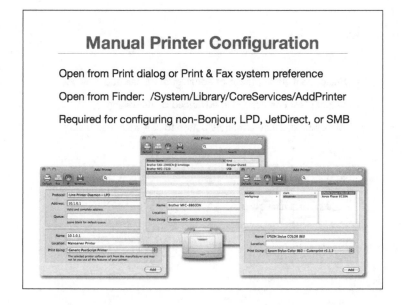

## Manual Printer Configuration

Open from Print dialog or Print & Fax system preference

Open from Finder: /System/Library/CoreServices/AddPrinter

Required for configuring non-Bonjour, LPD, JetDirect, or SMB

For detailed instructions, see "Configuring Printing and Faxing" in Chapter 9 of *Apple Training Series: Mac OS X Support Essentials v10.6.*

## Managing Printer Configuration

Adjust printer configuration
- Human name and location
- Selected printer driver
- Check supply levels
- Open dedicated printer utility

Print & Fax preference
- Options & Supplies button

Printer queue application
- Printer Setup button

For detailed instructions, see "Configuring Printing and Faxing" in Chapter 9 of *Apple Training Series: Mac OS X Support Essentials v10.6.*

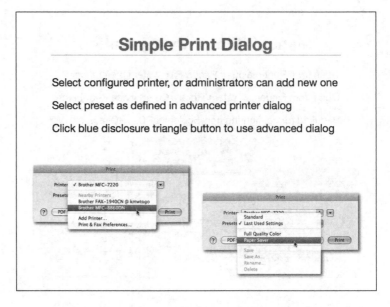

For detailed instructions, see "Managing Print Jobs" in Chapter 9 of *Apple Training Series: Mac OS X Support Essentials v10.6.*

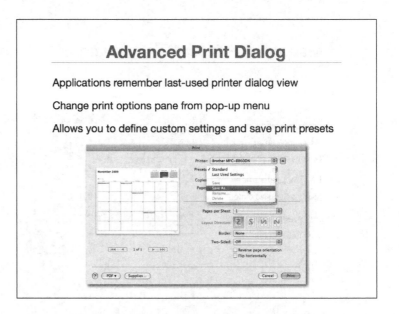

For detailed instructions, see "Managing Print Jobs" in Chapter 9 of *Apple Training Series: Mac OS X Support Essentials v10.6.*

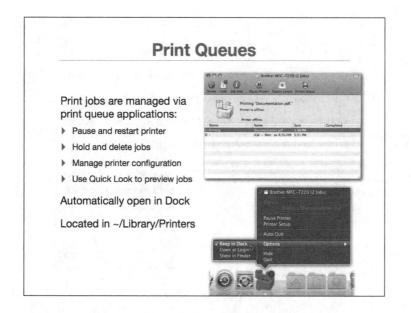

For detailed instructions, see "Managing Print Jobs" in Chapter 9 of
*Apple Training Series: Mac OS X Support Essentials v10.6.*

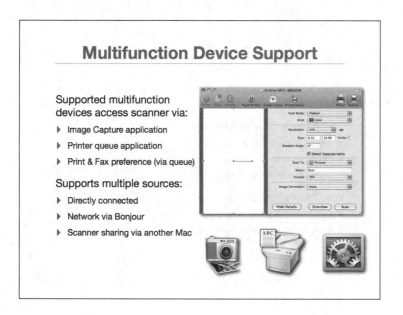

For detailed instructions, see "Managing Print Jobs" in Chapter 9 of
*Apple Training Series: Mac OS X Support Essentials v10.6.*

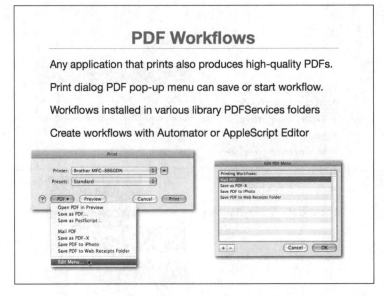

For detailed instructions, see "Using PDF Tools" in Chapter 9 of *Apple Training Series: Mac OS X Support Essentials v10.6*.

For detailed instructions, see "Configuring Fax Services" in Chapter 9 of *Apple Training Series: Mac OS X Support Essentials v10.6*.

## Sharing Local Printers

Printers and local faxing can be shared via IPP and Bonjour.

By default only local printers are enabled, but sharing is off.

Enable and manage printer sharing from Sharing preference

For detailed instructions, see "Sharing Printers and Faxes" in Chapter 9 of *Apple Training Series: Mac OS X Support Essentials v10.6*.

## CUPS Advanced Administration

CUPS printing commands

▸ Print PS or PDF file: `lpr path`

▸ Show print jobs: `lpq`

▸ Remove print jobs: `lprm`

CUPS web interface

▸ http://localhost:631

▸ Administer printers and jobs

▸ Allows for remote management

▸ Accounting via RSS subscription

For detailed instructions, see "Advanced Printing Management" in Chapter 9 of *Apple Training Series: Mac OS X Support Essentials v10.6*.

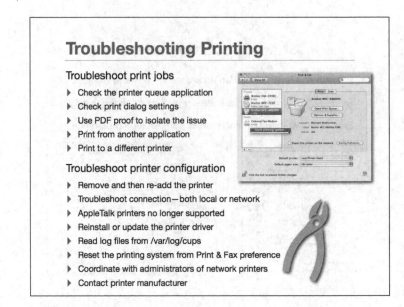

## Troubleshooting Printing

### Troubleshoot print jobs

▸ Check the printer queue application
▸ Check print dialog settings
▸ Use PDF proof to isolate the issue
▸ Print from another application
▸ Print to a different printer

### Troubleshoot printer configuration

▸ Remove and then re-add the printer
▸ Troubleshoot connection—both local or network
▸ AppleTalk printers no longer supported
▸ Reinstall or update the printer driver
▸ Read log files from /var/log/cups
▸ Reset the printing system from Print & Fax preference
▸ Coordinate with administrators of network printers
▸ Contact printer manufacturer

For detailed instructions, see "Troubleshooting the Printing System" in Chapter 9 of *Apple Training Series: Mac OS X Support Essentials v10.6.*

## Exercise 9.2.1
# Managing Printing

## Objective

- Set up a networked printer

## Summary

This lesson introduces you to basic printer configuration and the printing process. You will configure a network printer and print to it from TextEdit.

## Set Up a Networked PostScript Printer

In this exercise, you'll add a printer that is hosted on the instructor's server.

1   Log in as Chris Johnson.

2   Open System Preferences and then click Print & Fax.

3   Click the lock icon, and authenticate as Client Administrator.

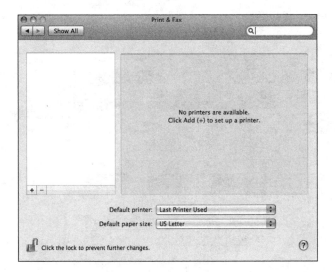

4  Click the Add (+) button to add a printer.

The Add Printer dialog appears.

5  Click the Default button in the Add Printer dialog's toolbar.

6  In the printer name list, click NewQueue.

The computer attempts to find a driver for the printer and defaults to Generic PostScript Printer. Notice the message that indicates that the driver may not give you access to all the printer's features.

7   Click Add.

A dialog slides down to ask about installable options for the printer.

8   Click Continue.

NewQueue now shows as the default printer in your printer list.

9   With the NewQueue entry selected, click the Open Print Queue button.

You can set more descriptive names for printers by using the Printer Setup button in a queue's window. For supported printers, you also have access to supply-level information and printer utilities from the queue window, in addition to being able to delete, hold, and restart individual jobs and pause and restart the whole queue.

10 To change the printer name, click the Printer Setup button in the toolbar.

11 In the Name field, type `Pretendco Network Printer`.

12 In the Location field, type `Instructor Server`.

**13** Click OK.

Print & Fax preferences now shows the Pretendco Network Printer in the list.

**14** Close System Preferences.

Notice that the queue window stays open.

**15** Close Pretendco Network Printer.

## Print to a Networked Printer

In this exercise, you will print to the network printer you just set up. Since this is a print queue on the server, and not a physical printer, you will not see printed output. Your instructor will display the status of the print queue so that you can see the document with your student number appear in the queue.

**1** Go to Chris's Documents folder, and open the My Document.rtf file. Use TextEdit to create this document, if you do not have one.

**2** Choose File > Save As.

3  In the name field, change the name to `My Document-n`, where *n* is your student number, then click Save.

| Save As: | My Document–17 | ▾ |
|---|---|---|
| Where: | 📁 Documents | ⬍ |

| File Format: | Rich Text Format | ⬍ |
|---|---|---|

Cancel   Save

4  Choose File > Print.

Pretendco Network Printer appears in the print dialog as the default printer.

| Printer: | Pretendco Network Printer | ⬍ | ▾ |
|---|---|---|---|
| Presets: | Standard | ⬍ | |

(?)  (PDF ▾)  (Preview)   (Cancel)  (Print)

5  Click Print and wait for your print job to appear on the instructor's server.

6  Log out.

Exercise 9.2.2
# Troubleshooting the Printing System

## Objectives

- Examine the CUPS log in Console
- Configure a CUPS RSS feed
- Reset the printing system

## Summary

Troubleshooting printing involves understanding what goes on during the print process. In this exercise, you will examine the logs that are available from the print system and configure the underlying printing system to provide RSS feeds whereby you can monitor it.

## Examine the CUPS Logs

Mac OS X tracks many different events, including printing, through logs. You can view logs of both system and user events in the Console application. In this exercise, you will use Console to view the available CUPS logs.

1   Log in as Chris Johnson.

2   In the Finder, choose Go > Utilities, then open Console. If necessary, click Show Log List in the toolbar to see the list of log locations.

3   Click the disclosure triangle next to /private/var/log to display the list of logs and then click the disclosure triangle next to cups.

Because the CUPS log is located in the directory /private/var/log in the Mac OS X file system, it is displayed under /private/var/log in the Console window.

4   Click access_log in the list.

If you have printed, as you did previously, you will see entries in the access log. There also will be entries in the page log for each job. The access log shows interactions with the CUPS service while the page log shows actual print jobs. Commands sent to CUPS will show here also, though not exactly as you entered them at the command line.

5   View the page_log.

*Question 6   From the entries in the log files, can you tell which user printed?*

6   If there is an error_log, view it.

7   Quit Console.

## Configure an RSS Feed from CUPS

CUPS uses HTTP as its transport protocol and provides a web-based interface for management. While most of CUPS's functionality is available through the GUI, a handful of useful things must be configured in the web interface. You will take a look at one of those useful features.

1   Open Safari.

2   Load http://localhost:631 using the address bar.

This opens the CUPS web interface. Localhost is another name for the computer you are sitting in front of. It should always refer to this computer. 631 is the port that CUPS listens on.

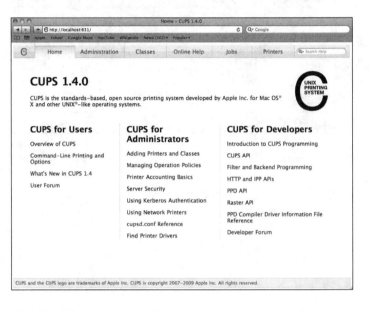

3   Click the Administration tab.

On this tab you can manage printers, classes (pools of printers), jobs, and various server configurations.

4   Click Add RSS Subscription.

A new page opens to allow you to edit the configuration of an RSS (Really Simple Syndication) feed.

5   Configure the RSS feed as follows:

- Name: Jobs-Client*n* (where *n* is your student number)

- Queue: All Queues

- Events: Job Created, Job Completed, Job Stopped, Job Options Changed

- Maximum Events in Feed: 20

6   Click Add RSS Subscription.

You are prompted to log in.

7   Log in as Client Administrator and select "Remember this password in my keychain."

A page is briefly displayed telling you that the feed was added successfully. The browser then loads the Administration page again. Notice the Jobs-Client*n* RSS feed is now available at the bottom of the page.

8  Click the RSS feed link.

Safari displays the (empty) RSS feed.

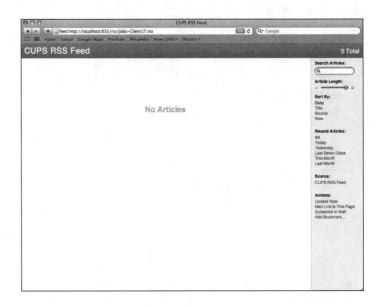

9  Switch to TextEdit, open ~/Documents/My Document-*n*.rtf and print the document.

10  Switch back to Safari and click the reload button or View > Reload Page.

Entries have been added to the RSS feed, reflecting the status of your job.

11  Quit Safari.

## Reset the Printing System

If you can't print to your printer, and you've tried other solutions, you can restore the printing system to "factory defaults" by resetting it. This process deletes all printers from your Printer list, deletes information about all completed print jobs, and deletes all printer presets. Because this completely resets information, it's likely to be your last option, rather than the first.

1 From the Apple menu, choose System Preferences and then click Print & Fax.

2 Hold the Control key and click in the printer list.

3 Click "Reset printing system" in the menu that appears.

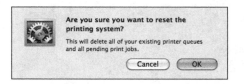

4 Click OK when asked to confirm, then authenticate as Client Administrator.

You can re-add your printers when the process is complete, if you like. It is not necessary for the remaining exercises.

5 Quit System Preferences.

6 Move My Document-*n*.rtf to the Trash.

7 Log out.

Exercise 9.2.3

# Creating a PDF Print Plug-in (optional)

## Objective

- Create a PDF workflow

## Summary

Applications generate PDF documents to send to the printing system to be rendered on the output device. Because printing starts with a PDF document, it is easy to take that document and do other useful things with it. In this exercise, you will create a PDF Print Plug-in (also known as a PDF workflow), hook it into the printing system, and use it to customize a PDF document output from an application.

## Create a Print Plug-in

PDF workflows can be used to perform multiple actions on files as part of a production environment. In this example, you will apply a grayscale filter to a file with a PDF workflow added to the Print dialog.

1   Log in as Chris Johnson and open Automator from the Applications folder.

Workflow is selected by default.

2   Click Print Plugin and then click Choose.

3   In the search field, type `quartz`.

As you have probably seen, this field filters all actions by the keyword you enter. This is a quick way to locate actions for your workflows.

4   Drag the action Apply Quartz Filter to PDF Documents into the workflow at the right of the window.

5   In the warning dialog that appears, click Add, so that the workflow creates copies of your files with the workflow applied, rather than changing your originals.

6   Click the To pop-up menu of the Copy Finder Items action and choose Other.

7   In the dialog that appears, click Desktop under Places in the sidebar.

8   Click New Folder, then name the folder `Grayscale Quartz`, and click Create.

9   When the folder has been created, make sure it is selected and then click Choose.

This sets the new folder as the location for files that have had the Quartz filter applied.

**10** In the Apply Quartz Filter to PDF Documents action, open the pop-up menu next to Filter and select Gray Tone.

The filter previews in the window to the right.

**11** Choose File > Save As.

**12** Name the plug-in `Gray Filter` and click Save.

Notice that it does not ask you where you want to save. This particular type of Automator workflow must be saved in a particular location in order for the print system to find it.

**13** Quit Automator.

Now you'll print a color file and apply the workflow from the Print dialog.

**14** In the Finder, navigate to the Chapter9 folder of the student materials.

15 Open the file Snow Leopard Prowl.jpg, then choose File > Print.

16 In the Print dialog, click the PDF button and then choose Gray Filter from the pop-up menu.

17 Open the Grayscale Quartz folder on the desktop and then open the file Snow Leopard Prowl.jpg.pdf.

You can see that the gray-scale filter has been applied. You may want to rotate it to get the full effect (Command-R or Tools > Rotate Right).

18 Quit Preview.

19 Log out.

# 10

# System Startup

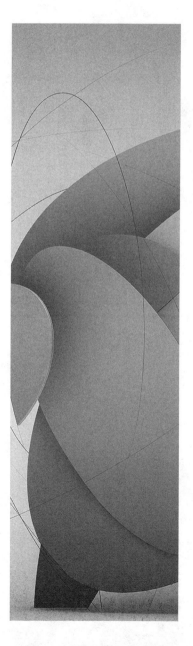

# 10.1 Understanding and Troubleshooting System Startup

It may seem counterintuitive to end the course with system startup, but this choice is deliberate, as you need the requisite knowledge covered in previous chapters to truly understand the Mac OS X startup process. For instance, to properly grasp the startup sequence you need to understand how the Mac system is organized as covered in Chapter 5, and how to monitor running processes as covered in Chapter 6, and finally how to navigate the command line as covered in Chapter 3. As always, the ultimate goal for understanding the technologies involved in system startup is for you to have the appropriate experience to effectively troubleshoot any issues that may arise during this process.

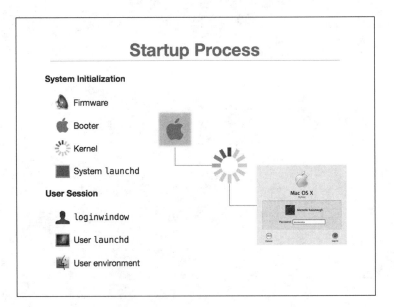

For detailed instructions, see "Understanding the Startup Sequence" in Chapter 10 of *Apple Training Series: Mac OS X Support Essentials v10.6*.

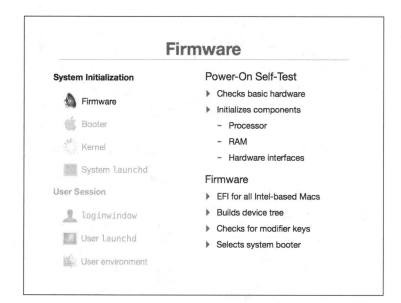

**Firmware**

**System Initialization**

- Firmware
- Booter
- Kernel
- System launchd

**User Session**

- loginwindow
- User launchd
- User environment

**Power-On Self-Test**

▶ Checks basic hardware
▶ Initializes components
  - Processor
  - RAM
  - Hardware interfaces

**Firmware**

▶ EFI for all Intel-based Macs
▶ Builds device tree
▶ Checks for modifier keys
▶ Selects system booter

For detailed instructions, see "Understanding the Startup Sequence" in Chapter 10 of *Apple Training Series: Mac OS X Support Essentials v10.6*.

**Booter**

**System Initialization**

- Firmware
- Booter
- Kernel
- System launchd

**User Session**

- loginwindow
- User launchd
- User environment

/System/Library/
CoreServices/boot.efi

Loads core kernel environment and necessary extensions for starting up the system

Typically loads kernel and extensions using cache to improve startup times

For detailed instructions, see "Understanding the Startup Sequence" in Chapter 10 of *Apple Training Series: Mac OS X Support Essentials v10.6*.

**Kernel**

System Initialization

- Firmware
- Booter
- Kernel
- System launchd

User Session

- loginwindow
- User launchd
- User environment

Initializes the I/O kit for management of hardware and peripherals

Loads necessary additional kernel extensions from /System/Library/Extensions

Starts the primary system launchd process

For detailed instructions, see "Understanding the Startup Sequence" in Chapter 10 of *Apple Training Series: Mac OS X Support Essentials v10.6.*

**System launchd Process**

System Initialization

- Firmware
- Booter
- Kernel
- System launchd

User Session

- loginwindow
- User launchd
- User environment

Manages all system processes

- ▶ Provides fast system initialization by starting various launch daemons simultaneously
- ▶ Many processes only start when needed
- ▶ Starts WindowServer process which shows "blue screen" during system startup
- ▶ Eventually starts the loginwindow process resulting in appearance of the login screen

Locations for system launchd items:

- ▶ /System/Library/LaunchDaemons
- ▶ /Library/LaunchDaemons
- ▶ Also starts legacy /Library/StartupItems

For detailed instructions, see "Understanding the Startup Sequence" in Chapter 10 of *Apple Training Series: Mac OS X Support Essentials v10.6.*

For detailed instructions, see "Understanding the Startup Sequence" in Chapter 10 of *Apple Training Series: Mac OS X Support Essentials v10.6*.

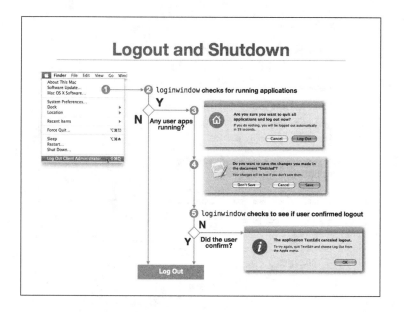

For detailed instructions, see "Sleep Modes, Logout, and Shutdown" in Chapter 10 of *Apple Training Series: Mac OS X Support Essentials v10.6*.

## Startup Modifiers

| | |
|---|---|
| C | Start up from system volume in optical drive |
| D | Start up from diagnostic system in optical drive or hardware ROM |
| N | Start up from default NetBoot system image |
| T | Start to FireWire target disk mode |
| Option | Start to Startup Manager, allowing for system selection |
| Command-Option-P-R | Reset nonvolatile memory settings |
| Eject Key or Mouse | Eject optical media during startup |
| Shift | Start up Mac OS X using Safe Boot |
| Command-V | Start up Mac OS X with Verbose Mode |
| Command-S | Start up Mac OS X in Single-User Mode |
| 6-4 | Force Mac OS X to use 64-bit kernel if hardware is supported |
| 3-2 | Force Mac OS X to use 32-bit kernel if set for 64-bit as default |

For detailed instructions, see "Startup Modifiers" in Chapter 10 of *Apple Training Series: Mac OS X Support Essentials v10.6.*

## Safe Boot and Safe Mode

Safe Boot startup:

▸ Forces a system volume directory check

▸ Only loads required kernel extensions

▸ Moves font caches to the Trash

Safe Mode is the state of your Mac after performing a Safe Boot:

▸ Only loads launchd items in /System/ LaunchDaemons and /System/LaunchAgents

▸ Does not load StartupItems

▸ Disables autologin

▸ Disables all non-system fonts

▸ Disables all login items

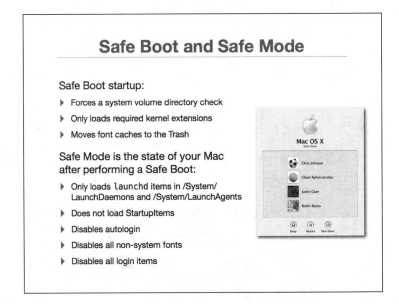

For detailed instructions, see "Troubleshooting Startup" in Chapter 10 of *Apple Training Series: Mac OS X Support Essentials v10.6.*

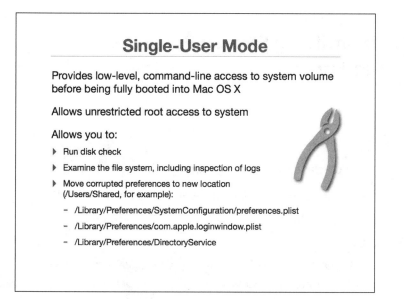

# Single-User Mode

Provides low-level, command-line access to system volume before being fully booted into Mac OS X

Allows unrestricted root access to system

Allows you to:

▸ Run disk check

▸ Examine the file system, including inspection of logs

▸ Move corrupted preferences to new location
  (/Users/Shared, for example):

  – /Library/Preferences/SystemConfiguration/preferences.plist

  – /Library/Preferences/com.apple.loginwindow.plist

  – /Library/Preferences/DirectoryService

For detailed instructions, see "Troubleshooting Startup" in Chapter 10 of *Apple Training Series: Mac OS X Support Essentials v10.6.*

Exercise 10.1.1

# Identifying Startup Processes and Items

## Objectives

- Understand the visual cues displayed onscreen during startup
- Understand process hierarchies associated with `launchd`

## Summary

As Mac OS X starts up, it gives auditory or visual cues as to which step of the startup process is currently being performed. If the startup process fails to complete, identifying the step where it halted can help illuminate the cause of the problem. In this exercise, you will identify steps in the startup sequence using audible and visible cues. You will then examine the processes that activate automatically when you boot your computer. After completing this exercise, you will be able to identify the sequence of startup events that occur during Mac OS X startup.

## Identifying Steps in the Startup Process

In this exercise, you will watch the startup process in a standard startup and in single-user mode. You will find that the startup process moves through some steps very rapidly, while other steps will only flash on the screen, such as an icon that blinks to indicate a component loading. Some steps will be displayed onscreen for a significant amount of time only if the underlying process does not start properly.

1   If your computer is on, shut it down. You can use the buttons on the login window or the Apple menu to shut it down.

2   Start up your computer.

3   As the computer is booting up, note in the table below the major steps occurring during the startup process (from power on until the user environment has appeared). Keep in mind that certain steps may not apply, since we are not testing hardware problems or problems where the boot device cannot be found.

Write down the startup process associated with each visible or audible stage of the startup process. Refer to Chapter 10 of your reference guide or slides from this lesson. When you reach the login window, log in as Chris Johnson.

| Visual or auditory cue | Startup step, or process executing at the startup step |
| --- | --- |
| Startup chime | |
| Gray screen with Apple logo | |
| Gray screen with Apple logo and spinning gear | |
| Blue screen | |
| Login window appears | |
| Desktop and Dock appear | |

## View the Process Hierarchy

The launchd process is an essential part of Mac OS X v10.6. It is responsible for starting and managing much of what goes on in the background of Mac OS X. It is important to understand that there is a hierarchy of tasks in the core operating system. The kernel starts launchd, launchd starts a number of other processes, those processes start other processes, etc. It can be useful, in the event of a problem, to understand this parent-child relationship or hierarchy in order to identify parent tasks, like launchd, that spawn multiple children to do their work.

1   Ensure you are logged in as Chris Johnson.

2   Open Activity Monitor in /Applications/Utilities.

3   Choose All Processes, Hierarchically from the pop-up menu near the top.

4  Click in the PID (Process ID) column header to display the processes in the order they launched (ascending order by process ID). You want the triangle, indicating the sort order, to be pointing up. If it is not, click the column header again.

5  Click the disclosure triangle next to the launchd process with a process ID of 1 to reduce the view to just kernel_task and launchd.

You can see that in the Process ID column, kernel_task is listed as a process. This represents the activity taking place inside the kernel. You can also see that launchd is process 1, meaning that it is the first task that is started by the kernel. This launchd process will not terminate until the system shuts down. All other processes will be numbered sequentially after these core tasks. The process ID (PID) is an unsigned 32-bit number with a maximum value somewhere in the neighborhood of 2,147,483,647. Rest assured, however, that should you ever run two billion processes without rebooting, the system would not crash when it reaches the maximum PID. It will simply start over again, using currently unused PIDs. To understand the task hierarchy, you need more information than the task name and ID.

6   Select launchd and click Inspect on the toolbar.

When inspecting a process, the name of the window will be the name of the process followed by the process ID in parentheses. The parent process is important when you are trying to evaluate processes during troubleshooting. You can also see various process statistics relating to performance, resource allocation, memory usage, and open files for processes you own. You may also quit a process (don't quit launchd at process ID 1, it will reboot your computer without warning) or sample a process. Sampling involves observing what is happening within the process and can be useful to developers if their application or other process is hanging.

Note that you can click the parent process and open an Inspect window for that task as well. This is very useful when you are working with higher-numbered tasks and you are tracing the process hierarchy backward.

**Note**  The statistical values in your window may differ from what is shown here.

7   Close the Inspect window.

8   Click the disclosure triangle next to launchd. Open some of the other disclosure triangles, too.

You will see the list of processes running on the computer. The low-numbered processes are generally daemons. *Daemon* is a term for a background process that acts on behalf of the system. *Agents* are background processes that act on behalf of a user. Daemons generally run as root (the System Administrator account) or another system user. Agents run as the user they are running on behalf of.

A parent-child relationship is indicated by an indent and a disclosure triangle.

9   Look for a second instance of launchd and click its disclosure triangle to show its child processes.

Check the launchd process for unexpected subprocesses that might affect the user environment. For example, this list would contain applications that were launched as login items for the current user, but hidden at startup. It also shows a disclosure triangle for processes that have subprocesses.

10  Quit Activity Monitor and log out.

## Exercise 10.1.2
# Using Single-User Mode

## Objectives

- Understand how to operate in single-user mode

- Run a file system check from single-user mode

- Identify the locations of items launched during startup

## Summary

When troubleshooting Macintosh startup problems that seem to be software-related, you might need to troubleshoot with the operating system started up in single-user mode. Single-user mode is a very primitive state of the operating system. The operating system has only loaded enough services to allow you to interact with it from the command line. It hasn't even mounted the startup disk read/write yet. Single-user mode is a low-level maintenance mode that allows you to bring the system up, look at log files, edit or replace configuration files, etc. In this exercise, you will boot your computer into single-user mode, then proceed to the user interface and identify various files used during startup.

## Using Single-User Mode

In this exercise, you will enter single-user mode, then continue booting to the login window.

1  Shut down your computer.

2  Boot your computer into single-user mode by pressing the power button and then holding Command-S until you see text appearing on the screen.

When your computer finishes booting into single-user mode, Mac OS X v10.6 displays instructions on how to remount the startup disk read/write and how to continue the boot process to multi-user mode, the usual run mode of Mac OS X or any other UNIX.

```
Singleuser boot -- fsck not done
Root device is mounted read-only

If you want to make modifications to files:
    /sbin/fsck -fy
    /sbin/mount -uw /


If you wish to boot the system:
    exit


:/ root#
```

Note that the user name in the prompt is root and the prompt ends with a # instead of the usual $. This tells you that you are logged in as the super user (root, or System Administrator). You have unfettered access to the disks and the rest of the system.

3  Force a check of the file system's integrity.

```
:/ root# /sbin/fsck -fy
```

The computer runs what's called a file system consistency check, correcting any errors that it finds and is able to repair. On today's large disks, this can take a while, especially if there are many files and folders in the file system. This is one of the advantages of file system journaling. Most of the time, a complete fsck does not need to occur, so startup is much faster.

Once that process is complete, you need to remount the disk read/write.

4   Use mount to remount the startup disk.

:/ root# `/sbin/mount -uw /`

You are given a new prompt a few seconds later. This command enables you to make changes to the disk. This command should not generate any output if all runs correctly. If it generates an error message, double-check your typing. The most common error with this command is to leave off the trailing /.

5   Try to ping mainserver.pretendco.com:

:/ root# `ping mainserver.pretendco.com`

```
ping: cannot resolve mainserver.pretendco.com:
Unknown host
```

The network has not been started yet, so you can't get name resolution.

6   Try to ping 10.1.0.1:

:/ root# `ping -c 2 10.1.0.1`

```
PING 10.1.0.1 (10.1.0.1): 56 data bytes

Ping: sendto: No route to host

Ping: sendto: No route to host

Request timeout for icmp_seq 0


--- 10.1.0.1 ping statistics ---

2 packets transmitted, 0 packets received, 100.0%
packet loss
```

The c option specifies how many times to try to ping. Not even IP addresses work for network communication. Your computer does not have any network software running, so it is completely isolated.

> **Note**  If you left off the c option to the ping command, you can tell it to stop pinging by pressing Control-C.

7   Get a process listing.

`:/ root# ps ax`

You see a much shorter list than you previously saw in Activity Monitor. At process ID 1, you see launchd. Process ID 2 is launchctl, which launchd uses in this case to manage the boot process. Process ID 3 is the command shell you are interacting with. The last process is your ps command. The OS is in a very primitive state.

8   Continue the boot process by exiting your shell.

`:/root# exit`

The computer exits your shell and continues starting the operating system, initializes the user environment, and shows the login window so that you can log in normally.

9   Log in as Client Administrator when the login window appears.

## Identify Locations of Items Started During Boot

In this exercise, you will view various locations where your computer finds items that are to be executed during a normal startup, as well as items that are affected by Safe Boot. When you troubleshoot startup problems, it is important to understand that Safe Boot is simply a way to turn off a number of services and drivers, bringing the system up with reduced functionality in the process. If the computer boots properly using Safe Boot, your understanding of where those items are located is essential for you to perform a split-half search (reducing the set of items that might be problematic) to determine what has caused the problem.

1   In the Finder, navigate to /System/Library/LaunchDaemons.

These are property lists (settings) for the tasks that are run at startup by launchd. It's important to know that LaunchDaemons have their own property lists, because they will still launch in Safe Boot.

2   Use Quick Look to view com.apple.backupd-auto.plist.

This is the configuration file that tells `launchd` to run Time Machine every hour. It consists of a number of key-value pairs that tell `launchd` what to call the configuration (Label), what to run (ProgramArguments), when to run it (RunAtLoad and StartInterval), etc. There are a few other `launchd` configuration files relating to Time Machine.

Taken as a whole, the items contained in /System/Library/LaunchDaemons reflect the core daemons of the system. When `launchd` first starts, it examines the files in this folder and finds all the ones that are enabled. Of those, it collects the ones that should be started at boot (as opposed to under other conditions like when a file exists or when a network connection is received) and then starts them.

`launchd` provides "a fully asynchronous bootstrap." *Boot* is short for *bootstrap*. The system is pulling itself up by its bootstraps from only the logic contained in firmware to a full-blown, modern operating system. Because of the asynchronous nature of the boot process, it is difficult to determine the order in which these items will be started.

Feel free to use Quick Look to examine more of these files and to use the manual (launchd.plist) to research the various configuration options.

3   Use the Finder to view the contents of /System/Library/
    LaunchAgents.

    As mentioned before, agents run on behalf of a user, rather
    than the system. Some or all of the items in this folder are used
    to start various background processes as the user logs in. Feel
    free to use Quick Look to examine some of these.

4   Scroll through the /System/Library folder to the StartupItems
    folder.

5   Select the StartupItems folder to see its contents. It is empty
    because no applications with startup processes have been
    installed yet. StartupItems and the SystemStarter process that
    runs them were deprecated in Mac OS X v10.4, but continue to
    work. Various third-party applications and background services
    (like databases) continue to use them, especially in their
    older versions.

    During a normal startup, launchd starts the SystemStarter
    process. SystemStarter reads through the StartupItems folders
    (there is another one at /Library/StartupItems) and determines
    their proper order of execution, then starts these items
    accordingly. Some startup items start background processes,
    some check for particular hardware components, and some
    perform configuration steps and stop executing.

    During a Safe Boot, no startup items are launched. When you
    troubleshoot startup problems, remember that your computer
    checks several places for its startup configuration.

6   In the Finder, navigate to /Library/LaunchDaemons.

    This folder is empty. This is where third parties should install
    their launchd configuration files for daemons. Items in this
    folder are not loaded during a Safe Boot.

7   Use the Finder to navigate to /Library/LaunchAgents.

    This is where launchd finds third-party launch agent
    configuration files. None have been installed on your computer,
    so it is empty.

8  Now navigate to /Library/StartupItems.

This is where third parties should put their startup items. Unfortunately, some third parties place their startup items in /System/Library/StartupItems, so be alert to non-Apple-provided items appearing in /System/Library. This can happen with `launchd` configuration files too, but is much less common.

The folder is empty because you haven't installed any third-party applications, but this is an important place to check when troubleshooting startup problems. Items located in /Library/StartupItems are also disabled during a Safe Boot.

9  Log out.

Exercise 10.1.3

# Removing a Corrupt Startup Item

## Objectives

- Examine how Mac OS X evaluates suspect Startup preferences
- Identify the cause of startup problems based on information displayed at startup
- Resolve startup problems using single-user mode

## Summary

When troubleshooting Macintosh startup problems, you may come across a problem with a corrupt startup item. When you work with third-party utilities, especially in network environments where your end users might download and install startup items, it is especially useful to be able to identify and resolve startup item problems. In this exercise, you will install a problematic startup item to see how you can fix problems caused by a bad startup item.

## Install a Corrupt Startup Item

In this exercise, you will install some faulty software that causes problems for your users. You will then isolate the problem and fix it.

1 Log in as Client Administrator.

2 Navigate to the Chapter10 folder in the student materials folder.

3 Double-click the Pretendco installer.

4 In the Installer's introduction window, click Continue.

5 In the Standard Install on "Macintosh HD" screen, click Install.

6 Authenticate as Client Administrator.

7 When you are informed that the install will require a reboot, click Continue Installation.

8 When the installation is complete, click Restart.

## Evaluate and Resolve a Problematic Startup Item

You will use your knowledge of the startup process from the last exercise and identify the correct problem resolution. You will log in to your computer, resolve the problem, and then restart to ensure that the problem has gone away.

1  Follow the startup process to identify when problems begin.

| Visual or auditory cue | Startup step, or process executing at the startup step |
|---|---|
| Black screen | |
| Startup chime | |
| Gray screen with Apple logo | |
| Gray screen with Apple logo and spinning gear | |
| Blue screen | |
| Login Window appears | |
| Desktop and Dock appear | |

Allow the computer to reboot and watch it again. Is it consistent? Feel free to do this a few times to get a feeling for what is going on.

Ask yourself what startup task was executing, if any, when the system failed. Is it user initiated? Is some background process causing it?

In this case, you know what you did to the computer (installed a package), but understanding the startup process and what is happening at any given time is very useful in resolving problems.

2  Restart the computer using a Safe Boot (hold down the Shift key just after the chime until you see a progress meter on the screen).

Is the problem still there? Give it some time.

The computer does not seem to exhibit the same problem. If that is the case, you now know that the problem has to be with one of the things that the system does not load during a Safe Boot.

3  Log in as Client Administrator.

**4**   Open the Pretendco installer package from Chapter10 of the student materials again. *Do not install it.*

**5**   Choose File > Show Files.

**6**   Click the two disclosure triangles to show what files are installed by the two components of the package.

You see two files that were installed. One looks like it might be a `launchd` configuration file, based on the name. Unfortunately, Installer does not tell you where it installed the files.

**7**   Click the Spotlight menu and enter `com.pretendco.funkytown.plist` (the name of one of the files).

Because you are in safe mode, the Spotlight menu doesn't work. The services that provide Spotlight search are among those not started during a Safe Boot.

**8**   Open the Terminal application.

**9**   Use the command-line tool find to find the file that was installed.

`client17:~ cadmin$ sudo find -x / -name com.pretendco.funkytown.plist`

**10**  Provide your password when prompted.

find will now perform a brute force search of the file system to find that file. You may see some errors while you wait. These can be safely ignored.

After a little while, find outputs:

`/Library/LaunchDaemons/com.pretendco.funkytown.plist`

It looks like that is the file and it makes sense that Safe Boot would fix the problem if it is caused by that configuration file because `launchd` won't load from /Library/LaunchDaemons while in safe mode.

11 Press Control-C to stop the search.

12 Change your working directory to /Library/LaunchDaemons.

13 Use `less` to view com.pretendco.funkytown.plist.

14 Disable the `launchd` job using `launchctl`, the `launchd` management tool.

`client17:LaunchDaemons cadmin$` `sudo launchctl unload -w ./com.pretendco.funkytown.plist`

You will get an error while unloading it. This is because `launchd` doesn't actually have it loaded currently because you are in safe mode. However the `-w` option will cause `launchctl` to disable the item so that it will not load when you reboot.

15 Reboot the computer, looking for a repeat of the previous behavior.

The problem appears to be gone. It is a good idea to remove the faulty software so that it does not get reactivated.

16 Use the Finder to navigate to /Library/LaunchDaemons.

17 Use Quick Look to view com.pretendco.funkytown.plist.

18 Take note of the path to the funkytown program; it is contained in the ProgramArguments section of the property list file.

19 Move com.pretendco.funkytown.plist to the Trash. When asked to authenticate, provide Client Administrator's credentials.

20 Use the Finder or Terminal to move the funkytown file that you found referenced in the `launchd` configuration file to the Trash or to delete it.

## See How Mac OS X Evaluates Suspect Startup Preferences

1  In the Finder, drag com.pretendco.demo.plist from Chapter10 of the student materials to /Library/LaunchDaemons.

2  Authenticate as Client Administrator when prompted.

3  Open Terminal.

4  Make your working directory /Library/LaunchDaemons.

5  Get a long listing of /Library/LaunchDaemons.

Note from the directory listing that the preferences file for demo is owned by cadmin.

6  Tell `launchctl` to load com.pretendco.demo.plist into `launchd`. Provide your password if necessary.

```
client17:LaunchDaemons cadmin$ sudo launchctl load -w
com.pretendco.demo.plist

launchctl: Dubious ownership on file (skipping): com.
pretendco.demo.plist

nothing found to load
```

The job is not loaded because `launchd`/`launchctl` don't like the ownership on the file. It would be a serious breach of security if any user could load a daemon process job into `launchd`.

7  Change the ownership of the configuration file.

```
client17:LaunchDaemons cadmin$ sudo chown root:wheel com.
pretendco.demo.plist
```

This changes the owner and group on the file.

8  Type:

```
client17:LaunchDaemons cadmin$ ls -l
```

Note that the ownership has changed.

9  Run the `launchctl` command again. You can do this by pressing the Up arrow until the command sudo launchctl load -w com. pretendco.demo.plist appears, or just type it again.

This time the job loads successfully.

# Answer Key

## Chapter 1

*Question 1* *What is the processor type and amount of RAM in the example above?*

In the example above, the computer has 4 GB of RAM and an Intel Core 2 Duo processor running at 2.53 GHz.

*Question 2* *Does this computer meet the qualifications to run Mac OS X v10.6?*

Yes.

*Question 3* *Which BootROM version is installed on this computer?*

MBP51.0074.B01

*Question 4* *What SMC version is installed on this computer?*

1.33f8

*Question 5* *What is the minimum amount of hard drive space necessary to install Mac OS X?*

5 GB

*Question 6* *What is the minimum amount of memory required by Mac OS X?*

1 GB

## Chapter 2

*Question 1* *Which password unlocks the keychain now? Why?*

The password is chris. This password works because when Chris Johnson reset his password, the login keychain's password and the account password were the same so System Preferences was able to change both at the same time.

## Chapter 3

*Question 1  Why does grep not find any results?*

The command-line environment is generally case-sensitive. The pattern "mac" does not occur in AppleHardwareInfo.txt. The pattern "Mac" does, however, occur.

*Question 2  How did sort order the list?*

It sorted lines starting with capital letters before those starting with lowercase letters.

## Chapter 4

*Question 1  How do your answers compare to those you found in the graphical interface?*

While units of measure sometimes differ, the same information is available from both the graphical and command-line environments.

*Question 2  What permissions do users other than the owner have for the Desktop folder?*

The desktop folder is read/write for the owner and no access for others. Other users of the computer can see that the desktop folder exists, but not view or alter its contents.

*Question 3  Can you see inside the folder? Can you open the Secret Bonus List file?*

Yes, files and folders created by users in their home folders are read only for others.

*Question 4  Can you open the file? Save changes to the file? Why?*

The home folder is read only by default for others. Users should be aware that files they create or leave in their home folder are readable by others. However, while default permissions do allow anyone to read a file, users besides the owner cannot save to it.

*Question 5  Can you open the folder?*

Robin Banks has a FileVault-protected home folder. Although you can leave files for other users in their ~/Public/Drop Box folders, there is no access to a FileVault user's Public folder when they are not logged in.

*Question 6  Has anything changed? If so, what and why?*

The file is now owned by cadmin. TextEdit performed an atomic or safe save. It wrote the changed document into a new file, deleted the old file, and renamed the new file to the old filename. Because this is a new file created by cadmin, cadmin owns the file.

*Question 7  Are you able to copy this file?*

No. Because the permissions on the Public folder have been changed, the drop box is not available.

*Question 8  Are the permissions for this folder set as you would expect? What tools can you use to find the answer?*

Normally, you would expect the Public folder in any home folder to be read only, so that other users can access files stored there and in the drop box. You can tell the permissions have been changed to no access, because the Public folder now has a red minus sign (do not enter) badge on the icon. You could also go to Get Info and check Sharing & Permissions. Finally, you could open Terminal, navigate to Chris's home folder, and use the `ls -l` command to check permissions at the command line.

*Question 9  Were you able to change the permissions?*

Because you performed `chmod` using `sudo`, the command worked.

*Question 10  Were you successful?*

Now that the permissions have been changed to Read Only for the Public folder, Mayta can copy a file into Chris's drop box.

## Chapter 5

*Question 1*  *What do you think these files are for?*

These are the help files for the German localization. Generally, this is the same information as the English localization, but translated into German.

*Question 2*  *What does this command do?*

This command creates a file named Prefs.txt on the desktop that lists the contents of the current directory.

*Question 3*  *What does clicking the Change All button do?*

This changes the default application for .txt files to SubEthaEdit. All .txt files will now open in SubEthaEdit. This is stored in Launch Services' preferences.

*Question 4*  *In which application does it open?*

It now opens in SubEthaEdit.

*Question 5*  *What is different in the two directory listings?*

The com.apple.LaunchServices.QuarantineEvents file keeps track of downloaded files. A downloaded file is flagged with metadata that points to this database. It was created when you downloaded SubEthaEdit from the Pretendco.com website. The com.apple. LaunchServices.plist file keeps track of Launch Services' preferences. It was created when you clicked the Change All button in step 20. You may also see preferences files for Safari, WebKit (Safari's rendering engine), and SubEthaEdit.

*Question 6*  *How has the com.apple.LaunchServices.plist file changed?*

The entry for text files (public.plain-text) has changed its default application to Console (com.apple.console).

*Question 7*  *What happens?*

The archive is expanded (the Logs folder appears on the desktop) and the archive is moved from the desktop to the Trash.

## Chapter 6

## Chapter 7

*Question 1  What happens with the domain name service when setting service priority?*

DNS is handled by the service with the highest priority.

*Question 2  What differences do you see?*

The router and the subnet mask are different.

*Question 3  Why didn't the websites load?*

Unable to determine at this time, but given that Safari keeps complaining about proxy settings, that seems like a likely candidate.

## Chapter 8

*Question 1  What message did your partner receive at this attempt?*

The operation can't be completed because you don't have the necessary permission.

*Question 2  Which users' Public folder share points did you not see?*

Robin Banks, the FileVault user, and Mayta Mishtuk, whose home folder we copied out of a disk image.

*Question 3  Why would you have a firewall enabled on your computer if you already have a network firewall?*

A firewall on your computer can protect it from threats originating within your local network. Most network firewalls protect the boundaries, but do little to examine traffic within the network.

*Question 4  Why do you not have any tickets?*

There are no tickets because Chris Johnson is a local user and did not authenticate with the Kerberos server.

## Chapter 9

*Question 1  What do you think it would mean if the mouse (or other device) did not appear in the list?*

If the device did not appear in System Profiler, it would indicate the computer did not recognize the device as being connected. Troubleshooting steps would include power issues, cables, or other hardware connection issues. This is a different issue than whether the operating system has drivers for the device.

*Question 2  List the CD media formats your computer can burn.*

With Disc Burning selected, you can view the media types listed next to CD-Write and DVD-Write.

*Question 3  Can your computer burn DVDs? Single or dual layer?*

Media types that include RW indicate that the optical drive can burn that media. DL indicates dual layer.

*Question 4  Can you drag it to your desktop?*

Because the normal write-only permissions of Mayta's drop box are circumvented, you are allowed to copy this file. This makes target disk mode both useful for data recovery and a security risk.

*Question 5  Can you see what is in Chris's drop box now? Why or why not?*

Now that the volume is respecting permissions again, no, you cannot. You have to navigate away and then back because the Finder will have certain information about the folder/volume cached and may not immediately reflect the changes in permissions, though it will still be bound by them.

*Question 6  From the entries in the log files, can you tell which user printed?*

Yes, the user's short name is the third field in both the access and page logs.

## Chapter 10